Product Design

Paul Rodgers and Alex Milton

Laurence King Publishing

LAURENCE KING

Published in 2011 by
Laurence King Publishing Ltd
361–373 City Road
London EC1V 1LR
United Kingdom
email: enquiries@laurenceking.com
www.laurenceking.com

A catalogue record for this book is available
from the British Library.

ISBN: 978 1 85669 751 4

Portfolio series design concept by Jon Allan,
   TwoSheds Design
Design by Vanessa Green, The Urban Ant Ltd.
Senior editor: Zoe Antoniou
Picture research: Fredrika Lökholm
Copyeditor: Nicola Hodgson

Printed in China

Frontispiece: (p. 4) Clouds, designed by Ronan &
Erwan Bouroullec for Kvadrat, 2008.

Chapter openers: (p. 5) Ruminant Bloom by Julia
Lohmann; (p. 19) Add-On Radiator by Satyendra
Pakhalé; (p. 55) mood board by Tom Harper; (p. 77)
Blown fabric lanterns by Nendo; (p. 107) Algue by
Ronan & Erwan Bouroullec; (p. 167) Pewter Stool by
Max Lamb; (p. 201) page from sketchbook by Tom
Harper; (p. 229) Z. Island by Zaha Hadid Architects.

Front cover: Tide, by Stuart Haygarth, 2005.
Back cover: cobi™ chair by PearsonLloyd designed in
conjunction with Steelcase Design Studio.

Introduction

What is product design? **6** / What does a product designer do? **12** / Creating a product **14** / The main stages of product design **15** / Interview: Julia Lohmann **16** / About this book **18**

1. Historical and cultural context

The Industrial Revolution: 1750s to 1850s **20** / The Great Reform movements: 1850s to 1914 **21** / Modernism to pre-war luxury and power: 1900s to 1945 **25** / The post-war period: 1945 to 1970s **30** / Post-Modernism: 1970s to present day **38** / Interview: Satyendra Pakhalé **48** / Emerging twenty-first century design trends **50** / Timeline **52**

2. Research, brief and specification

Product design research **56** / Research methods **56** / The brief **64** / Identifying customer wants, needs and demands **67** / Interview: Stuart Haygarth **70** / The Product Design Specification (PDS) **72** / Common elements of the PDS **74**

3. Concept design

What is a concept design? **78** / Concept generation **78** / Concept generation methods **79** / Drawing techniques for product design **83** / Technical drawing **91** / Interview: Nendo **96** / Modelling **98** / Prototyping **101** / Concept evaluation and selection **105**

4. From manufacture to market

Detail design **108** / Design and manufacture **111** / Common materials **113** / Manufacturing processes **128** / Interview: Raw-Edges Design Studio **154** / Marketing and selling **156**

5. Contemporary issues

Green issues **168** / Interview: Max Lamb **182** / Ethical issues **184** / Inclusive design **190** / Emotional design **196**

6. Design education and beyond

Studying product design **202** / Design rights **209** / Interview: Tim Brown, IDEO **212** / Developing your design skills **214** / Engaging with industry **216**

••• Glossary **230** / Bibliography **233** / Further resources **234** / Useful addresses **235** / Index **236** / Picture credits and Acknowledgements **240**

Related study material is available on the Laurence King website at
www.laurenceking.com

It is fair to say that we live in an almost completely designed world. We are surrounded by a multitude of designed products, spaces, systems, services and experiences that have been created in response to some physical, emotional, social, cultural or economic need. In its simplest definition, product design is the design of products, but it also has a wider meaning that includes the generation of ideas, the development of concepts, product testing and manufacturing or the implementation of a physical object, system or service. The role of a product designer encompasses many disciplines, such as marketing, management, design and engineering, and also combines art, science and commerce in the goal of producing tangible artefacts.

What is product design?

Product design regularly blurs the boundaries between specialist areas such as lighting, furniture, graphic, fashion, interaction and industrial design. It can encompass the design of products such as spectacles, scissors, cameras, fly swats, waste bins, vases, fruit bowls, telephones, door mats, clothes hangers, razors, bottle stoppers, kettles, cigarette lighters, fire extinguishers, cutlery, salt and pepper shakers, shelving systems, MP3 players and computers. From chairs and lights to consumer and environmental objects, product design is about enriching quality of life, whether in the home, workplace or public domain. Product design is also a commercial activity that can help businesses by ensuring they create and sell products that appeal to, please or challenge consumers. It can provide ways of answering unmet needs, improving function and appearance, or offer new ways of critically engaging with objects. Design is fundamentally about making things better: better for consumers and users, better for business, and better for the world.

The Industrial Revolution, which began in Britain during the eighteenth century, saw the emergence of mass production, with the production of goods revolutionized by new manufacturing processes and the division of labour. Historically, products had been conceived and manufactured by craftspeople, and were often the work of an individual operating within an aesthetic tradition. Manufacturers rapidly identified the competitive advantages designers could bring to their products through divorcing designing and making, and positioning designers as the planners of a complex process. The full integration of design into the industrial production process saw product design become an identifiable discipline, one that has evolved to play an important role in the wider process of developing new products of every type. In some cases this is for high-volume (mass) production, but it can also be for smaller batch production or even one-off products, with designers re-engaging with the notion of neglected craft traditions.

The activity of product design is always relevant to any company manufacturing physical products, and especially consumer (or consumer-facing) products. The word 'product' is widely, and confusingly, used to describe everything, from a life insurance scheme to a new savings account.

Opposite
Product designers are directly involved in the creation of a wide range of products. Clockwise from top left: Blanke Ark by Blueroom Designstudio, Innovativoli Industridesign & Kadabra Productdesign, 2008; Craftsman power tool by IDEO for Chervon, 2006; iPhone 3GS by Jonathan Ive and Apple Design Studio, 2009; Girls Ski Helmut by Per Finne for Kari Traa AS, 2008; My Beautiful Backside by Doshi & Levien for Moroso, 2008; Picturemate Printer by Industrial Facility with Epson Design, 2005; and retro design Fiat 500C by Roberto Giolito, 2009, alongside original 1957 model by Dante Giacosa.

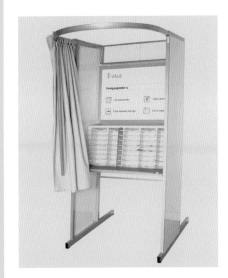

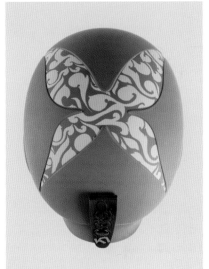

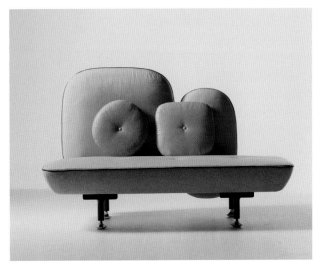

But, wherever 'hardware' and people interact, there you will find product design relevance. Perhaps less obviously, many manufacturers of industrial products benefit greatly from the integration of designers, design thinking and design process into their normal development activities. This is especially true of any manufacturer whose products need an edge in a competitive climate.

For any company involved in the manufacture and marketing of products, the design of the product affects nearly every aspect of the company's business – most obviously and directly on marketing, research and development (R&D), and new product development, but also upon logistics, distribution, sales, public relations (PR) and customer services. This is why senior management typically exerts such interest and influence over the process. Most crucially for a company, the design of its products is invariably the single most important manifestation of its brand.

Public services also make use of product design. This may involve the design of furniture, street furniture, interactive facilities (such as public information points), transport systems and public service equipment (such as fire, police and ambulance), as well as medical, health and even military hardware. They may focus on improving learning, services, environments or other facilities, or simply on enhancing the quality of life for the products' users or operators.

Product design is increasingly being seen as an important strategic tool in creating preference and deeper emotional values for the consumer. Its benefits for the consumer include products that are more usable, attractive, reliable and cost-effective, and that enable greater emotional ties. These benefits may result in the consumer having increased loyalty to the product in question.

Types of products

Product design covers the range of different types of products outlined below. These classifications are not intended to be viewed as unique or complete, but as fluid and overlapping. Individual products may appear in one or more classification or cross the boundaries.

Consumer products

The largest category of objects, by some margin, that a product designer is directly involved in is that of **consumer products**. Such products cover a wide range of designed objects including lighting, domestic appliances, medical products, audio-video equipment, office equipment, motor cars, personal computers and furniture. Consumer products need to work on a number of levels: they need to work well (function), they need to look good (aesthetics), and they need to be made available at a suitable cost (to both the client and the customer). A feature of many of these types of product is that they possess numerous components and are, therefore, designed by a team of people including mechanical and electronic engineers, **ergonomists** (who assess the fit between a person and their work, considering the job being done and the demands on the worker, the equipment used, how appropriate

it is for the task, and the information used) and manufacturing specialists. A vital feature of modern consumer products is that they have an appropriate appearance and operability; they must also project the right brand values of the product and of the manufacturing (or selling) company.

One-off artistic works

Some classic designed products are considered as much works of art as the works of a designer. The iPod, the Coca-Cola® bottle and the Volkswagen Beetle car are frequently cited examples in this regard. However, the creation of actual one-off limited-edition designed products has been a growing area for product designers in recent years. Many designers regularly create one-off pieces for the yearly design shows at locations throughout the world, such as the Milano Salone, the ICFF (International Contemporary Furniture Fair) in New York, and the London Design Festival. Within the confines of this type of product, appearance is the primary driver; functionality tends to be less important.

Z. Island by Zaha Hadid Architects, 2006, an example of one-off artistic product design, is a radical innovation in kitchen design that features an intelligent environment for browsing the internet, watching television, or listening to music while cooking.

 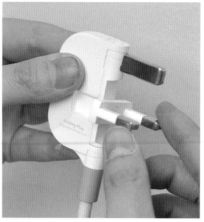 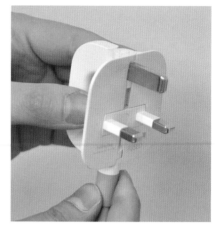

Consumables

The next group of products is **consumables** such as packaged butter, motor oil, bottled water, newspapers or fizzy drinks. Here, the focus for the product designer is mainly in the design of the packaging, branding and advertising campaigns. Product designers tend not to be involved in the design of the consumable itself – be that butter, oil or a soft drink – but in the product's packaging, branding, advertising and marketing.

Bulk or continuous engineering products

The term '**bulk products**' (also known as continuous engineering products) generally covers raw materials used in the manufacture of other products. This includes metal rolled sections, **rod** and **bar stock plastics**, woven sheet and foil, and laminates. Product designers may occasionally be involved in the processes and manufacturing of these products, such as in **embossing** (the process of creating a three-dimensional image or design in paper and other ductile materials), surface texture and finishes for other products.

Industry products

Industry products are items or assemblies that are bought by a manufacturing company for assembling into their own products. The appearance of this type of product is secondary to the primary requirements of functionality and performance. These products include ball and roller bearings, electric motors and controllers, circuit boards, crane hooks and gas turbine engines for aircraft.

Industrial equipment products

Industrial equipment products are self-contained devices (i.e. machines) that perform a complex function and are intended for use within industry. Again, the appearance of this type of product is secondary to its functioning and performance. Among these types of products are industrial work-stations, machine tools, goods vehicles, earth-moving machinery and passenger aircraft.

Above
Folding Plug, designed by Min-Kyu Choi, 2009, 2010 Brit Insurance Design of the Year winner. This ingenious space-saving plug demonstrates how designers can transform an everyday impractical object into something more innovative.

Below
Perrier water bottle, an example of a consumable and packaging design.

Special purpose products

Special purpose products include jigs, bespoke tooling, fixtures, special purpose robotics machinery, and specialized manufacturing and assembly machinery. This type of product is usually produced to order as single items (one of a kind) or a small series. The design and development of these products generally takes place specifically for one customer. Product designers involved in the development of this type of product need to be flexible, as the types of tasks change rapidly from one contract to the next. The majority of product design companies involved in this class of product are small to medium-sized enterprises (SMEs).

Industrial plant

Industrial plant consists of industrial equipment products and devices to provide control and connections between them. The plant and devices are usually designed to special order and bought from specialist suppliers. This type of product typically incorporates other products, and the task of designing them, and their associated components, is usually the suppliers' responsibility. Examples of this type of product include plant and components for water purification systems, electric power station equipment and telephone networks.

Above left
Jet engine, an example of an industry product.

Above right
Airbus A380 passenger jet, an example of an industrial equipment product.

Below left
A purified water-filling plant, an example of industrial plant.

Below right
KR5 Arc Hollow Wrist robotic arm from Kuka Automation + Robotics, 2008, an example of a special purpose product.

What does a product designer do?

Product designers design many of the things that we commonly use in our day-to-day activities, from toothbrushes to kettles, DIY tools to mobile phones, vacuum cleaners to laptops. A product designer's role includes making things easier to use, perhaps by improving particular aspects of a product's function; making products more efficiently, by exploiting the latest manufacturing and technological developments; making products cheaper to produce by utilizing new and innovative materials; or enhancing a product's emotional appeal through exploring and pushing new aesthetic boundaries.

The work of the product designer involves at its core some form of problem-solving. It typically starts with a problem statement given to the designer by the client, or the company involved can initiate the statement in-house. Generally speaking, product design problems have a set goal, some constraints within which the goal should be achieved, and some criteria by which a successful solution can be judged.

There are three main categories of product design: routine, where everything the designer needs to know is provided; **variant**, where some aspects of a brief are open to development; and **creative**, a more unusual scenario where new products or inventions are required.

Product designers are heavily involved in the process of taking a product from a description of users' needs and wants to a developed brief, making initial sketches, preparing detailed drawings, making models and working **prototypes**. In recent years, the role has moved beyond its traditional **hard skills** of concept modelling, new product development, styling and product graphics to embrace newer **soft skills** such as branding, **CAD (computer-aided design)**, trend and forecasting, and graphical user interface (GUI) products based on the foundation of qualitative user and market research.

In general, a product designer today observes people, listens and asks questions, holds conversations with people (end-users, manufacturers, clients, managers, engineers and so on), generates design ideas, communicates them to others, explores and evaluates, makes and tests prototypes, produces detailed drawings, and possibly becomes involved in the final manufacture of the product(s) itself.

Finally, another important aspect of design to be emphasized is the role of the client. The client expects the designer to interpret the problem set before him or her and contribute to it perhaps by highlighting sub-problems and opportunities that the client has initially overlooked. The client also expects the designer to resolve these problems, while at the same time dealing with issues of form, materiality, aesthetics and manufacturing, among others. The client–designer relationship works in two ways: the client expects the designer to consider other problems that may arise during the design process, and the designer expects a certain degree of freedom and flexibility to interpret and define new problems and issues that the client may not have considered. For this reason there is always, not unsurprisingly, an element of tension between

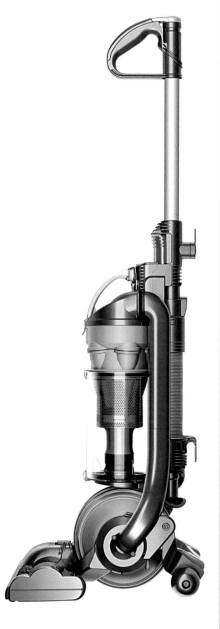

the two. Both are dependent on each other and both are anxious about the other exerting too much control. The harmony of their relationship is therefore a hugely important factor in the successful development of new products.

Are product designers artists?

It can be hard to separate design from art. This is particularly difficult today given the rise in the number of 'celebrity designers' producing one-off pieces for design shows and auction houses across the world, or even to exhibit limited-edition pieces in galleries, just as artists do. The products of design are often seen by the public as works of art and designers themselves are often referred to as artists. In recent years, the creative processes involved in art and design practice, and the talents required to participate in them, have undoubtedly come closer.

Opposite
The DC24 Dyson Ball™ upright vacuum cleaner is a good example of variant design, where some aspects of the design brief were open to development.

Left
The Tournament, designed by Jaime Hayon, 2009, a leading proponent of DesignArt. Here, 32 handcrafted ceramic pieces are created in a oversized chess set, which was launched at the London Design Festival. Hayon's work regularly blurs the boundaries between design and art.

Creating a product

Typically, the creation of a new product begins with an idea and ends with the production of a physical artefact. The creation of any new product is a collaborative venture involving many individuals working together as a team. There are many different disciplines involved in the process. Some of the key people involved include product designers, engineers, anthropologists (who study the origin, behaviour, and the physical, social and cultural development of people), marketing personnel, sales staff, ergonomists, manufacturers, clients and customers.

Four key functions are almost universally involved in new product design and development:

Design

The design team is responsible for the overall physical form of the product that will best meet the customers' needs. Design, in this sense, can mean the engineering design (i.e. mechanical, electrical, software and so on), and the product design (i.e. aesthetics, ergonomics, user interface and so on).

Research

Increasingly, researchers such as anthropologists and **ethnographers** (ethnographers study culture and cultural processes using multiple ways to research, observe and document people, events or artefacts) are asked to support the design and development of new products by bringing their expertise and knowledge of observing and recording how consumers interact with the designed world. Typically, research staff are more involved towards the front end of the process, exploring the real needs and desires of end-users.

Marketing

The marketing department is the point of contact between the company developing the product and its customers. Marketing individuals often facilitate the identification of product opportunities, help define market segmentation, and support the design team with the identification of customer needs, wants and desires. Typically, the marketing department also oversees the launch of the product, helps set the price plans and negotiates communication between the company and its customers.

Manufacturing

The manufacturing team is responsible for designing and operating the production system that produces the product. Sometimes, the manufacturing department also undertakes tasks associated with the purchase of raw materials and the distribution and installation of the new product.

The main stages of product design

In summary:
This chart shows the breakdown of the elements involved in the process of designing and producing a product design. It is important to remember, however, that some stages may occur in a different sequence or may even be omitted altogether, as each product has its own unique set of requirements and the product designer's role may, as a result, vary.

Research
- background stage
- exploratory stage

The brief
- identifying customer needs
- completing the Product Design Specification (PDS)

Concept design
- generation of ideas
- sketches, drawings and renderings
- evaluation of concept

Design development
- technical drawings
- prototypes

Detail design
- exploring materials
- exploring manufacturing techniques
- testing and refinement

Production
- marketing
- supply
- disposal

INTERVIEW
Julia Lohmann

Biography
Julia Lohmann's work explores provocative contemporary issues such as the contradictions in our relationship to animals as sources of food and materials. The German-born, London-based designer regularly transforms the practice of product design into a rich and complex medium of social investigation and debate. By working with off-cuts of leather and other meat industry waste products, she probes those contradictions while giving value to leftovers. Her work is often polemical, but everything Lohmann designs is intended to be useful.

Interview

What is your definition of product design?
I have a very wide definition of product design; or rather, I do not really believe in the segmentation of design into different disciplines. Design in its widest sense is about identifying problems and addressing them. Product design concerns itself with the three-dimensional world and our interaction with objects.

What do you do in this field?
With my products I trigger thoughts about our interaction with products. How do we sustain ourselves? How much do we know about the objects we buy and consume? The objects I make have a dual function: you can use them as objects in the established sense, for example, by sitting on them, but also as objects that help you consider and define your own position towards the man-made world. A writer once described them as 'Ethical Barometers'.

How do you start to design a product?
I usually start by identifying an area of thought that intrigues me; for example, a question I have been asked or a fundamental one facing our society. Why do we accept something? Where are we going? A fascination with a particular material, such as seaweed, is another starting point. Nature, science, travel or social interaction can all spark off projects. The final outcome of the process from inspiration to production is not predetermined. I do not sit down planning to make another chair or light; the object becomes a chair or light because I believe it to be the best possible way of communicating a particular thought or concept.

What problems do you commonly have to address?
I address the same problems that every designer is faced with: Can it be made? What should it be made of? How do I source materials? Who can help me make it? What happens with it when it breaks? Can it have another life or function? How can I design out waste? I also address questions through the concept behind the design: Why are we acting like we do? Have we made the most of this material? Do we understand how and why we like something? What does an object say about its origins, maker, user and life cycle? I am trying to design the story the object tells just as carefully as the object itself.

Opposite top left
Kelp Constructs, 2008. These seaweed lamps are one of the first experiments with kelp by the designer.

Opposite top right
Ruminant Bloom, 2004. These flower-like lights are made of preserved cow and sheep stomachs perhaps provoking mixed feelings somewhere between attraction and aversion.

Opposite bottom
Cowbenches, 2005. These benches explore the threshold between animal and material.

About this book

The aim of this book is to bridge the gap between traditional product design education and the fast-moving world of contemporary product design practice by demystifying the discipline and offering a variety of routes to a successful product design career. The text provides a general framework for the study and practice of product design, intended for use as a starting point for devising personal product design strategies.

Over the years, many models of the design process have been developed. There are descriptive and prescriptive models and many of these historical models suggest a strict linear design process. This book, however, stresses that the modern design process is highly flexible, iterative, dynamic and often overlapping, and certain tasks may well be ignored, repeated and conducted out of sequence.

Chapter 1 provides a brief historical and cultural context for product design from 1750 to the present day and introduces some key figures in the discipline. Chapter 2 goes on to explain the early stages of the design process, from research to brief to **Product Design Specification (PDS)**. Chapter 3 explores the concept design stage and details the tasks associated with drawing up a number of different viable concept designs that satisfy the requirements outlined in the PDS. Chapter 4 covers the key stages of detail design, manufacture, marketing, branding, visual language development and sales. Chapter 5 explores and explains some of the more significant issues – green, ethical, inclusive and emotional – that surround modern product design practice. The final chapter covers a range of topics relating to design education and beyond, such as preparing for product design presentations and assessment, engaging with industry, and getting that all-important product design job in one of the most rewarding industry sectors in the world.

Each chapter is richly illustrated with examples of product design projects, artworks and diagrams. Boxes are included that provide useful information, guidelines and advice, and a number of interviews discuss key design issues with leading figures from the world of product design. A glossary, a list of valuable product design resources and a comprehensive further reading list are provided at the end of the book.

1.

Product design, as we understand it today, is a relatively young discipline.
It is generally recognized that it emerged as an activity during the Industrial
Revolution of the mid-eighteenth century. Until then, what is now commonly
described as craft production had existed as the sole means of producing
objects. Makers of objects were the originators of that design, or guardians
of a design handed down through generations of designer-makers, often
remaining unchanged or unquestioned. Since the emergence of product
design as a profession, the discipline has been characterized by a spirit of
reform. A number of individual designers, self-styled movements and writers
have attempted to establish its role in society. This chapter examines the
profession's development within a social, theoretical and cultural framework
from 1750 to the present day.

The Industrial Revolution:
1750s to 1850s

The Industrial Revolution heralded mass production. This industrialization
was characterized by factory owners commissioning specialists to supply
drawings and instructions that could be interpreted and manufactured by
semi-skilled or unskilled factory workers, producing goods in large numbers
far more economically than the previous craft methods. As the production
process became increasingly complex, and the business of making became
ever more divorced from the role of determining a product's form, a
profession known as 'product designer' emerged whose primary role was
to give form to these mass-produced items.

The mid-eighteenth century saw a number of significant industrial
developments. For instance, in 1752 Benjamin Franklin (1706–90) discovered
electricity and, by 1765, James Watt (1736–1819) had developed the steam

Josiah Wedgwood

Josiah Wedgwood (1730–95) spent most of his life in the Wedgwood family's
pottery business, which was based in Staffordshire. He was responsible for
revolutionizing pottery-manufacturing techniques in order to increase production
and sell to a wider market during an era largely characterized by handwork.
Faster production led to wider availability and increased affordability. Wedgwood
transformed the pottery industry and established a mass-manufacturing
production system, where he exploited advertisement by royal association
that elevated his pottery's status. Wedgwood's approach to manufacturing split
areas of labour into a production-line concept, which distinguished design from
manufacture and production. *Jasperware vase, twentieth century (right).*

engine, which enabled the rapid development of efficient semi-automated factories on a previously unimaginable scale. Without some notable earlier inventions, however, including the spinning jenny and the flying shuttle, some of the later achievements such as Watt's steam engine might never have been possible. Industrial mass production heralded the production of all sorts of consumer goods and modern transportation systems. The division of labour enabled factory owners to produce goods cheaply, eventually resulting in the workforce being paid low wages and regularly working long hours in horrendous and often dangerous conditions. Inevitably the drive for more and more goods at lower prices led to bitter poverty, poor living conditions and a miserable life for the working classes.

In the process of transition from handwork to industrial production, the planning of an object began to be separated from work by either hand or machine. Pattern books and portfolios were widely distributed in the mid-eighteenth century in order to solicit and secure orders. Furniture, for example, was produced in advance and offered for sale as finished pieces in larger magazines and sales catalogues. The first known pattern books of the early industrial era in Britain came from Thomas Sheraton (1751–1806) and Thomas Chippendale (1718–79), both of whom were to have a major influence throughout Europe. Design had, therefore, acquired significance not only for production but also for sales. Josiah Wedgwood (1730–95) founded his pottery factory in 1769 in Stoke-on-Trent in Staffordshire, Britain, to serve not only the aristocracy but to feed a wider market among the middle classes with more everyday pottery.

The Great Reform movements: 1850s to 1914

By the middle of the nineteenth century, the awful conditions in factories led to widespread worker unrest and the formation of workers' unions and parties. In 1867 Karl Marx (1818–83) wrote *Das Kapital*, one of the most important socio-economic books ever produced, in which he analysed the new structures of industrial production and society. The increasing mechanization of the Industrial Revolution encompassed not only production methods but the products themselves. The nineteenth century was the time of the engineer, and by the middle of that century the United States had taken over the leadership of engineering developments. In 1869, the east and west coasts of America were united by the Union Pacific Railway, and in 1874 the first electric streetcar debuted in New York. The following year, Thomas Edison (1847–1931) developed the incandescent light bulb and the microphone. Since 1851, Isaac Merrit Singer (1811–75) had been producing the household sewing machine, and Alexander Graham Bell (1847–1922) exhibited a working telephone at the Philadelphia World's Fair in 1876.

In Europe, at around the same time, a great deal of mechanical furniture
was being produced, including swivel chairs and space-saving folding
furniture for the increasing number of hair salons and offices that were
emerging. In Munich in 1854, Michael Thonet (1796–1871) presented his first
bentwood chairs, and by 1859 the Thonet chair No. 214 became the model
for all bentwood chairs and a prototype for modern mass-produced furniture.

Towards the end of the nineteenth century, a second wave of industrialization
spread across Europe. The technical advances of the century resulted in new
methods of production, new commodities and equipment with new functions.

Arts and Crafts: 1854–1914

A number of significant reform movements emerged during the second half
of the nineteenth century that advocated a return to nature and handcraft as
an answer to the excessive development of industry, large cities and mass
production. William Morris (1834–96), the father of the Arts and Crafts
Movement, was the most important voice for the renewal of artistic handwork.
Morris, along with the art critic and philosopher John Ruskin (1819–1900) and
the painter and illustrator Walter Crane (1845–1915), took inspiration from the
Pre-Raphaelites (a group of English painters, poets and critics, founded in 1848
by Dante Gabriel Rossetti and others) in their pursuit of a return to nature as well
as to clear and simple organic forms. Morris and Ruskin also campaigned for a
better quality of life for those living in an industrialized society.

William Morris

William Morris (1834–96) was, among many things, a poet and dreamer, a businessman and a political campaigner. He had great design and craft skills and executed several pieces of work of outstanding beauty in wallpapers, in printed, woven and embroidered textiles, and in book production. Morris founded a firm, Morris & Co., to retail furnishings produced in his own workshops, where craftsmen were given free rein. The firm's products, however, while intended to brighten the lives of ordinary people, were too expensive to sell to any but the wealthy.
Anemone wallpaper, nineteenth century (right).

Art Nouveau: 1880–1910

Around the turn of the century, Art Nouveau, a reform movement shaped by the Arts and Crafts philosophy, developed into a fully formed international movement in many of the key centres of Europe, including Paris, Nancy, Brussels, Vienna, Barcelona, Glasgow, Darmstadt, Munich, Dresden, Weimar and Hagen. Art Nouveau was known by many names throughout Europe. In Britain it was called Decorative Style, in Belgium and France Art Nouveau, in Germany Jugendstil ('youth style'), in Italy the Stile Liberty, in Austria Sezessionsstil, and in Spain Modernista.

A significant amount of Art Nouveau work was influenced by geometrical forms drawn from Japanese art as the Western world discovered Asian culture. This was due in some part to a trade treaty being agreed, in 1854, between the United States and Japan that approved the import of Japanese

Writing desk and chair, by Henri van de Velde, 1897–98. The design displays an organic aesthetic common to Art Nouveau.

Christopher Dresser

Christopher Dresser (1834–1904) is generally acknowledged as being one of the first independent product designers. Born in Glasgow, he won a place at the newly established Government School of Design at the age of thirteen. This new art training system was set up to improve the standard of British design for industry by joining the disciplines of art and science. Dresser championed design reform in nineteenth-century Britain, while embracing modern manufacturing techniques in the development of a range of products from textiles, ceramics, glass, furniture and metalware. He was a household name, famed for his promotion of product design as a force for furnishing ordinary people with well-made, efficient and engaging goods. His commercial success is all the more remarkable as he also pioneered what we now recognize as the spruce, simple, modern aesthetic. Some of Dresser's products, notably his 1880s metal toast racks, are still in production today. *Geometric teapot, 1880 (right).*

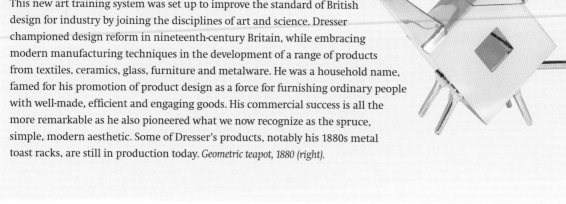

art after almost 200 years of isolation. At this time, much Japanese art used imagery from nature – birds, insects and botanical studies of plant life – as primary sources of inspiration. Moreover, Japanese art's use of flat perspectives and block colouring was a revelation to many Western artists. One of the main aims of Art Nouveau was to transcend the boundary between pure and applied art. Practitioners were supposed to design not just 'art' but jewellery, wallpaper, fabric, furniture, tableware and more. As a response to mass-produced wares, the movement strove for a comprehensive artistic reformation of all areas of life.

Victor Horta (1861–1947) and Henri van de Velde (1863–1957) were two of the most famous representatives of Art Nouveau in Belgium. Horta utilized the new materials of iron and glass that had been exploited in the building of London's Crystal Palace in 1851 and the Eiffel Tower in Paris from 1884 to 1889. He used the floral ornamentation of Art Nouveau as both a surface decoration and a construction element. Among Horta's most important works are the Maison du Peuple (1896–99), the Tassel House (1893) and villas Solvay (1894). Henri van de Velde enjoyed more success than Horta in his work as a theoretician and furniture designer. He demanded a stronger relationship between organic ornamentation and function in the theories that he disseminated through various publications and lectures.

Modernism to pre-war luxury and power: 1900s to 1945

The first half of the twentieth century was a time of political and economic upheaval across much of Europe and also in Asia. At the end of World War I, Germany signed the Treaty of Versailles, which resulted in the loss of a significant part of its territory, limited the size of the German army and imposed massive reparations. It was not until 1933, when Adolf Hitler (1889–1945) became the leader of Germany and democracy was abolished in favour of Fascism, that a massive rearming process took place. In Russia, the Civil War (1918–21) led to the creation of a Soviet government headed by Vladimir Ilyich Lenin (1870–1924) and later to the Communist regime of Joseph Stalin (1879–1953). In Italy, Benito Mussolini (1883–1945) seized power as a Fascist dictator, promising to create a 'New Roman Empire'.

The history of China in this period was also one of political turmoil and endless wars. Decades of struggle preceded the establishment of the Communist Party in 1921 and followed it with fighting between the Communists and the ruling Nationalist party, the Kuomintang (KMT). Throughout the 1930s, the increasingly militaristic Japanese empire also continued its push into Chinese territory.

Above
Wenger Swiss Army Knife, 1970. The multi-functional knife and tool was originally developed in 1908. The knife is held in the permanent collection of the Museum of Modern Art in New York.

Deutscher Werkbund: 1907–35
The Deutscher Werkbund was founded in 1907 in Munich as a response to widely held worries that Germany's rapid industrialization and modernization were coming at the cost of its national culture. It involved artists, architects, craftsmen, industrialists, politicians and designers. Its main leaders were Hermann Muthesius (1861–1927), Henri van de Velde, Peter Behrens (1868–1940), Karl Ernst Osthaus (1874–1921) and Friedrich Naumann (1860–1919).

Peter Behrens

Peter Behrens (1868–1940) initially worked as a painter, illustrator and bookbinder. At the turn of the century, however, he was one of the leaders of architectural reform and was a major designer of factories and office buildings in brick, steel and glass. In 1907, AEG (Allgemeine Elektricitäts Gesellschaft) retained Behrens as artistic consultant. He designed the entire corporate identity (including logotype, product design and publicity) and for that he is considered the first industrial designer in history. Behrens was never an employee for AEG but worked in the capacity of artistic consultant, and in 1910 designed the AEG Turbine Factory. *Fan (model GB1), 1908 (right).*

The Werkbund was primarily interested in the link between the artistic and the economic aspects of mass production. It was against revivalism and believed that architecture should be a representation of the zeitgeist, or 'spirit of the age'. Industrial development was very much the spirit of Germany at this point and this was reflected in the works of the Werkbund. With this in mind, it set out to produce architecture that utilized mass production but still made use of craftsmanship. Handcraft and art were still to be used, but in a way that complemented the spirit of modern Germany. The founders set out to prove that through cooperation between the applied arts and industry a national style in tune with the modern age could be developed.

Above
Alvar Aalto vase, 1936, produced by Iittala. It was first shown in the Finnish Pavilion at the International Exhibition in Paris, 1937.

Marcel Breuer

Marcel Breuer (1902–81) is best known as one of the early twentieth century's most influential furniture designers. At the Bauhaus, Breuer became one of the first apprentices to join the new furniture workshop. His first piece was the hand-carved and painted Romantic Chair (also known as the African Chair). By 1923 his work, most notably the Wood-slat Chair, was increasingly influenced by the abstract aesthetic of De Stijl. Firmly established as one of the most prolific members of the Bauhaus, and a protégé of its director Walter Gropius, Breuer eventually ran the furniture workshop at the new Bauhaus in Weimar, where one of his first projects was the 1926 Steel Club armchair (later renamed the Wassily, after the Bauhaus teacher Wassily Kandinsky). *Wassily Chair (model B3), 1927 (right).*

Ludwig Mies van der Rohe

Ludwig Mies van der Rohe (1886–1969) was one of the most important designers of the Modern movement, and his architecture is famous for its transparency and clarity. He designed one of the most influential buildings in history, the German pavilion at the World Exhibition in Barcelona in 1929, and also created the Barcelona Chair, a design icon made of flat strips of chromed steel welded together by hand and with leather upholstery. Between the 1940s and 1960s, van der Rohe designed some of his most famous buildings, including the Farnsworth House, Illinois (1946–50), the Lake Shore Drive Apartments, Chicago (1950–52), and his masterpiece, the famous 37-storey bronze and glass Seagram Building in New York (1954–58). *Barcelona Chair, 1929 (right).*

Bauhaus: 1919–33

The Bauhaus, which translates literally as 'building house', opened in Weimar in 1919 and, under its first director Walter Gropius (1883–1969), integrated magnificently the disciplines of art and design under one roof. The Bauhaus made an invaluable contribution to the Modern movement in design because it brought highly creative and talented thinkers and practitioners together in one place.

Several of the most important individuals in the history of design were instrumental in the running of the Bauhaus at one time or another, such as Gropius, Marcel Breuer (1902–81), Ludwig Mies van der Rohe (1886–1969), Johannes Itten (1888–1967), Wassily Kandinsky (1866–1944) and Hannes Meyer (1889–1954). By 1923, the Bauhaus had staged a landmark exhibition that featured a number of important designs including Gerrit Rietveld's Red/Blue chair of 1918 to 1923 and graphics incorporating the New Typography inspired by the Dutch art movement De Stijl and Russian Constructivism. This success was relatively short-lived and, when the Bauhaus' budget had been slashed by half in 1924 and the Nazis seized power in Weimar in 1925, the Masters voted to break up the school and relocate it to Dessau.

With Nazism on the ascent, political pressure mounted, and in 1928 Gropius resigned. Both of his successors, Meyer and van der Rohe, spent most of their directorships mired in political strife before agreeing to dissolve the Bauhaus in 1933. Many of the Bauhaus Masters emigrated to the United States to escape persecution. In 1938, a retrospective of Bauhaus design was held at the Museum of Modern Art, New York, which reinforced the school as the most important design institution of the twentieth century.

Modernism – The International Style: 1914–39

Modernism was the dominant force in twentieth-century Western culture, influencing art, music, literature and design. The main characteristics of this movement were its emphasis on experimentation, formalism and objectivism. As the century began, the Modern movement in design believed it was necessary to create buildings and products that expressed the spirit of a new age and that would surpass the styles, materials and technologies of earlier work. The aesthetics of the Modern movement in architecture and design differed radically from what had gone before. Modernist designers felt nineteenth-century architecture and design was usually either oppressively bound to past styles or annoyingly picturesque and eclectic.

Some architects, enraptured by the powerful machines that were developed in the late nineteenth century, sought to devise an aesthetic that conveyed the sleekness and energy of a machine. This aesthetic crystallized in the International Style of the 1920s and 1930s. 'Truth to materials' and 'form follows function' were two of this movement's most representative mottos. Modernism gained momentum after World War II, when its theories were particularly influential in the planning and rebuilding of European towns and cities that had been destroyed in the war, and also in the building of North American cities.

Art Deco: 1920–39

Art Deco was an eclectic decorative arts style that first appeared in Paris in the first half of the twentieth century. Characteristics of the style manifested themselves in a range of decorative arts and architecture from as early as 1910, and spread across the Western world until the 1940s. The Art Deco style made its first large-scale public appearance, drawing an estimated audience of over 16 million, at the Exposition Internationale des Arts Décoratifs et Industriels Modernes held in Paris in 1925. The fact that the name 'Art Deco' was drawn from the title of this exhibition highlights the significance attributed to the event in launching the style.

The Art Deco style drew inspiration from an eclectic range of sources including the Bauhaus, avant-garde movements such as Cubism, Russian Constructivism and Italian Futurism, American developments in industrial design and architecture, and even the principles of aerodynamics. The range of material affected by the Art Deco style was as eclectic and far-reaching as the influences that shaped it – interior and product design, textiles, furniture, jewellery, fine art, sculpture, photography, film and architecture all exploited, and in turn furthered, the remit of the style. The 1980s witnessed the revival of much of Art Deco's excess and exuberance in the works of Post-Modern designers such as Robert Venturi, Hans Hollein and Charles Jencks.

Radio Wireless, Ekco AD-65, designed by Wells Coates, 1932. Bakelite, named after its inventor Leo Baekeland, was the first plastic to be used for making radios, and was ideal for the Art Deco-style designs of the 1920s and 1930s. It was useful for its mouldable and good electrical insulating properties.

Streamlining: 1930s

Streamlining evolved in the United States in the 1930s, a decade that has often been referred to as the 'streamlined' decade. Streamlining – literally, the shaping of an object, such as an aircraft body or wing, to reduce the amount of drag or resistance to motion through a stream of air – was applied to a vast array of products, from buses to prams, coffee machines to pencil sharpeners, and was widely employed by designers. Key figures during the era were Raymond Loewy (1893–1986), Norman Bel Geddes (1893–1958), Henry Dreyfuss (1904–72) and Walter Dorwin Teague (1883–1960).

The use of streamlining in the design of products quickly became widespread and the main designers involved became household names. Harold van Doren, for instance, observed in 1940: 'Streamlining has taken the world by storm' and Raymond Loewy became the first designer to be featured on the front cover of *Time* magazine with the strapline 'He streamlines the sales curve' (see p. 160). Streamlining added value to products at little or no extra cost and helped American manufacturers stimulate their sales figures and regain healthy profits during the difficult years of the Depression following the Wall Street Crash.

The post-war period: 1945 to 1970s

The post-war period, and particularly the 1950s, witnessed deep changes in politics, the economy and design. In Germany, Italy and Japan the main focus was on recovery and their efforts were on basic needs – food, shelter, rebuilding their economies, their countries and their governments. The United States, on the other hand, survived the war relatively unscathed, which allowed it to quickly establish itself as an economic and design leader well into the 1950s. Post-war, the influence of American culture (i.e. design, music, movies) spread wide into Europe, particularly to Germany and Italy – Coca-Cola® and Lucky Strike cigarettes quickly became symbols of a new international lifestyle. In China the Communists seized power with the founding of the People's Republic of China in 1949. After over a century of fighting on China's territories, the conditions for the development of a national industry and economy finally existed in the mid-1950s, some two centuries later than many Western nations.

The food, clothes and fuel shortages caused by World War II resulted in something of a post-war wave of consumption in the early 1950s. Around this time, however, most key needs had been met and industry found itself having to revive consumer demand through new models, forms and technical improvements, particularly in the United States and Western Europe. In an effort to safeguard continual sales and sustain the escalating economy, the role of advertising increased. The sales of automobiles and domestic electrical appliances boomed during this time, and the rapid development of television and transistor technology promised continually growing markets. Notable designers of this time included Henry Dreyfuss, Norman Bel Geddes and Raymond Loewy. Although Japanese electronics manufacturers appeared as early as the 1950s as competition to American manufacturers, the American economy was prosperous and looked optimistically to the future.

Raymond Loewy

Raymond Loewy (1893–1986) has been described as the 'father' of the American design profession. Beginning as a fashion illustrator, he soon dedicated his talent to the field of product design. Working as a consultant for more than 200 companies, he created product designs for everything from cigarette packs and refrigerators, to cars and spacecraft. Loewy's first design commission, in 1929, was for Gestetner, a British manufacturer of duplicating machines. He was commissioned to improve the appearance of the Gestetner Ream Duplicator 66 machine and in three days he designed the shell that was to encase Gestetner duplicators for the next 40 years. It has been suggested that Loewy's success is largely due to the fact that he knew industrial (product) design was basically about advertising and selling and not about truth to materials and honest functions. *Pencil Sharpener, 1933 (right).*

Charles and Ray Eames

Charles (1907–78) and Ray (1912–88) Eames were responsible for some of the most important examples of twentieth-century design work. Between them they created more than 200 designs for furniture, toys, exhibitions, films, graphics and architecture over the course of almost half a century. The Eames are widely regarded as setting the standard for design excellence and are perhaps best known for experimenting with wood moulding that led to many products, including bedside chairs and other furniture, and they also designed using materials such as fibreglass, plastic and aluminium. Their 1956 Lounge Chair, constructed in leather and plywood, became a design icon of the 1960s and 1970s. *Ottoman 671 armchair and footstool, 1955 (right).*

The Marshall Plan of 1947, designed to aid European economic recovery, provided Germany and other countries with a share of over $12 billion. With this financial support Germany began the German *Wirtschaftswunder* ('Economic Miracle'). Perhaps the most significant design-related development in post-war Germany was the establishment of the Ulm Academy for Design in 1953. Max Bill (1908–94), the first director, saw the Ulm Academy as a successor to the Bauhaus in its teaching, philosophy, methodology and politics and, more generally, the belief that design had an important role to play in society. From the early 1960s to its closure in 1968, under the leadership of Tomás Maldonado (from 1964 to 1966) and Herbert Ohl (from 1966 to 1968) the Academy focused its design programme on technical problem-solving and the theory of information and technical systems. Near its eventual demise the academy worked in close collaboration with companies such as Kodak and Braun.

Italy, after World War II, emerged as one of the foremost design nations. The flexibility of the Italian workforce coupled with relatively low wages and financial aid from America helped Italy become a major design force in post-war times. While American design tended to be market-led and German design tended to be theoretical, Italian design after the war was characterized by improvisation and a culture that did not separate art, design and economics. Arguably the best-known products to appear from Italy were the Vespa scooter and the Fiat 500, although furniture and fashion soon became Italian export successes. A number of leading Italian furniture companies were established around this time, including Zanotta, Cappellini, Arflex, Kartell and Cassina.

Dieter Rams

Dieter Rams (1932–) was one of the most influential product designers of the late twentieth century. As head of design at Braun, the German consumer electronics manufacturer, he developed and maintained an elegant, legible, yet rigorous visual language for all its products. Rams is particularly well known for his ten principles of 'Good Design', that a product is: innovative; useful; aesthetic; helps us to understand it; unobtrusive; honest; durable; is consequent to the last detail; is concerned with the environment; and is as minimally designed as possible. Rams remained design director of Braun until 1995, when he was succeeded by Peter Schneider. During his 40 years at Braun, Rams developed products to be manufactured at vast scale and used daily by millions of people through his quest for 'Good Design'.
Braun SK55 stereo radiogramme, 1956, by Rams and Hans Gugelot (right).

'Good Form': Mid-1950s to 1968

In the early 1960s, 'Good Form' was characterized by functionality, simple forms, utility, durability, timelessness, order, clarity, solid workmanship, suitable materials, finished details, technology, and environmental responsibility. This stylistic principle, which emanated largely from the Ulm Academy, began to stimulate serious criticism of functionalism by the mid-1960s. Advances in technology, transportation, communication, materials, manufacturing processes, and even space travel, inspired designers to experiment in the creation of new products and systems. By the late 1960s, consumer taste and designers' ideologies combined into a counterculture that stood against mass consumption. During this time design drew more and more energy and ideas from the student protests in Europe and the United States, from pop art, pop music and film. Italy emerged as the leading design nation in the world. Prominent designers of this time included Dieter Rams, Marco Zanuso (1916–2001), Richard Sapper (b. 1932), Ettore Sottsass (1917–2007), Mario Bellini (b. 1935), Verner Panton (1926–98), and 'Cesare' Joe Colombo (1930–71).

Many of these designers made a name for themselves through their experimental work with the new man-made materials being used in furniture and product design of the time, such as polypropylene, polyurethane, polyester and polystyrol. Some of the most iconic design pieces ever created were produced during this period: Joe Colombo's 4860 stackable plastic chair, Verner Panton's Panton chair, Mario Bellini's Divisumma 18 electric calculator, Richard Sapper's Tizio lamp, and Ettore Sottsass and Perry A. King's Valentine typewriter.

Above
Valentine typewriter, designed by Ettore Sottsass with Perry A. King for Olivetti & Co., 1969. This iconic 'anti-machine' machine was designed for use 'anyplace but an office'. A design classic, it expresses the mood of its time with its new mobility in a light, modern, plastic casing made from ABS.

Experimentation and anti-design: 1965–76

The oil crisis of 1973 and subsequent price controls and rationing was a turning point for design. Until then, plastic was viewed as modern and high-tech, but it quickly became seen as cheap, tacky, tasteless and environmentally harmful. Set against the economic turmoil of the early 1970s, protests against the war in Vietnam, and student unrest in major European and American cities, the role of design in capitalist societies was being increasingly questioned. Many designers at this time perceived their roles as pawns of industry, perpetuating value systems that no longer served a useful social purpose. Some opted to work independently and experimentally for themselves, and many incorporated political statements and embraced social concepts into their work.

A number of the leading design counter-movements were formed in Italy. By the end of the 1960s, a new generation of Italian designers were dissatisfied with their working conditions and with the consumption-led 'good form' of many designed products. These designers protested against established design norms and the obsession with consumption. The main centres of this 'radical design' movement were to be found mainly in Milan, Turin and Florence and included the design groups Superstudio (established in 1966), Archizoom Associati (1966), Gruppo 9999 (1967), Gruppo Strum (1966), and Alchimia (1976). By the mid-1970s, most of the counter-movements had disbanded and Italian avant-garde design languished in uncertainty until the start of the 1980s.

Pratone, designed by G. Ceretti, P. Derossi and R. Rosso, 1971. The chair is made from polyurethane foam and is intended to recreate the effect of lounging about in a large grassy meadow.

Joe Colombo

Joe Cesare Colombo (1930–71) was a prolific and illustrious Italian designer intent on creating visionary products, interior and furniture designs. In 1962, Colombo, in collaboration with his brother Gianni, developed the Acrilica desk lamp for Oluce. Later that year, Colombo opened his own design practice in Milan and initially focused on architectural and interior design projects – mostly mountain hostels and ski resort hotels. He designed many products and interiors for a long list of clients, including Kartell, Alessi, Alitalia, Bieffeplast, Flexform and Boffi. A common theme in his work was multi-functionality and adaptability such as the Additional Living System (1967–68), the Tube chair (1969–70), and the Multi chair (1970), all of which were configurable by the user. Colombo received ADI (Associazione per il Disegno Industriale) awards in 1967 and 1968 as well as a Premio Compasso d'Oro in 1970. *4867 chair, 1968 (right).*

High-tech miniaturization: 1972–85

High-tech design brought together materials and prefabricated industrial elements in new relationships to create furniture and other products. High-tech is an acknowledged stylistic term to describe designs that emphasize technological aspects in their appearance. A famous example from the world of architecture is the Pompidou Centre in Paris, where the internal fixtures and fittings were positioned visibly on the exterior of the building. High-tech products drew upon visual references from the worlds of science, technology and/or electronics in their appearance, such as Norman Foster's Nomos furniture system or Matteo Thun's Container Cabinet (1985).

Opposite top
BeoSound 9000, designed by David Lewis, was launched by Bang & Olufsen in 1996.

Opposite bottom
Nomos Desking System, designed by Foster and Partners in collaboration with and manufactured by Tecno, 1987. The idea originally dates back to 1981 when the architects wanted something that could be used for a number of different functions – a meeting table, drawing board, or a stand to display models.

Achille Castiglioni

Achille Castiglioni (1914–2002) was one of the masters of twentieth-century Italian design. He was the main figurehead of the design triumvirate that included his brothers and partners, Pier Giacomo and Livio, with whom he designed many of his most iconic pieces. Livio left the partnership in 1952, but Achille and Pier Giacomo continued to work together until Pier Giacomo's death in 1968. Endearing symbols of their design approach are evident in their famous Mezzadro stool, which incorporated a tractor seat, and the Sgabello per Telefono stool (1957), which utilized a bicycle seat. The playful experimentation and the joy of the designed results became a trademark of the Castiglioni brothers' work. *Mezzadro stool, 1957 (right).*

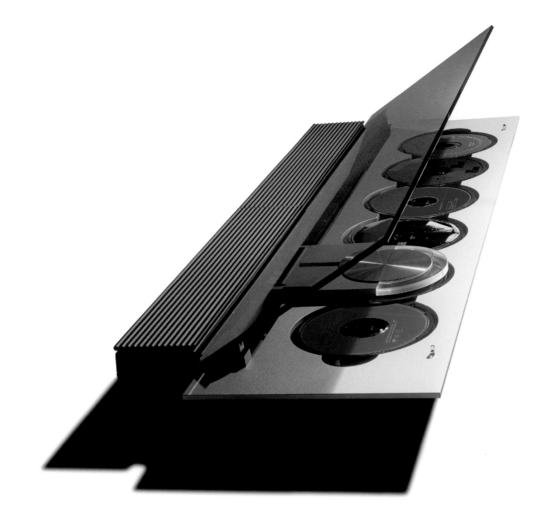

Richard Sapper

Richard Sapper (1932–), widely considered a leading twentieth-century designer, was born in Munich, where he studied philosophy, anatomy, graphics, engineering and economics at university. In 1956, he worked briefly in the design division at Mercedes-Benz before going to Milan, where he worked with Alberto Rosselli and Gio Ponti. From 1958, Sapper was employed in the practice of Marco Zanuso, considered a significant figure in post-war Italian design because of his experimentation and exploitation of new materials and production processes. Sapper and Zanuso continued their prolific collaboration until 1977, creating extraordinarily innovative furniture, lamps and electrical appliances. Their work included the Lambda chair, made of die-cast steel, for Gavina (1959–64); the 4999/S stackable children's chair of pressure-moulded polyethylene for Kartell (1961–64); the Brionvega TS502 radio (1964) and the Doney (1964) and Black Box Brionvega portable television (1969); and the Grillo telephone for Siemens (1966). In 1972, Richard Sapper designed the Tizio lamp for Artemide, an enormously successful high-tech task light, which has proved to be one of his most popular products.
Tizio Table Lamp, 1972 (right).

Design in Asia: 1930s–70s

Shanghai, which had functioned as the key trade port of China since the mid-nineteenth century, became even more significant by the 1930s as the main advanced manufacturing hub of the country. Cotton spinning and weaving were two of the most important industries based in the city, together with a rapidly developing printing and graphic design industry. The main design industry at this time concerned the packaging and printing of wrapping paper, comic cards for cigarette packs, and cardboard box packaging for products such as matches, soap, needles and thread. Shanghai became known as the 'Paris of the Orient', but this golden age was wiped out suddenly by the Japanese occupation of 1938.

Product design developed at a much slower rate than other forms of design in China, such as graphic design and interior design. This is chiefly because China continued to experience dramatic shortages in domestic products up until the 1980s. Up to this point the main concern for the country was to produce large quantities of goods; the manufacture of most products in the 1950s was the responsibility of engineers, who were in charge of everything from mechanical function to appearance. Occasionally artists, known as *Mei Gong* or 'art workers', would be brought into the factories to decorate and beautify products. Design was deemed less important and many manufacturers used the same design of products – such as telephones, pens, electric fans and bicycles – for two or three decades without making any changes.

Opposite top
Walkman, 1981. The first Walkman was built in 1978 by engineer Nobutoshi Kihara for the Sony co-chairman Akio Morita. Morita wanted to be able to listen to music during his frequent travelling. The original Walkman was marketed in 1979 as the Walkman in Japan, the Soundabout in other countries including the USA, the Freestyle in Sweden, and the Stowaway in the UK.

Opposite bottom
Casio watch, 1999. Casio is a multinational electronic device manufacturing company founded in 1946, with its headquarters in Tokyo. It is best known for its calculators, audio equipment, cameras and watches. In 1974, the company released the Casiotron, a watch that featured a fully automatic calendar.

The Chinese motor vehicle industry was set up in the late 1950s in Changchun, Jiling province in Manchuria, with financial assistance from the Soviet Union. The first product manufactured there was a 1.5-ton Jiefang truck that was based heavily on the prototype of the Soviet Union GAZ truck. It was in production from 1957 to 1984 without any change of design (breaking the Ford Model T's record of continuous production between 1907 and 1925). In 1958, China began producing its own cars with a model called the Dong Feng (East Wind), made not on a production line but manufactured individually in a workshop in Beijing. China's car production continued to develop and, in 1962, the country produced its first limousine, the Hong Qi (Red Flag), influenced by the design of the Russian Seagull limousine with its V8 engine, heavy, wide body, black paintwork and bullet-proof glass windows. In the early 1960s, the first totally original Chinese-designed car, the Shanghai, was produced by engineers with no artists involved. Similar in appearance to the Russian Volga car, the Shanghai had a very bad maintenance and repair record and production of it ceased in the early 1980s. At present, a number of joint automotive production ventures exist with Chinese and foreign manufacturers such as Volkswagen and Skoda.

By the end of the 1960s, two key South Korean companies began to make significant advances in electronic product design and development. The first was Samsung Electronics, which, in 1969, started producing televisions, mobile phones, radios, computer components and other electronic devices. The other was LG Electronics, established in 1958, which has since made a number of advances in the design and manufacture of many digital home appliances such as radios and televisions.

Meanwhile, in other parts of Asia, Sony is one of Japan's most recognized companies in the West and is synonymous with high-tech electronics and good design. The company was originally established as Tokyo Telecommunications Engineering in May 1946, but in 1958 it changed its name to the Sony Corporation. A large part of the success of Sony is attributed to the inspirational chairman, Akio Morita. From its modest beginnings, Sony has developed into a multinational brand leader with one of its most famous products being developed in 1979 – a personal stereo system called the 'Walkman' followed later by products such as the Watchman (1984), a television counterpart of the Walkman, the Camcorder (1983), a hand-held video recorder, and the Discman, a portable CD player.

Post-Modernism: 1970s to present day

Post-Modernism has its roots in the 1960s when several design movements were emerging, most notably in Italy, such as the Anti-Design and Radical Design groups Archizoom, Superstudio and Gruppo Strum. The 1960s was a decade of rebellion in many walks of life in politics, music, art and literature, and this extended to the world of design. Designers involved in many of the radical groups of the period included Ettore Sottsass, Michael Graves, Alessandro Mendini, Robert Venturi and Charles Jencks, who all started to produce work that made ironic comments on modern design by applying heavy decorative motifs that made reference to historical styles. Post-Modern designs typically embrace a wide range of cultural emblems from contemporary society that transcend geographical boundaries. Thus, forms and symbols commonly used by Post-Modern designers are usually drawn from past decorative styles such as Art Deco, but they also utilize imagery from significant historical moments in art, such as Surrealism.

9093 water kettle, designed by Michael Graves for Alessi, 1985. This is one of the Italian company's best-selling items and is widely considered a modern design icon.

Ettore Sottsass

Ettore Sottsass (1917–2007) worked for several major manufacturers, including the office equipment company Olivetti, the domestic products company Alessi, the furniture companies Knoll and Artemide, and the glass company Venini. Sottsass is perhaps best known for his design of the Valentine typewriter for Olivetti in 1969. He was at the forefront of avant-garde design practice in Italy for most of the second half of the twentieth century. His rejection of Modernism in the 1950s was followed by his involvement with the Anti-Design movement of the 1960s and 1970s, with Studio Alchimia from the late 1970s, and Memphis during the 1980s. From the mid-1960s he worked for Poltronova, designing experimental furniture that drew on many references to popular culture such as Disney's Mickey Mouse. Sottsass's work has been exhibited at major venues around the world for three decades and features prominently in the contemporary design collections of all major museums. *Yemen blown glass vase, 1994 (right).*

Memphis: 1976–88

It is widely acknowledged that the first objects of Post-Modern design were pieces of furniture produced by the Italian groups Studio Alchimia and Memphis. The roots of these two groups lay in the Italian 'radical design' movement of the 1960s, where they vehemently opposed the indifferent functionality of modern mass-produced designs. By the 1980s, Studio Alchimia was respected as one of the most important design groups in the world. The studio included the designers Alessandro Mendini, Andrea Branzi, Ettore Sottsass and Michele de Lucchi, among others, and participated in many major exhibitions, such as the trailblazing 1980 Forum Design held in Linz, Austria. Ettore Sottsass, one of the group's key players, left to co-found the Memphis group – a Milan-based collective of furniture and product designers – with Andrea Branzi and Michele de Lucchi. Memphis dominated the early 1980s' design scene with its Post-Modernist style. By 1981, bolstered by the addition of George Sowden and Nathalie du Pasquier, Memphis had completed more than a hundred drawings of furniture, lamps and ceramics. There was no set formula. 'No-one mentioned forms, colours, styles, decorations,' observed Barbara Radice (Sottsass' partner). That was the point. After decades of Modernist doctrine, Sottsass and his collaborators longed to be liberated from the tyranny of smart but soulless 'good taste' in design.

Above
Casablanca sideboard, designed by Ettore Sottsass for Memphis, 1981. It featured in the very first Memphis exhibition of that year.

Daniel Weil

The work of Daniel Weil (1953–) has been heralded as moving design from a Modernist to a Post-Modernist era. Weil originally qualified in architecture from the University of Buenos Aires, Argentina, in 1977, but relocated to London to study industrial design at the Royal College of Art, where he received his MA (RCA) in 1981. After he designed and manufactured a range of his own products, he then joined the Pentagram design company as a partner in 1992. His many projects have included product, packaging, interiors and art direction and his clients include Swatch, Lego, EMI and Cass Art London. Weil is best known for the series of digital clocks, radios and lights that he designed from 1981 for Parenthesis. Encased in soft, pliable plastic, these products are brightly coloured with all their working parts revealed. *Bag Radio, 1981 (right).*

'New Design': 1980s

Memphis became a catalyst for many designers based throughout Europe and led to a range of anti-functionalist developments gathered under the umbrella term 'New Design'. Many of this loose group of individual designers are influenced by sub-cultures and anti-authoritarianism and share common philosophies: a focus on experimental works, use of their own production and distribution networks, the creation of small series and unique pieces, a mixing of styles, utilization of unusual materials, the use of irony, wit and provocations, and the manipulation of the boundaries between art and design. Designers often associated under the heading of 'New Design' include Shiro Kuramata (1934–91), Borek Sipek, Ron Arad, Jasper Morrison and Tom Dixon among others.

Ron Arad

Ron Arad (1951–) has emerged as one of the most influential designers of our time. In 1989, Ron Arad Associates was established in London. Much of Arad's early design work captured London's 1980s spirit of rugged individualism and post-punk nihilism, particularly in his Rover Chair, his stereo cast in concrete (1983), and his beaten steel Tinker chair (1988). His well-documented opposition to orthodoxy is evident in the way he set out, during the early years of his career, to challenge the principles of mass manufacture in the furniture design industry by creating a number of one-off pieces. Arad has also completed a number of architectural commissions for retail and restaurant interiors such as the Belgo restaurants in London in 1994 and 1995, and the Y's store for Yohji Yamamoto in Tokyo in 2003. His largest built project is the 1994 Tel Aviv Opera House. *Bookworm, 1994 (right).*

Philippe Starck

Philippe Starck (1949–) is one of the best-known product designers in the world. He has not only received public acclaim for his amazing building interior designs but has also proved to be an accomplished architect and product designer. Much of his work produced in the 1980s and 1990s was influenced by fashion and novelty. In the twenty-first century his approach to design seems to have changed. Starck has recently promoted the ethos that honesty and integrity should be at the core of design – products should not be created as 'throw away artefacts', only surviving for as long as they remain in fashion but should ideally have longevity and durability. He believes designers need to be both honest and objective. In the field of product design, Starck has been responsible for the creation of a wide variety of objects in the O.W.O. series, noodles for Panzani, boats for Beneteau, mineral-water bottles for Glacier, kitchen appliances for Alessi, toothbrushes for Fluocaril, luggage for Louis Vuitton, 'Urban Fittings' for Decaux, office furniture for Vitra, as well as vehicles, computers, doorknobs and spectacle frames. *Louis Ghost chair, 2002 (right).*

Neo-Modernist design: 1990s to present

Neo-Modernism, as the term implies, has many ideological links with the Modernist attachment to a functional aesthetic and rejection of past styles, but it mainly evolved as an alternative to the **blob architecture** of the 1990s. Neo-Modernist design acknowledges the significance of an *individual* aesthetic as a 'functional' dimension of design, rather than the search for universal solutions associated with the Modernist ideal. Neo-Modernism, therefore, seeks to recover the sometimes stark functionalism of Modernism but taking into account its critique. Moreover, it offers a response to the more whimsical elements of what was considered Post-Modern design, in an effort to restore design for the people. Neo-Modernist design tends to be experiential rather than theoretical, and poetic rather than literal.

Droog and ready-mades: 1993 to present

Droog, founded in Amsterdam by the product designer Gijs Bakker and the design historian Renny Ramakers, has been at the cutting edge of design and the discourses connected to it since it launched in 1993. Droog products and projects have featured extensively in design journals and the general press throughout the world. Droog has championed the careers of internationally respected designers such as Hella Jongerius and Marcel Wanders, while at the same time defining a new approach to design by mixing materials and interacting with the user.

   The core of Droog's work is its collection of more than 120 products such as lamps, napkins, bird houses, chairs, tables and dish mops, which were either created by one of its group projects or commissioned from their

Marcel Wanders

Dutch designer Marcel Wanders (1963–) is one of the most prolific and celebrated designers today. He is based in Amsterdam, where his studio designs products and interiors for various international clients such as Moooi, Cappellini, Mandarina Duck, Flos, Boffi and Magis. Wanders also collaborates in other design-related projects, such as the Vitra Summer Workshop, and acts as a juror for various international competitions, including the Rotterdam Design Prize. He is best known for his Knotted Chair, where macramé meets high-tech, and his work is included in some of the most important design collections and exhibitions around the world. *Knotted Chair, 1996 (right).*

designers by Bakker and Ramakers. 'The criteria are flexible and shaped by developments in product culture and the designers' own initiatives,' states Droog. 'The only constant is that the concept has validity today; that it is worked out along clear-cut, compelling lines; and that product usability is a must. Within this framework literally anything goes.'

Ready-made products is a term that covers designed objects that are created by combining often mundane and utilitarian products, such as bicycle seats and car headlights, in a new context. The tradition of using and reappropriating everyday objects can be traced back to the artist Marcel Duchamp's (1887–1968) early ready-mades. In design this approach has been well used: from Achille and Pier Giacomo Castiglioni's Mezzadro and Sella stools in the 1950s, to Ron Arad's Rover Chair in the 1980s to Tejo Remy's Milk Bottle lamp and Rag chair for Droog in the 1990s. However, a recent trend towards design that addresses the social and political issues of today has begun to emerge. Tord Boontje's Rough and Ready series of furniture made from materials such as plywood, blankets and newspapers scavenged from the street aims to create an uncomfortable edge, presenting deliberately unresolved solutions that question society's notion of consumer products. If designers merely cater for those wealthy enough to afford the latest 'designer' furniture, what is left for those who can't or don't wish to aspire to such design?

Opposite top
Tree-trunk Bench, designed by Jurgen Bey for Droog, 1999. The bench strikingly illustrates that a fallen tree can serve as a good seat. Bey's addition of bronze classical chair backs makes it an amazing piece of furniture, which straddles somewhere between nature and culture.

Opposite bottom
Rough and Ready, designed by Tord Boontje, 1998. This is part of the Ready-made collection which featured furniture made from salvaged and recycled materials. Boontje made the designs easily available to the public by providing free blueprints of each, with tens of thousands distributed to date.

Jonathan Ive

Jonathan Ive (1967–) is widely regarded as one of the most important product designers of his generation. Ive studied design at Newcastle Polytechnic, now Northumbria University, before co-founding Tangerine, a design consultancy where he developed everything from power tools to televisions. In 1992, one of his clients, Apple, offered him a job at its headquarters in Cupertino, California. Working closely with Apple's co-founder, Steve Jobs, Ive developed the iMac. As well as selling more than two million units in its first year, the iMac transformed product design by introducing colour and light to the drab world of computing. Apple have since applied the same lateral thinking and passionate attention to detail to the development of equally innovative new products such as the Cube, the iPod, the PowerBook G4 and much more. *iPod touch, 2009 (right).*

DesignArt: 2004 to present

Today, it is often difficult to make a clear distinction between art and design. Increasing overlap has provoked serious concern from art critics who fear that it signals the demise of critical space. At the same time, a growing number of artists are using the intersection of art and design as a site for experimentation, exploring how the interchange might provide a unique vehicle for critical intervention in the commercial sphere. Contemporary art, in all its various manifestations, involves the conception and production of objects, experiences, performances, concepts and images, which, like designed products, can be commercial activities.

Alex Coles supports the concept of DesignArt and the notion that it is art itself that is inevitably 'designed'. The problem is no longer the difference between art and design, therefore, but rather the collusion of art, design and commerce. Artists and designers who exploit this fuzzy line between art and design include Donald Judd, Scott Burton, James Turrell, Jorge Pardo, Hella Jongerius, Marcel Wanders, Zaha Hadid, Ron Arad and Tord Boontje.

Opposite
Crystal Candy Set, designed by Jaime Hayon for Baccarat, 2008. These limited-edition glass vases cross the boundary between product design and art.

Campana Brothers

The brothers Fernando (1961–) and Humberto (1953–) Campana combine found objects with advanced technologies to create vibrant, energetic design art inspired by Brazilian street life and carnival culture. Since 1983 Fernando, who graduated in architecture, and Humberto, who studied law, have worked together in the field of design, somewhere between art and design. In their joint studio in São Paulo, Brazil, they develop furniture, products and industrial goods. Their clients include Cappellini and Alessi. *Corallo Chair, 2003 (right).*

The rapid growth of design in Asia

In 1978, the Four Modernizations policy (agriculture, industry, science and technology, and national defence) was outlined, marking the beginning of China's reform era. Around this time, foreign investment and the import of foreign products such as VCRs, computers, cars and cosmetics gathered pace, giving Chinese people their first taste of modern commodities and modern design.

Of all design activities in China, advertising, graphic and interior design have had a comparatively faster development than product design, which still lags behind. However, new design centres are now being built in cities such as Beijing and Shanghai that include product design. China is focusing its attention on being an innovation-led country, spending greater amounts of money on research and development activities, and building a capability based on high-level skills and knowledge. A growing number of Chinese manufacturers are aware that the future of design in China depends on understanding better the way that Chinese people live and behave and designing and developing products that meet their needs and desires. At the forefront of these innovative approaches to new product design and development are companies such as the computing and electronic giant Lenovo, Philips China, mobile phone manufacturer Ningbo Bird, and China's largest white goods producer Haier. Moreover, during the next decade China will enter the global market as a key player in the design and development of products including automobiles, mobile phones, gaming and entertainment.

Today, South Korean companies such as Samsung and LG Electronics continue to design and produce innovative technologies, unique products and cutting-edge designs. LG Electronics is now a global leader and technology innovator in home entertainment, mobile communications, home appliances, consumer electronics and business solutions, employing more than 84,000 people around the world. Similarly, Samsung continues to grow as a major international brand and has now overtaken the likes of Sony, Canon and Apple in *Business Week*'s yearly analysis of global brands. Samsung's products are regularly reviewed as being among the best on the market, especially their mobile phones and televisions.

Opposite top
HD-31100EG Microwave, produced by the Chinese white goods manufacturer Haier.

Opposite bottom
Samsung Go N310, 2009. The company continues to grow as a major international brand.

INTERVIEW
Satyendra Pakhalé

Biography

Satyendra Pakhalé is an industrial designer who was born in India but now lives in Amsterdam. He set up his own design practice in Amsterdam in 1998. His design emanates from cultural dialogue, synthesizing new applications of materials and technologies with great ingenuity. He conveys a message that could be defined as 'universal' through his designs. Since 2006, the Design Academy Eindhoven, NL, has invited him to devise and head the Master Programme in Humanitarian Design and Sustainable Living. His works are in several public collections, including the Stedelijk Museum, Amsterdam and Centre Pompidou, Paris, among others.

Interview

Where do you look for inspiration?

Inspiration is a strange thing. Often one idea leads to another and one project leads to another. Sometimes it could be an image, a thought or a discussion with a friend; a passing remark or an observation of a new situation. All of this and more could inspire or motivate me to create or think of a new way of doing something. But I would like to mention another important source of inspiration has been closely collaborating with industrialists, such as Paolo Avvanzini of Erreti, Eugenio Perazza of Magis, Alberto Alessi of Alessi, Giulio Cappellini of Cappellini and Vittorio Livi of Fiam. These are very inspiring personalities in the design industry.

What have you learnt from other designers, past and present?

There are many, many people, such as Setsu Yanagi, Daisetz Suzuki, Isamu Noguchi, Ettore Sottsass, Issey Miyake, Frederick Kiesler and Shiro Kuramata. I have been fascinated by their life-long commitment to creation and the idiosyncrasy of their huge body of work.

What is your favourite product and why?

It is difficult for me to give you just one favourite product. There are many, from simple objects of utility to pure poetic pieces filled with symbolic meanings and associations. There are many objects and products that I think are really great. I especially like everyday products that work very well and become part of the user's life without them even realizing it. I also like products that defined a new era and created their own culture and therefore new traditions. These might include the first Beetle car for Volkswagen by Ferdinand Porsche; the first Macintosh for Apple by frog design, and the first Vespa for Piaggio by Corradino D'Ascanio.

Which designers do you admire?

I don't believe in creating 'gods'. I have been fascinated by many people; thinkers, engineers, reformers, industrialists, artists, filmmakers, writers, poets, architects, social workers, scientists and many more. To give just one name is very hard for me. But if you insist, one name that comes to mind as one of the greatest designers is Ettore Sottsass. I had the great privilege of knowing him personally during my formative years. He successfully created works ranging from clay to computer and everything in between, and his body of work is enormous. I continue to be impressed with, and fascinated by, his ability to consistently create great works in ceramics, glass and technological products, all the way to architecture – and let's not forget his wonderful writing, photographs and drawings.

Opposite top left
Add-On Radiator, 2004, designed for Italian manufacturer Tubes.

Opposite top right
Amisa door handle, 2004, for Colombo Design, manufactured in die-cast brass.

Opposite bottom
B.M. Horse Chair, 1998. The limited-edition cast-metal chair is produced through lost-wax casting.

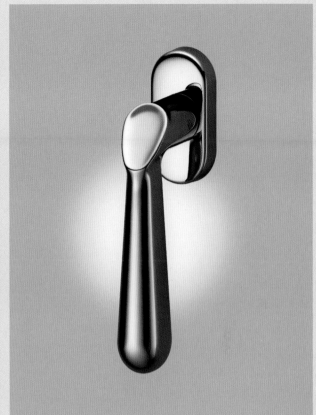

Emerging twenty-first century design trends

A number of developments in the way designers work, in information and communication technologies, and in socio-economic opportunities, has altered the practice of design at the beginning of the twenty-first century. Professor Anthony Dunne, Head of Interaction Design at the Royal College of Art, London, has claimed that: 'New hybrids of design are emerging. People don't fit in neat categories; they're a mixture of artists, engineers, designers, thinkers. They're in that fuzzy space and might be finding it quite tough, but the results are really exciting.'

Critical design products

Critical design, as defined by Anthony Dunne and Fiona Raby is an alternative approach to established product design practice that challenges and reveals the current situation by producing artefacts that embody alternative values and ideologies. One of the key aims of critical design is to provoke reflection on cultural values that might involve the process of design, the actual object produced, and the reception by an audience of such an object. Critical design products are not intended for mass-market; critical designers are free to pursue their individual goals and not those of a client.

In this sense, the concept of critical design is closer to conceptual art. Dunne and Raby, however, dismiss the notion that they are producing works of art when they say: 'It is definitely not art. It might borrow heavily from art in terms of methods and approaches but that's it. We expect art to be shocking and extreme. Critical design needs to be closer to the everyday, that's where its power to disturb comes from.'

Above
Robot 4: Needy One, from *Technological Dreams Series: No. 1, Robots*, by Dunne and Raby, 2007. Over the coming years, robots are destined to play a significant part in our daily lives. This series asks how we will interact with them, rejecting commercial solutions and instead aiming to spark a discussion about how we would like our future robots to relate to us. Do we want them to be subservient, intimate, dependent or equal?

Ross Lovegrove

Ross Lovegrove (1958–) began his design career working for the design group frog design in West Germany, where he designed products including Walkmans for Sony and computers for Apple. He moved to Paris and worked with Knoll International, where he designed the highly successful Alessandri office system. He was a member of the design group Atelier de Nîmes, which included Philippe Starck, Jean Nouvel and others, and designed work for Louis Vuitton, DuPont and Hermès. Upon returning to Britain, Lovegrove initially set up a design office with Julian Brown in 1986 before establishing his own design practice, Studio X, in 1990. He has since completed projects such as the Figure of Eight chair for Cappellini and the Supernatural chair for Moroso. Many of Lovegrove's designs are inspired and influenced by the natural world and his interest in state-of-the-art materials and manufacturing technologies. *Study for the Eye Digital Camera, 1992 (right)*.

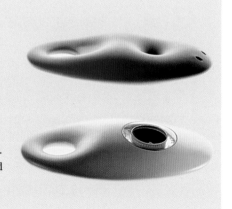

Bokka table lamp, designed by Karim Rashid for Kundalini, 2005. This is a classic and iconic expression of 'blobism'.

Blobjects

A **blobject** is a colourful, mass-produced, plastic-based, emotionally engaging consumer product with a curvilinear, flowing shape. This fluid and curvaceous form is the blobject's most distinctive feature. The word is a portmanteau of 'blobby' and 'object' and was coined by design critic and educator Steven Skov Holt in the early 1990s. Blobject designers have produced a wide range of work, including typographic fonts (Neville Brody), furniture (Karim Rashid), clothing (Rei Kawakubo), buildings (Future Systems) and sculpture (Hadeki Matsumoto).

Blobjects can be made of any material in any size or scale for the home, office, car or outdoors, but the most common materials used in fabricating blobjects are plastic (especially polycarbonate, polypropylene or polyethylene), metal and rubber, with the aim being to give a more organic and animate feel. Karim Rashid was an early leader in creating blobjects, along with the likes of Marc Newson, Philippe Starck and Ross Lovegrove.

TIMELINE: A century of product design

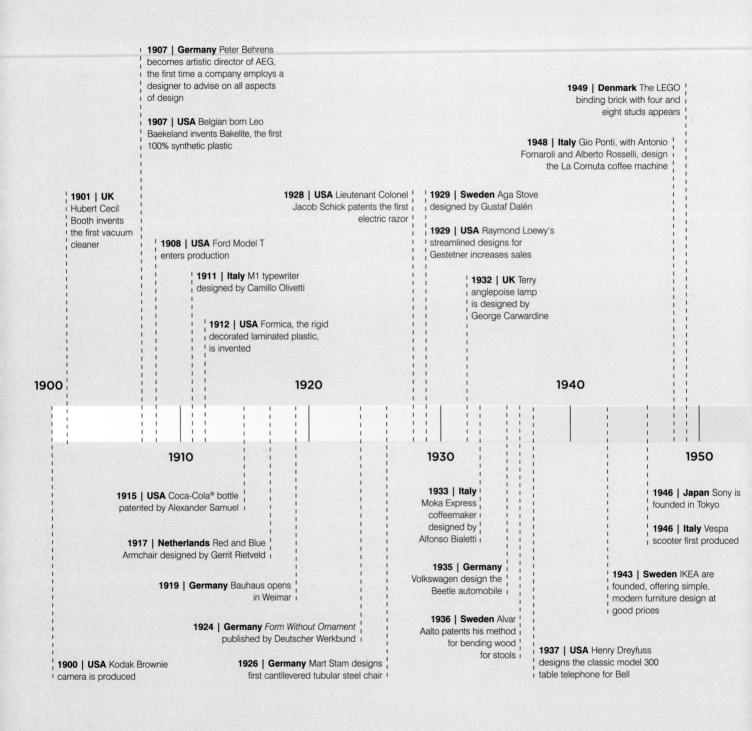

1907 | Germany Peter Behrens becomes artistic director of AEG, the first time a company employs a designer to advise on all aspects of design

1907 | USA Belgian born Leo Baekeland invents Bakelite, the first 100% synthetic plastic

1949 | Denmark The LEGO binding brick with four and eight studs appears

1948 | Italy Gio Ponti, with Antonio Fornaroli and Alberto Rosselli, design the La Cornuta coffee machine

1901 | UK Hubert Cecil Booth invents the first vacuum cleaner

1928 | USA Lieutenant Colonel Jacob Schick patents the first electric razor

1929 | Sweden Aga Stove designed by Gustaf Dalén

1908 | USA Ford Model T enters production

1929 | USA Raymond Loewy's streamlined designs for Gestetner increases sales

1911 | Italy M1 typewriter designed by Camillo Olivetti

1932 | UK Terry anglepoise lamp is designed by George Carwardine

1912 | USA Formica, the rigid decorated laminated plastic, is invented

1900

1920

1940

1910

1930

1950

1915 | USA Coca-Cola® bottle patented by Alexander Samuel

1933 | Italy Moka Express coffeemaker designed by Alfonso Bialetti

1946 | Japan Sony is founded in Tokyo

1917 | Netherlands Red and Blue Armchair designed by Gerrit Rietveld

1946 | Italy Vespa scooter first produced

1919 | Germany Bauhaus opens in Weimar

1935 | Germany Volkswagen design the Beetle automobile

1943 | Sweden IKEA are founded, offering simple, modern furniture design at good prices

1924 | Germany *Form Without Ornament* published by Deutscher Werkbund

1936 | Sweden Alvar Aalto patents his method for bending wood for stools

1900 | USA Kodak Brownie camera is produced

1926 | Germany Mart Stam designs first cantilevered tubular steel chair

1937 | USA Henry Dreyfuss designs the classic model 300 table telephone for Bell

1976 | USA APPLE I personal computer appears, soon followed by the APPLE II

1979 | Japan SONY launches its Walkman, model TPS-L2, the first personal stereo

1981 | Italy Memphis design studio in Milan is formed, led by Ettore Sottsass

1981 | UK Daniel Weil designs his Radio in a Bag

1983 | Switzerland Swatch create a new fashion-driven agenda to the watch industry

1985 | Japan Super Mario Bros computer games created by Nintendo, announcing the arrival of virtual design

2009 | USA *Objectified: A Documentary Film* directed by Gary Hustwit, providing an insight into the world of product design, is released

2009 | UK Philippe Starck fronts a reality BBC2 TV show called *Design for Life*, where he hopes to discover the next generation of British design talent

1958 | Japan HONDA launch the 50cc moped, one of the most successful motor vehicles ever

1958 | Denmark PH5 light fitting by Poul Henningsen launched and becomes a classic

1959 | UK Morris Mini Minor is designed by Alec Issigonis

1960 | USA Henry Dreyfuss publishes his *The Measure of Man*

1961 | UK Jaguar E-Type is launched, becoming an icon of the 'swinging sixties'

1968 | Japan SONY Trinitron colour TV developed

2005 | USA $100 wind-up computer introduced

2005 | Worldwide Term 'DesignArt' gains popularity, as decorative arts and limited editions are back in vogue

1999 | UK The term 'critical design' is first used in Anthony Dunne's book *Hertzian Tales*

1950   1970   1990   2010

1960   1980   2000

1951 | Denmark Arne Jacobsen designs Ant chair for Fritz Hansen

1950 | Italy Marcello Nizzoli produces Lettera typewriter for Olivetti

1969 | Italy Ettore Sottsass and Perry A. King's Valentine portable typewriter is launched

1969 | USA Internet first appears as ARPANET (Advanced Research Projects Agency)

1989 | Japan Nissan Figaro car launched, announcing the arrival of 'retro' design

1990 | France The iconic Juicy Salif is designed by Philippe Starck

1972 | Italy Tizio table lamp designed by Richard Sapper

1971 | Italy Achille Castiglioni designs the Spirale ashtray for Alessi

1971 | USA Victor Papanek's *Design for the Real World* published

2007 | USA Apple launch the iPhone

1998 | USA Google search engine launched

1997 | China S. Point, the first private product design company, starts in Shanghai

1993 | UK Dyson DC01 bagless vacuum cleaner launched

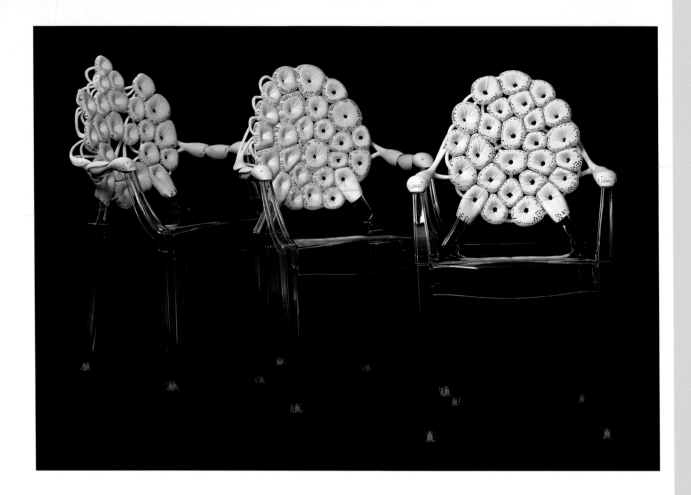

Advances in computer-aided design and manufacture, information visualization, **rapid prototyping**, materials, and **injection moulding**, have given designers the chance to use new shapes and to explore transparency and translucency without significant extra production costs. Blobjects are the period objects of our time. They are the physical products that the digital revolution brought to the consumer shelf and were impossible to create until the early 1990s. Blobjects have even been divided into a variety of blob categories such as 'proto-blobjects', 'kandy-kolored', 'fluid', 'cutensils', 'bio/exo/derma' and 'chromified'.

Individualized products

Individualized production involves the manufacture of bespoke products. An example of this type of product is the focus for Lionel T. Dean, a researcher at the University of Huddersfield, who launched FutureFactories, a digital manufacturing concept for the mass individualization of products. FutureFactories explores flexible design and manufacture made possible by digital technologies (principally, but not exclusively, rapid prototyping). FutureFactories' aim is the individualized production of one-off products via an element of computer-generated random form.

Holy Ghost Chairs, designed by Lionel T. Dean for Kartell, 2006. The chairs use the latest rapid prototyping technology to produce morphed versions of Philippe Starck's classic Louis Ghost chair (see p. 41).

2.

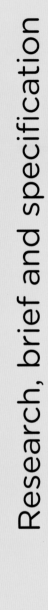

Research, brief and specification

This chapter examines the early stages of the design process and provides practical and appropriate methods and techniques commonly used in design research, constructing and analysing a design brief, identifying customers' needs, and establishing a comprehensive Product Design Specification (PDS). Examples, images and tips from a variety of product design projects reinforce the essential aspects of how to progress a project from inception to PDS. Generally speaking, these early stages of the design process progress chronologically, but it is not uncommon for there to be some flexibility in the order that product designers carry out these activities.

Product design research

In recent years, there has been an increasingly lively debate about research methods in design practice. Design research is a relatively young discipline and does not possess a well-established knowledge base when compared to the sciences, humanities and other more recognized scholarly disciplines. Thus, a lot of design research has tended to draw on existing methods, techniques and approaches from the physical and the social sciences. This connection with science has troubled many design researchers in recent years. While a scientific research is more analytic, therefore, recent developments in design research are more constructive, and seek to find new answers and knowledge in a constant drive to improvement.

There is another distinction with design research that needs to be clarified, and this lies between the academic and commercial worlds. A lot of design research conducted in commercial product design projects is highly confidential and is used to drive creative endeavours that are likely to result ultimately in new products coming on to the market. Most academic research in product design ends up in either conference or journal publications.

Research methods

There are numerous research methods commonly used in contemporary product design. This section covers a range of these: observing people to find out what they do (rather than what they say they do); enlisting people's participation to obtain information for your project; learning how to analyse information collected to identify insights and patterns; and creating simulations to help empathize with your target population and to evaluate design proposals. An explanation is also included of the impact of personal and contextual inspiration on a design project, with descriptions of a variety of project triggers, such as interviews, literature reviews, questionnaires and surveys, focus groups, shadowing and ethnography.

Typically, the aim of product design research is to ask, observe, think and learn (with objectivity) from people who interact on a day-to-day basis with

2.

products, spaces and systems. Most research methods utilized in product design involve people, so it is vital you have empathy with your research participants. The following guidelines are useful when dealing with people:

- Make sure you treat people with courtesy at all times during your research.
- You must clarify to your participants your research intentions, what you are looking to find out, why, and what this information will be used for.
- You should describe how you are going to use the information you are collecting and its value to you as a product designer.
- You must gain permission from your participants *before* collecting any photos or videos of them.
- You need to ensure that the information you collect remains confidential, unless you have agreement with your participants beforehand.
- You must inform your participants that they can decline to answer specific questions or stop the research at any time *before* the research commences.
- You must ensure that you retain a consistent non-judgmental, relaxed and harmonious relationship with your participants throughout your research activities.

Once you have completed your design research, you are usually expected to produce new knowledge or understanding that will improve the world, be that from an economic, social, cultural or environmental perspective (typically by designing a new product, environment, service or system). The product design research methods used in the early stages of the design process have been categorized in this section. Research methods for a third stage, the concept stage, are covered in Chapter 3.

Design students discussing design research at the start of a project.

Background stage

The background stage referred to here includes the gathering of information from users, clients and other individuals likely to be involved during the creation of the product. Methods of gathering this information include interviews, questionnaires and surveys. The information sought embraces potential users' wants, needs and desires along with evaluations of competitors' products.

Interviews

One of the simplest ways to explore whether or not users are happy with a product is to ask them. Interviews basically comprise a series of questions that are posed directly to the participants. They are a good way to get users to comment on how they feel about products. When interviewing, for example, product designers can ask users how they feel when using the product, whether it is easy or difficult to operate, if they enjoy using it or if it is frustrating or annoying to use. There are three broad categories of interviews: unstructured, semi-structured and structured.

In an unstructured interview, the interviewer asks users a series of open-ended questions and the users are free to steer the content of the interview to cover the issues relevant to them. This type of interview is best used in situations where the product designer has little idea of what the users' concerns and needs might be. With a semi-structured interview, the interviewer will typically have a clearer idea of what he or she wishes to cover during the interview. In this type of interview, then, users will be more constrained than in an unstructured interview, as the interviewer will have a set agenda to cover. With a structured interview, the interviewer has a much clearer idea of the issues that need exploration. Structured interviews typically comprise a pre-determined list of values that the user is asked to select from. Interviews are a versatile method for gathering information throughout the design process, but product designers should be mindful that it can be time-consuming to arrange, conduct and process the information collected during them.

Literature review

A literature review is the effective evaluation of selected documents on a particular topic. This is a useful early-stages method that enables the design team to develop an informed point of view. A good product design literature review should include a review of published articles and papers, **patent** searches, a survey of competitors' products, and an analysis of historical trends and **anthropometric data.**

Cross-cultural comparisons

Cross-cultural comparisons can often reveal important differences in users' preferences and how they interact with certain products. Analysing personal or published accounts of users' interactions with products or systems across cultures can help product designers design for unfamiliar or global markets.

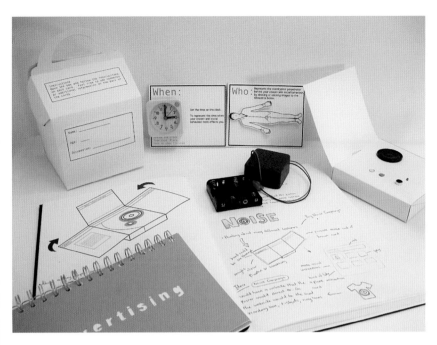

Cultural probes

Cultural probes are typically made up of a kit of products that might contain items such as a camera, a notebook and instructions. Cultural probes are a creative way of collecting and assessing users' perceptions and interactions with designed products, spaces and systems. They are one way to access environments that are difficult to observe directly and also to capture more of a user's actual life. Selected volunteers are given cultural probe packs and asked to use the items in the pack over a period of a few days or weeks and then return the pack to the researchers. The cultural probe items in the pack depend largely on the specific circumstances of the project, but the probe is designed to stimulate thought as well as capture product-user experiences.

Questionnaires and surveys

Questionnaires and surveys are an effective way to elicit responses from a large number of people. However, one major disadvantage of written questionnaires is the possibility of low response rates. Another disadvantage of questionnaires is the inability to probe responses and, when nearly 90% of all communication is visual, gestures and other visual cues are potentially lost. This method can be useful, however, for ascertaining particular traits and values of many users relatively quickly. Questionnaires and surveys can be conducted via email, by the internet, by post, by telephone and by researchers asking people for responses on the street, in their workplace or at their home.

Above left
Noise Bomb, by Jenny Kelloe, an example of a cultural probe pack for research on digital interaction design.

Above right
Example of a questionnaire.

Exploratory stage

The stage involves the product designer/researcher working much more closely with their intended end-users, creating tools and techniques for gathering information, and using props or prototypes to gauge responses from potential end-users. For example, end-users may be given specific tasks to carry out with prototypes and 'narrate' their thoughts as they use them.

Camera journals

Camera journals involve users recording their daily activities via a written and photographic diary. This is a useful method for getting users to reveal real insights into their daily patterns of behaviour. Camera journals are a highly effective method for recording visual evidence of how people interact with products, spaces and systems.

Narration

Narration is a valuable method for identifying users' concerns, desires and motivations when using specific products, systems and services. Narration involves asking users to think and describe aloud while they are performing a specific activity or operating a product in a particular context.

Focus groups

Focus groups are a form of group interview that capitalize on the communication between participants in order to generate information. Although group interviews are often used as a quick and convenient way to collect information from several people simultaneously, focus groups explicitly

Photographic storyboard capturing the sequential process of making a bag, by Andy Murray Design.

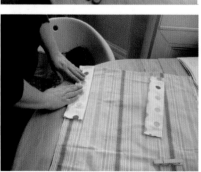

use group interaction as part of the method. Focus groups typically involve around ten to twelve consumers who are led by a moderator for anything up to two hours in duration. The group works to a tightly scripted discussion. This is an effective way to generate ideas and develop understanding on particular themes without having to reach consensus.

Shadowing

Shadowing is a research method that involves the product designer tagging along with people to observe and gain a good understanding of their day-to-day routines. It is a useful method for identifying potential design opportunities and learning first-hand how users interact with designed products, systems and services. There are a number of other product design research methods that fall under the general heading of shadowing:

- 'fly on the wall' (for observing and recording users' behaviour without interfering with their daily routines);
- 'guided tours' (involves designers accompanying users on a tour of their relevant designed spaces, products and regular systems);
- 'a day in the life' (a method for identifying the tasks and experiences of users throughout a full or part day).

Ethnography

Ethnography has its origins in anthropology; it is a research approach that is usually defined as the description and explanation of the culture of a group of people. Recently, however, ethnography has been recognized as a creative process that is about discovering cultural patterns and developing models

Observing user working methods and behaviour – an example of ethnography.

to explain those patterns. Used in this way, ethnography is employed as a front-end design research method to investigate everyday social life and culture as a context for innovation and creativity. The commercial success of this approach has been proven and documented by many leading product design and development companies, including Intel, Microsoft, BMW and IDEO. Ethnography does not aim to study people, but instead observes people in order to examine everyday experiences, situations, environments, activities, relations, interactions and processes in rich detail. Various options are: field ethnography (a group of people are observed by a researcher while they go about their normal lives); digital ethnography (using digital tools including digital cameras, PDAs and laptops to speed up the process without compromising the quality of the data collected); photo ethnography (a camera is used to capture images of their day-to-day life that are annotated with textual descriptions); and rapid ethnography (designers spend time with people in their regular habitats to understand first-hand their habits and rituals).

Isabelle Johnson

Aged 36

Arts Administrator

Isabelle is a 36-year-old Arts Administrator for a critically acclaimed independent gallery in the United Kingdom. Isabelle works with about 10 staff and is responsible for the smooth day-to-day running of the gallery.

Isabelle likes meeting new people at her job and does so regularly, mixing with exhibiting artists, visitors and the press. She enjoys the daily challenges that are involved in the running of a

small independent gallery. Her ultimate objective is to one day work in a larger organization such as the Tate Modern in London.

The downsides to Isabelle's job, she states, are the rude people she often comes across and her sometimes uncooperative colleagues. She often gets frustrated by the repetition in her work and by the mountain of paperwork that she needs to deal with.

An example of a user persona.

Personas

Personas are archetypal users with specific objectives and needs based on real research. Personas typically include:

- personal details – name, age, gender
- interests and hobbies
- experience and education
- a photograph
- demographic characteristics
- personality details (shy, timid, outgoing)
- barriers and/or challenges
- specific goals, needs and motivations

Personas are a useful method during the exploratory stages of the design process. They allow product designers to gain a good understanding of their customers' expectations and needs in a relatively cheap and straightforward manner.

Branding research

You need to evaluate your rival products and brands and compare and contrast your product against them by asking the following questions:

- Is the product true to the brand?
- Is it relevant and credible in the context of its product field?
- How does it motivate its target consumers?
- Is it distinctive in the competitive context?
- Have you struck the right balance between the buyers and users?

Market research

This can be achieved by observing how rival products are advertised, fitted into the brandscape and retailed by asking the following questions:

- How is this product field merchandised overall?
- What's the immediate brandscape of competitive brands surrounding your own?
- How orderly or chaotic is the overall visual impression of the sector?

Retail research

The last step is to observe how people shop in a particular sector:

- Do they devote browsing time to the category, or is it a case of grab and go?
- Which elements of the design language in this marketplace seem to be the critical ones used by the consumers in making brand choices?
- Is this a market balanced between buyers and users, for example, a sector featuring adults buying for children?
- Does this product sector seem to represent an 'easy buy' for consumers, or do they find it confusing or difficult?

Mood board mapping the market, aesthetics and user comments of cleaning products, by Tom Harper (see p. 223).

The brief

This section looks at the product design brief, which is typically a statement of intent. This is an essential part of the design process, helping the designer understand the business problem he or she is required to solve. The brief also sets out the terms under which the designer can do this, including budgets and deadlines. However, although the brief states the problem, it isn't enough information with which to start designing, although it may come before your research, and so will play a more prominent role from the start.

Getting the product design brief right is important; without a clearly defined brief it can prove almost impossible to go on and design and develop a successful product. The first thing that needs to be done when creating it is to start by clearly defining all of the aims and objectives identified through research and/or discussions with the client. Writing the brief is best conducted as a knowledge-sharing activity. Involving all relevant parties, including designers, client, engineers, marketing, end-users and manufacturers, at this early stage in development helps to inform the brief and reduces the chance of misunderstandings. The brief can be complex or, equally commonly, somewhat vague and ambiguous. It is rare to find a really comprehensive brief. It is also uncommon for the brief to be a single coherent document – rather it is usually a file containing a record of all relevant issues and documents.

When writing a brief, try to consider the following important questions:

Who is the product aimed at?
Carefully define your market. Failure to do this may result in a brilliant product that appeals to entirely the wrong market sector. Or it may appeal to the right group of end-users, but have inappropriate functionality, visual language or material properties. If your product crosses between user groups, it may require more than one variation.

What are the anticipated production volumes?
Knowing how many of the proposed products you intend to make has a profound effect on the choice of manufacturing and production processes and materials usage. This will impact on the product development process, the time to market and the business investment.

Does it have to conform to any statutory or voluntary standards?
If you don't understand or address this area, you may develop a product that you are not legally allowed to sell. Failure to integrate the requirements of any standards will almost always incur expensive redevelopment.

What does it do and how does it function?
Although this may be obvious to the inventor of the technology or the engineering team, as a product designer you must fully understand the functionality of the device and how and where the end-user is likely to use it.

Why is it better than your competitors' products?

Having an accurate awareness and understanding of this aspect of your product is essential – and not just for marketing purposes. If the design team understands the uniqueness of your product and where the differences lie, this will influence their approach.

Which components are contained within the product?

Switching parts, assemblies and components during the design phase can lead to delays and possibly expensive modifications. You may not be able to pin down all your component choices at an early stage, but you should do as much as you can and always have a contingency plan.

Is the product a stand-alone item or part of a larger group or system?

Once again this will affect the choice of visual language used. Products in a range may need to have a similar look to fit in coherently. For example, if you look at Apple's iPod, even without the logo it is easy to spot that it is a product from Apple's range.

Are there environmental considerations (life cycle, recycling, waste, energy use in production)?

This is an area of increasing importance and can have an enormous impact upon material choice and production methods.

Structuring the brief

Typically the product design brief will comprise input from three key product development perspectives, namely marketing, technical and sales:

- The marketing part of the brief describes the anticipated product, its functionality and its market positioning with respect to the product's main competitors and brand imperatives. It may also have a 'wish list' of functions and features, as well as customer 'must haves'. It will also either refer to, or enclose, recent consumer research findings.
- The technical part of the brief specifies the constraints on investment for new tooling, existing parts or components that need to be reused, a preliminary PDS covering performance, cost and intended manufacture, and standards that need to be respected. It will usually clarify or define key functional criteria that are likely to influence a future design.
- The sales part of the brief will typically cover all aspects relating to sales and distribution, including the product's Return on Investment (ROI) and sales planning (targets and forecasts). In addition it may cover key account needs and commercial implications for the new product in the context of other products in the manufacturer's line-up. Typical outputs would include documents and reports that illustrate research into social, economic and technological matters.

It should be pointed out that not all products are created as a response to a brief. Some designers do not work to a brief, while others rise to the challenges inherent in a tightly restrictive brief. Many designers also set and shape their own design briefs in self-initiated projects. It is common for designers to work in this way in the lead-up to the major annual design festivals now held throughout the world. Whatever the approach and style, this key document wil be tested and explored according to the customer's or client's needs, as the next development stage.

An unusual brief: the Citroen 2CV (1948)

Pierre Boulanger's design brief – said by some to be astonishingly radical for the time – was for a low-priced, rugged 'umbrella on four wheels' that would enable two peasants to drive 100kg (220lb) of farm goods to market at 60km/h (37 mph), in clogs and across muddy unpaved roads if necessary. As a design brief, creating a car that would carry a basket of eggs across a ploughed field without breaking was more than a little odd.

Identifying customer wants, needs and demands

'Recognizing the need,' Charles Eames stated, 'is the primary condition for design.' Early in their careers together, Charles and Ray Eames (see p. 31) identified the need for affordable yet high-quality furniture for the average consumer – furniture that could serve a variety of uses. For 40 years they experimented with ways to meet this challenge: designing flexibility into their compact storage units and collapsible sofas for the home; seating for stadiums, airports and schools; and chairs for virtually anywhere.

This section concentrates on methods and tips to help you, as a product designer, focus on connecting your creative output with the customers most likely to appreciate and value it. It covers ways in which a product designer can best go about defining what their customers really want.

Identifying customers' needs, wants and/or demands can be a very challenging and complex task. Often a client or a customer will express these in their own linguistic style of expression, which can be too unclear or ambiguous for a designer to proceed with. The main task that the designer faces at this point is translating what the customer wants or needs, derived from the information collected during the research stages, into a set of statements about what the product has to do.

The following four stages of identifying customers' needs should help you progress from an initial vague customer statement to establishing clear and unambiguous design specification targets:

Stage 1: Interpret and analyse the information from customers

Interpreting the statements of the customer and expressing them in a manner that is useful for the design team to progress is the first step. A useful chart can be constructed with this information by placing questions posed to the customer in the left-hand column, the customer statement in the middle, and the interpreted design objective in the right-hand column.

There are five steps to develop vague customer statements into defined design objectives:

- Try to express the design objective in terms of *what* the product has to do, not in terms of *how* it might do it.
- Try to express the customer statement as specifically as the design objective.
- Try to use positive, not negative, statements.
- Express each customer need as an attribute of the product.
- Try to avoid the terms *must* and *should* as they imply a level of importance for the need.

Stage 2: Organize the customers' needs into a hierarchy of primary, secondary and tertiary design objectives

The design objectives need to be organized into a hierarchical list that comprises a set of primary needs, a set of secondary needs, and possibly a set of tertiary needs. Usually, the primary design objectives are the most general needs while the secondary and tertiary design objectives are expressed in more detail.

Here are six steps for developing the hierarchical list of design objectives:

- Print or write each design objective on a separate card or sticky note.
- Eliminate redundant design objectives, group the remainder together and treat them as a single objective. Take care to group only objectives together that are identical in meaning.
- Group the sticky notes together according to the similarity of the design objectives. The key objective of this process is to address the needs of the customer in the design objectives hierarchy. Some design teams have been known to invite the customer to help in this process.
- Select a heading for each group of design objectives.
- If there are fewer than 20 groups of design objectives then a two-level hierarchy of primary and secondary design objectives is sufficient. If there are more than 20 groups then you may need to create a third level in the hierarchy.
- Reflect on the design objectives hierarchical list created and, if appropriate, review and edit the lists or groups.

Stage 3: Establish the relative importance of the customers' needs

You will need to determine the relative importance of each individual design objective translated from the customers' needs. There are a number of ways of conducting this activity. The design team could meet and discuss the importance of each objective and assign relative ratings for each on a consensus basis, or it could be completed after further discussion with customers, perhaps during a focus group activity. Another way of defining the relative importance of design features can be conducted using the **pairwise comparison method** (see p. 69) or by using a **relative importance survey**.

Pairwise comparison allows designers to determine the relative order (ranking) of a group of product objectives. This is often used as part of a process of assigning weights to objectives in product design concept development. First arrange the objectives in a row along the top and in a row along the side. Pairs of objectives can then be compared systematically against one another by entering a 1 or 0 against each objective depending on whether the first objective is considered more or less important than the second and so on. Continue working along each row of the matrix, entering a 1 if the objective is deemed more important and a 0 if the objective is considered less important, until you come to the end. When all the comparisons have been made with the pairs of objectives the row totals indicate the rank order of the objectives.

2.

Pairwise comparison for a power drill						
	Low Weight	High Comfort	Low Cost	High Durability	Low Maintenance	Row Total
Low Weight	X	O	1	O	O	1
High Comfort	1	X	O	1	O	2
Low Cost	O	1	X	1	O	2
High Durability	1	O	O	X	O	1
Low Maintenance	1	1	1	1	X	4

Relative importance surveys are another effective way of identifying the relative weightings of individual product objectives. Typically, a scale of 1 (the product feature is undesirable and customers would not consider a product with this feature), through 3 (the product feature would be nice to have but is not crucial), on to 5 (the product feature is critical and customers would not consider a product without this feature) can be used to describe the importance of each product objective.

Stage 4: Reflect on the results and the process
The final step in translating the customers' needs into clear and unambiguous design objectives is to reflect on the process and the results. It is important that you challenge and reflect on the results that you have arrived at and evaluate them against the needs expressed by the customers.

Consider the following questions during and after this process:
• Have we communicated with our target customers?
• Have we managed to encapsulate any latent needs of our target customers that may currently not be addressed in existing products?
• Are there any areas we need to follow up in future interviews?
• Of these customers, who would be good to use in future projects?
• What have we learned that we didn't know at the start of this project?
• Are we surprised by any of the results during this project?
• Did we omit anyone that we should include in the next project?
• How might we improve this process in the next project?

INTERVIEW
Stuart Haygarth

Biography
Since 2004, Stuart Haygarth has worked on design projects that revolve around collections of objects. These objects are normally gathered in large quantities, then categorized and assembled in a way that transforms their meaning. Haygarth's work is about giving banal and overlooked objects a new significance, with the finished pieces of work taking various forms such as chandeliers, installations, functional and sculptural objects.

Interview

How do you initiate projects?
My projects are generally initiated by finding existing everyday and banal objects that inspire me. My immediate interest in the object is driven by its aesthetic quality, function, narrative and perhaps where it was found. Only after a period of time with these objects does the concept grow and a piece of work evolve.

What research methods do you employ?
Once my concept and idea is finalized in my sketchbook, I normally try to find visual reference through books and Google images. However, the majority of my research is given towards how my work is physically put together. The scale of the work is calculated by building scale models, and much time is spent finding materials and products on the internet. Also, depending on what kind of piece I'm working on, I spend a lot of time sourcing found objects from car boot sales, markets and specific beaches.

What is different about your personal design process?
I only have my personal design process. Obviously, with work that is commissioned for public spaces there are factors and restraints that have to be taken into consideration during the creative process. I really operate in the same way as an artist.

What is important in the early stages of the design process?
To let an idea settle for a period of time in a sketchbook and come back to it at a later stage. If the idea still excites you then it is probably worth pursuing.

Opposite top left
Tail Light (Fat), 2007, was created from carefully selected vehicle light lenses. The lenses are grouped by style and size and attached to acrylic boxes to form robotic structures. These are hung from the ceiling and illuminated by one 60w fluorescent white tube. Illuminated, they are reminiscent of stained glass.

Opposite top right
Raft (Dogs), 2009, consists of a pyramid of cat or dog figurines sourced from second-hand shops under a mushroom umbrella, creating an enchanting object out of previously considered valueless kitsch.

Opposite bottom
Aladdin (Amber), 2006, is a wonderful example of how Haygarth finds beauty in everyday discarded items, challenging perceived notions of what design finds precious and beautiful.

The Product Design Specification (PDS)

The next stage is to transfer all the information so far attained into one of the most important documents, the Product Design Specification. This section and the one that follows outline the tasks involved in creating the PDS to ensure a product designer produces a product design solution that reflects a true understanding of the actual problem and the needs of the user. The PDS is a document listing the design problem in detail; a product designer should constantly refer back to it to ensure his or her design proposals are appropriate.

A PDS splits the problem up into smaller categories to make it easier to consider. The customer or end-user group should be consulted as fully as possible while the PDS is being drawn up as their requirements are of major importance. Any numeric properties in the PDS should be specified as exactly as possible, together with any tolerances allowed on their value.

The PDS is an essential part of all design activity for disciplines such as architecture, product design and graphic design. In an increasingly competitive global market, product design teams need to produce comprehensive and clear-cut PDSs. It should be noted that the absence of one can cause problems throughout all the subsequent stages of the product development, even up to the final stage, its positioning in the marketplace. Moreover, a poorly constructed PDS will usually lead to a poor design, whereas a good PDS will give the design team a good chance of producing a product that the customer will want to buy and use.

What is a PDS and why write one?

A PDS is a document that sets out exactly what is required of a product, before it is designed. It is essential in the design process; it not only helps the people who design and make the product, but also those who eventually use it. Engineers sometimes overlook the needs and wishes of the customer, but those very people think critically about the products they buy. They may take an interest in design or engineering for its own sake. They certainly will not hesitate to criticize a product if it does not do, efficiently and reliably, what they expect it to. A PDS is therefore also an analysis of what the market will demand of the product.

Things to consider before you start writing a PDS

A PDS specifies a problem, not a solution. A PDS does not pre-empt the design process by predicting its outcome. Rather, it defines the task by listing all the conditions the product will have to meet. This can involve a good deal of research – into market conditions, competing products, and relevant literature including patents. When you write a PDS, you are defining something that does not yet exist.

Everybody must get involved in the PDS

Once a PDS has been written, it becomes the principal reference for all those working on the design. The PDS must therefore be written in terms that all parties can understand and must be endorsed by all.

A PDS is a dynamic document (subject to change)

A PDS has to be a written document, but it does not need to be engraved in stone. It can be changed. As a rule, the design follows the PDS. But if the emerging design departs from the PDS for some good reason, the PDS can be revised to accommodate the change. The important thing is to keep the PDS and the design in correspondence throughout the design process. In this way, the PDS ends up specifying not just the design, but the product itself.

Elements to cover in a PDS

A comprehensive PDS will comprise anything up to 32 elements (listed in the next section). It is therefore a good idea to write your PDS under these headings, leaving out only those that clearly do not apply. Some of the points overlap, but do not be tempted to skip any of them. Only by checking all of them can you be sure you will not overlook something important. In some projects, however, it may be appropriate to omit a number of elements as they may not be relevant, but if so, this will have been agreed in advance.

Each single PDS element consists of a **metric** and a **value**. For example, 'average time to clean clothes' is a metric and 'in less than five minutes' is the value of this metric. Values should always be labelled with an appropriate unit (e.g. seconds, metres, kilograms). These both form the basis of the PDS.

Guidelines for the development of a PDS

- The PDS is a dynamic document that can change over the course of the design process and will support the design team. It spells out in precise, measurable detail *what* the product has to do but not *how* it should be done.
- It is a user document to be used by the design team and others involved in the process. Thus, the PDS should be clear and succinct.
- Write the PDS using short, sharp precise statements under each heading.
- Add the *metrics* and *values* in each area of the PDS (e.g. weight, quantity and cost). If in doubt, estimate a figure.
- The relationships between PDS elements change from one project to the next. Try and vary the order of constructing each PDS that you write. This supports the flexibility of thinking that is crucial.
- Always ensure that you date your PDS and give it an issue number.
- Always ensure that you clearly record all amendments made to the PDS during a design project.

Common elements of the PDS

This sample of a PDS for a child's bicycle shows the types of information contained and how it is grouped.

Product: Fictional "X-Cross" Kids Bicycle		
Date: 21st April 2010	**Issue:** 2	**Creator:** Will Ernesto

1. Performance
1.1 Must be easy to operate – it is expected that the user age group is 5 to 13 years.
1.2 The product should withstand rough handling.
1.3 Operating conditions [see Environment].

The performance demanded of any product should always be fully and precisely defined.

2. Environment
2.1 Resistant to adverse weather conditions.
2.2 The product should perform in the temperature range -20°C (-4°F) to 70°C (158°F).
2.3 The product should be resistant to corrosion from salt water.
2.4 The product should withstand a shock load of 2268 kg (5000 lb).
2.5 The product should be able to withstand vandalism.
2.6 Dust and dirt should be easily cleaned from the product.

All aspects of the environmental conditions that the product is likely to come into contact with, and have a bearing on, need to be considered and investigated at the outset of the project. Environmental hazards may occur during a number of stages in the design and development.

3. Life in Service
3.1 A minimum of 10 years is required for this product and 15 years is desirable.

The service life of the product and how this is to be measured needs to be stated.

4. Maintenance
4.1 Screws, bolts and washers used must comply with British Standards.
4.2 Parts that require lubrication must be accessible.
4.3 The replacement of spare parts must be easily done.

You should be aware of the maintenance issues surrounding the product at all stages of its life, including the need for spare parts or special tools.

5. Target Product Cost
5.1 The product is aimed at the mid price range. Retail cost is £95.00 and target cost for manufacture is between £30.00 and £35.00.

Establish targets for production, supplier, contractor and retail costs as early as possible. Checking competitor or like products will help.

6. Competition
6.1 Raleigh BMX.
6.2 Hood BMX.
6.3 Apollo Urchin.

You will need to conduct a comprehensive analysis of competing and like products; this will typically involve literature searches, patent and product searches.

7. Packing
7.1 Size must be kept to a minimum.
7.2 Cost must be kept to a minimum.
7.3 Weight must be kept to a minimum.
7.4 Must be waterproof.
7.5 Must be easily unpacked by the customer.
7.6 Company logo must be clearly shown on package.

It is likely that the product being designed will need some form of packaging even if this is merely to protect the product while it is being transported from one place to another. The cost of packaging can have a significant impact on the final cost to the customer.

8. Shipping/Transport
8.1 Packages will be stored 10 to one box.
8.2 ISO containers will be used to carry the boxes.
8.3 Transport will be by sea then road or rail.

Do you envisage the products' delivery by land, sea or air? Consider the type of truck, pallet container, or aircraft.

9. Quantity
9.1 10,000 units to be produced annually initially.
9.2 Long production run expected.

Consider how many products you wish to manufacture, which will affect costs and schedule.

10. Manufacturing Facility
10.1 There are no constraints on the manufacturing facility.

Where is the product to be made and what facilities and expertise will be available?

11. Size
11.1 Length is not to be greater than 1800 mm (71 in).
11.2 Breadth not to be greater than 75 mm (3 in).
11.3 Height not to be greater than 500 mm (19½ in).

Are there any constraints on the size of the product? Ensure that the size and shape of the product make it easy for the end-user to handle and operate.

12. Weight
12.1 The weight of the product should be no greater than 10 kg (22 lb).

Consider weight: should you break down the manufacture into smaller modules if a problem?

13. Aesthetics
13.1 The "Fictional" brand values should be highly visible.
13.2 The company logo should be clearly seen in bold lettering at least 10 mm ($^1/_3$ in) high.
13.3 A robust image must be projected to the customer.

As a product designer, the colour, shape, form, texture and finish are major ingredients directly under your control that can lead to a product's ultimate success or failure.

14. Materials
14.1 The use of existing materials for manufacture is imperative.
14.2 The materials selected must withstand the environmental conditions.
14.3 The materials should not oxidize in any way.
14.4 All the materials should be non-toxic.

These must be readily available, easily processed, and comprise the required properties. If special materials are required, specify to the appropriate standard. Harmful materials, such as lead-based paint, must not be used in consumer products.

15. Product Life Span
15.1 This should be as long as possible with possible passing from one sibling to another.

How long will the product that you are designing stay on the market? The longevity of the product will affect important decisions including funding.

16. Standards/Specifications
16.1 BS EN 14872:2006 Accessories for bicycles.
16.2 BS EN 14764:2005, BS EN 14766:2005, BS EN 14781:20 Specification for safety requirements for bicycles.
16.3 BS EN 14766:2005 Mountain-bicycles. Safety requirements and test methods.
16.4 BS EN 14765:2005+A1:2008 Safety requirements for bicycles for young children.

Most products need to adhere to national and/or international standards. Bear in mind that standards are useful and essential in many areas but they should not be allowed to hinder real innovation.

17. Ergonomics
17.1 Controls must be positioned at a height suitable to the user.
17.2 Hand-operated controls must not need a force of more than 1 Nm to operate.
17.3 No sharp edges to be exposed [see Safety].
17.4 It is preferable if controls are different colours for easy use.

All products have a user-product interface. Ensure it is easy to operate, requiring little physical effort for both left-handed and right-handed people, for example. Ergonomic elements can also cover cognitive issues as well as physical ones.

18. Customer
18.1 It is expected that the customer will be a boy from age range 5 to 13 years.

Understand your customers' needs, wants and preferences as fully as you can.

19. Quality and Reliability
19.1 This product will be designed to comply fully with BS 5750.
19.2 The company will offer a 3-year full warranty with this bicycle.

Quality and reliability are difficult elements to assign measurable values to.

20. Shelf Life Storage
20.1 The product will be stored 10 units to one box within the company's warehouse.
20.2 The product will be packaged in their own individual box within retail units.
20.3 There are no limitations on shelf life as this is a non-perishable product.

Shelf-life storage is often overlooked in design specifications. Consider if products can stay unused for some time.

21. Processes
21.1 There are no limitations to the manufacturing processes [see Manufacturing].

Are special manufacturing processes required, such as plating or finishing requirements?

22. Timescale
22.1 Design Process complete – 1 June 2010
22.2 Commence Manufacturing – 1 December 2010
22.3 Delivery of first Bicycle – 1 March 2011

When you schedule your project, be sure to allow enough time at the beginning for the design phase.

23. Testing
23.1 Batch inspection to be used for the final product.
23.2 Batch test of 1 in every 1000 will be adopted.

After your product has been made, it will need a factory test to see whether it complies on every point with its PDS. You may also need to plan for acceptance and witness tests too.

24. Safety
24.1 The product must comply with all relevant parts of BS 3456 and the Home Safety Act (UK).

Consider all aspects of safety, such as statutory legislation and product labelling or instructions.

25. Company Constraints

25.1 There are no manufacturing constraints, so there should be no company constraints.

25.2 Depending on product sales, more production staff might have to be employed.

Ensure that the necessary expertise will be available within the company for each stage of the product's development.

26. Market Constraints

26.1 The product will be marketed on a worldwide basis.

Be mindful that local conditions, especially overseas, can constrain your design.

27. Patents

27.1 The following European Patent Office (EPO) patents should not be infringed:
B62K1/00 to B62K17/00
B62K19/06
B62M25/02
B62K19/36

You must search all relevant information, including patents, relevant literature and competitors' product information. You need to check that you are not infringing on other individuals' patents or products.

28. Political/Social Implications

28.1 The name of the product should be thoroughly checked when considering exportation to non-English speaking countries.

28.2 Logos and colours used in the product should be checked against individual countries' tastes.

28.3 Product should be manufactured to company's social and ethical guidelines.

Be sensitive to any political and social effects that your product might have in the country for which it is to be designed and manufactured. This includes local by-laws and regional trends.

29. Legal

29.1 Product adheres to company's product liability procedures and product liability legislation.

An important consideration is that of product liability legislation, particularly in terms of defects.

30. Installation

30.1 Product is ready assembled and does not require user assembly for use.

Many products form part of assemblies into larger products and systems or need to be installed.

31. Documentation

31.1 Product accompanied by appropriate comprehensive documentation for use and maintenance.

Product documentation is an increasingly important aspect of product design.

32. Disposal

32.1 Product and constituent components are able to be disassembled for disposal and recycling where at all possible.

32.2 Product components are clearly labelled for appropriate recycling/disposal.

The design of products has a significant effect on the environment. Your PDS, therefore, must include information on what is done with the product after its life. This will include things like how you best design for disassembly, dispose of any associated waste, and recycle the product.

Conclusion

This chapter has described a number of methods and techniques that will help you undertake research, construct a comprehensive design brief, identify customers' needs and establish a PDS. The next stage of the design process – concept design – is covered in the following chapter, where details of the tasks commonly associated with drawing up a number of different viable concept designs that satisfy the requirements of the PDS are explained.

3.

This chapter explains the concept design stage of the design process and details the tasks involved in drawing up a number of different viable concept designs – from concept generation to drawing, modelling to prototyping – that satisfy the requirements of the product outlined in the Product Design Specification (PDS). It also explains the techniques of concept evaluation and selection, showing how to choose and develop the most suitable concept.

What is a concept design?

A concept design is an approximate description of the technological, functional and aesthetic form of the product in development. A designer seeks to create a concise description of how a product will satisfy a customer's needs using sketches, models and descriptions. The importance of this stage in the design process cannot be underestimated. The quality of a concept largely determines the degree to which a product satisfies customers and can be subsequently successfully commercialized. While a good concept may be implemented poorly in the finished product, a poor concept can rarely be turned into a successful product. It has been estimated that 85% of all product costs, from manufacture to materials, are determined and committed at the concept design stage.

Concept design can adopt two distinct approaches:

- **Convergent thinking** – The designer follows an analytical process, developing a design in a sequential manner.
- **Divergent thinking** – The designer explores as many solutions as possible in a lateral manner, following all creative paths.

Concept generation

Successful designers use a variety of techniques for generating concept design proposals that address the requirements laid out in the PDS. These techniques involve extensive user research aimed at understanding functional needs and social/cultural interactions. Designers need to study the cognitive processes involved in the usage of their designs, the emotional issues surrounding a design, and investigate the events/ceremonies related to its context.

The methodologies explored in this section are based on the premise that designers must clearly illustrate the processes undertaken on design projects and demonstrate that the ability to model concepts abstractly and physically is a key part of a designer's professional armoury.

During the development of a new product, a designer needs to identify the context, depth and breadth of his or her design approach. This simple process is intended as a starting point that can help a designer clarify his or her personal design objectives, through the use of a flexible, client-centred concept generation methodology.

Concept generation methods

Methods are an integral element of the design process, enabling designers to structure the development process of a product. The most successful concept generation methods are deliberate thinking processes designed to help designers find the inspiration to build upon their research and produce new ideas and fresh insights. Below are some of the most successful techniques, which can help define concepts, aid communication across design teams and share viewpoints with all the stakeholders. None of these methods is guaranteed to solve a problem, but they can assist designers in finding ideas without having to wait for an uncooperative muse.

Brainstorming

Brainstorming is a technique used by design teams to generate ideas more rapidly and effectively. It is a highly efficient method of generating surprising and innovative concept proposals rather than the production of a list of familiar, orthodox ideas. Individuals can use brainstorming, but it works best when used by groups of people. Brainstorming is most effective if everybody involved keeps to the following simple ground rules:

- State the problem or scenario to be discussed clearly and concisely.
- Be visual – draw ideas or represent them with whatever is to hand.
- Number your ideas, and set a target of ideas to be generated.
- Stay focused on the task.
- Keep the ideas flowing.
- Approach the problem from different viewpoints.
- Defer judgment.
- Have one conversation at a time.
- Go for quantity, the more ideas the better.
- Every idea is valid.

Brainstorming concepts is said to promote the creative productivity of design teams by helping them generate and evaluate ideas through teamwork and collaboration. Here, the discussion by Stockholm designers Propeller focuses on a specific product, the Kapsel Media Centre.

Attribute listing

While brainstorming is a general idea generation method, **attribute listing** is a specific idea-finding technique in which you need to:

- Identify the key characteristics, or attributes, of the product or process in question.
- Think up ways to change, modify, or improve each attribute.
- Draw these changes and then compare and contrast them with the initial product or process.

Analogical thinking

Analogical thinking is the transfer of an idea from one context to another context. Direct analogical thinking brings together a problem from one domain with familiar knowledge of another domain as a way to gain insight. For example, Georges de Menstral invented Velcro after noticing plant burrs on his dog's fur.

While all designers refer to precedents in design through actual objects, books and magazines and think analogously all the time, analogical thinking can be a conscious technique if you deliberately ask questions like these:

- What else is like this?
- What have others done?
- Where can I find an idea?
- What ideas can I modify to fit my problem?

Below
Bone Armchair (left), 2008, and Bone Chair (right), 2006, by Joris Laarman. An example of analogical thinking, whereby the artist was inspired by the material and structural qualities of bone tissue to create a range of furniture. Using a biomimetic technique, the process takes its inspiration from the efficient way that bones grow, adding material where strength is needed and taking away material where it's unnecessary.

Idea checklists

There are a number of checklists written specifically to help solve problems creatively. Typical questions include:

- Combine – Blend? Combine components? Combine purposes?
- Modify – Change meaning, colour, form?
- Magnify – What to add? Extra value? Duplicate? Multiply? Exaggerate?
- Minimize – What to subtract? Miniaturize? Lighten? Split up?
- Put to other uses – New ways to use as is? Other uses if modified?
- Rearrange – Interchange components? Turn on its head?

Breaking the rules

This method enables a designer to temporarily rewrite the social, cultural or physical rules impacting on the problem at hand. To use this method you should:

- List all the taken-for-granted assumptions surrounding a problem and the unwritten 'rules' that govern your way of thinking.
- Find ways to challenge the rules by asking – Why not? What if? Take inspiration from nature and the world around you. In your problem-solving you could oppose, contrast, transfer, reverse, distort, contradict, substitute, superimpose, change scale, combine, empathize and so on.
- Escape these rules and free-associate to generate novel ideas, bypass a law against them, or imagine a different rule. Be playful and free yourself from conventions and preconceptions.

Lateral thinking

This series of techniques, popularized by leading design thinker Edward De Bono, attempts to change concepts and perceptions by rejecting traditional step-by-step logic. Popular lateral thinking techniques include:

- Challenge – Here you challenge the status quo, not to demonstrate that there is anything wrong with the existing situation but simply to enable you to explore concepts beyond those parameters.
- Random entry – A product is chosen at random and you attempt to draw parallels between that and the design issue you are working on.
- Focus – Here you carefully observe the inadequacies in existing products with the aim of creating better end results. For example, combining notebooks and desktops led to Personal Data Assistants (PDAs).
- Provocation – In this technique you make some provocative statements using exaggeration, reversal, wishful thinking and distortion to any given product.
- Escape – This is used to get away from expected product outcomes. Denying expectations can help you create better products.

Mind mapping

A mind map is a diagram used to represent ideas linked to, and arranged radially around, a central key word or idea. Designers use mind maps, sometimes referred to as concept maps, to generate ideas and help their problem-solving and decision-making processes. Mind mapping involves writing down a central idea and thinking up new and related ideas, which radiate out from the centre. By focusing on key ideas, and then looking for branches out and connections between the ideas, you can map out your knowledge in a manner that will help reframe your knowledge.

General rules for successful mind mapping include:

- A central multicoloured image that symbolizes the mind map subject.
- Themes that provide the main divisions.
- Lines that support each key word are the same length as the word and 'organically' connect to the central image.
- Printing to give each word used clarity.
- Single key words uncluttered by adjectives or definitions.
- Colour for vividness and memorability.
- Images each worth a thousand words.
- Enclosure of each theme with an outline that hugs the shape created by the branches.

Mind map, by Angela Gray. This diagram is used to represent words, ideas and tasks linked to, and arranged around, a central key word or idea. Mind maps are used to generate, visualize, structure and classify ideas, and are a useful creative tool for designers.

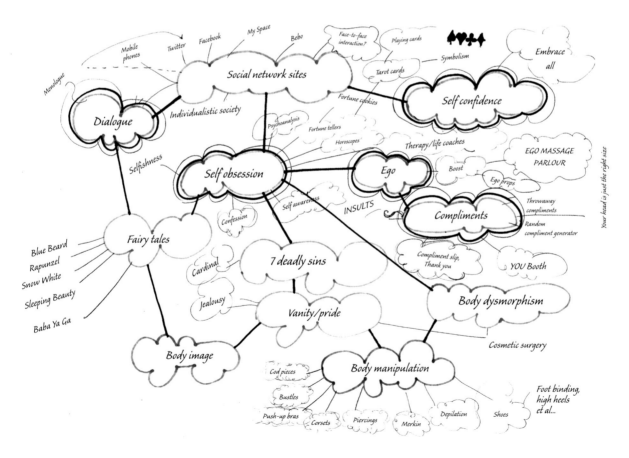

Drawing techniques for product design

The ability to explore large numbers of alternative concepts by externalizing thoughts on paper at the early stages of a design project is crucial. It will help to communicate your designs quickly and provide the client or fellow designer with a better impression of how a design would appear in reality.

Freehand drawing

When designers talk about drawing skills, what they most commonly mean is freehand perspective drawing ability. Fundamental to good drawing is the understanding and use of perspective technique.

There are three types of perspective drawings: one-point, two-point and three-point (see p. 91). Each type can either be drawn in an accurate, measured way using plans and elevations of objects as guides, or drawn freehand. The understanding of perspective and an ability to draw well is vital if a designer is to gain a command of three-dimensional form and be able to accurately visualize products from his or her imagination. The quicker you are able to sketch and develop designs, the greater the number of projects you will be able to work through in a given time period and the more money you will be able to bring in to either your own business, or the design consultancy for which you work.

Prototype Mini project drawing, by Alec Issigonis, 1958. A renowned draughtsman, this sketch shows the designer's thinking behind the original groundbreaking Mini design, with its front-wheel drive, transverse engine, sump gearbox, small wheels, and phenomenal space efficiency that still inspires car designers and engineers today.

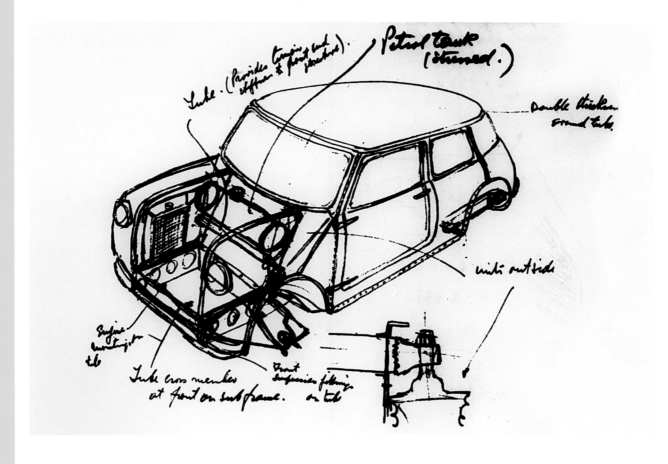

Concept sketching

Drawing enables designers to develop and evaluate their ideas on paper, storing concepts for later discussion, manipulation and iterative development. The act of drawing works as a means of firming up an idea, enabling designers to wrestle with design possibilities, and attempt to give form and meaning to an idea. During the concept stage, designers have to visualize through a variety of techniques as yet non-existent product concepts.

Usually designers will start generating their ideas with a pen or pencil and paper. Most designers utilize these tools at these early stages of the design process because of the immediacy of the sketching process, the freedom provided and the temporary nature (i.e. sketches can easily be erased, revised and redrawn) of pencils and paper. A designer also annotates his or her sketches, with the notes acting as aide memoires while also helping identify key points so that the ideas can be communicated to members of the design team and all the stakeholders involved. Concept sketches allow one to see the designer's mind at work. They fall into two broad categories: **thematic sketches** and **schematic sketches**.

Thematic sketches

These drawings are the initial exploratory visions of how a proposed design may look. They tend to be drawn in a wilfully fluid, dynamic and expressive manner, free from constraint. Thematic sketches should convey the product's physical form, characteristics and overall aesthetic. Such drawings often rely on a series of visual conventions that may need explanation to a client.

Schematic sketches

These drawings place less emphasis on the external styling or appearance of a design, and focus on defining and working within a 'package'. The 'package' is a term used to describe the fixed dimensional parameters of a design, including vital data such as off-the-shelf components to be used and ergonomic parameters.

Once a concept has been settled upon, the designer is able to move on to the production of presentation visuals to sell clients or investors the design, and then on to the **general arrangement (GA)** drawings, which act as the key to the large number of working technical drawings required for a design to be manufactured and assembled.

The GA is the master drawing, which describes the final form of the design and the layout of its components. It provides information relating to the overall dimensions and usually includes a parts list that refers readers to the other associated detailed drawings such as assemblies of components and individual detail drawings. These drawings include information detailing the materials the parts are made from, surface finishes and tolerances (dimensional accuracy required) of manufacturing. Traditionally produced by hand using technical pens on drafting film, they are now produced on screen using computer-aided design (CAD).

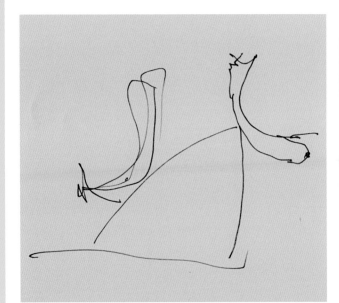

Rendering

Rendering is essentially the art of 'colouring in' a sketch. Since the birth of industrial design in the 1920s, rendering has evolved into a discipline full of distinctive approaches, techniques and conventions. The medium used in rendering is a more advanced form of the felt-tip pen, most commonly a Pantone Tria or Magic Marker. In addition to marker pens, chalk pastels in combination with talcum powder, coloured pencils and gouache paint are used to render drawings. The aim of a good rendering is to represent not only the colour of a product, its material and surface finish, but also how light is falling onto it.

Rendering is about giving an impression, rather than a true picture of reality. Provided enough information is supplied, the viewer's mind can draw on visual experience to fill in the gaps. Rendering requires a bold approach for best results. Because it is so fast and immediate, it is best to avoid the precious approach so often taken when constructing a drawing. Sometimes young designers become overly concerned with slightly blurred edges or straying over the edge of a line, but this approach produces dull, static drawings instead of the fluid and expressive visuals that designers should aspire to and that always look more effective.

The real secret to rendering is realizing that you should be as economical as possible with your marks on paper but still manage to create an informative visual. These techniques can be applied to simple visuals or complex drawings that explain the assembly of a design, through what are known as **exploded views**. Being able to render convincingly is vital for the designer to be able to communicate design concepts quickly and in the presentation of concepts to clients.

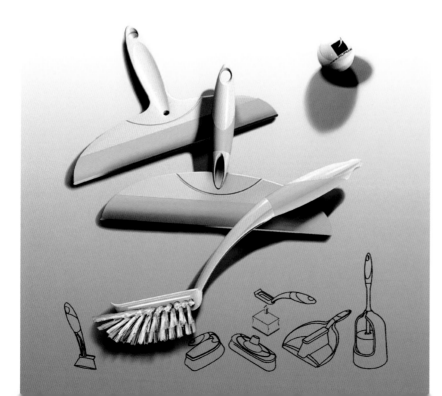

Left
LINEA Collection, designed by pilipili for PDC Brush NV in Izegem, Belgium, 2003. Computer-rendered images of 3D models of household cleaning tools.

Opposite top
Concrete, by Jonas Hultqvist of Jonas Hultqvist Design, 2003. This is a project for Tretorn Sweden AB, a swedish shoe company with a history of innovation in rubber-made products, and these renderings show how they develop their new footwear concepts for internal and focus group evaluation.

Opposite bottom
Ford Ka, 2008. This rendering of the second-generation model demonstrates the continued use and value of using traditional markers and pastels to quickly present design concepts.

Presentation visuals

During the concept generation phase, a product designer will often make hundreds of quick sketches while working on his or her designs for a new product. When a designer needs to present these ideas to the client and others, and communicate effectively the intentions of size, shape, scale and materials, he or she will need to tidy up the rough sketches and present something more visually seductive. The product designer has to shift from a three-dimensional idea into a two-dimensional sketch, and then back again into a three-dimensional representation of that idea. It is here that the product designer must ensure that his or her two-dimensional flat drawing on a piece of paper conveys three-dimensional qualities and jumps out of the page at a client.

Software 'Paint' packages that enable image manipulation have transformed the production of visuals in the design industry. Photoshop is the current market leader and the flagship product of Adobe Systems. It has been described as the industry standard for graphics professionals and played a large role in making the Apple Macintosh the designer's computer of choice during the 1990s.

Although there are software packages specifically designed for two-dimensional sketching, which use styluses or graphic tablets for inputting data, most designers still draw on paper and then scan in their originals to be cleaned up and coloured using Paint software. These packages enable the designer to use layers, and offer a variety of tools and filters that mimic traditional techniques, such as airbrushing, along with the ability to erase all steps. This is a method that designers in the past, with their laborious marker renderings, would undoubtedly have envied.

Drawing on computer

Drawing is a means to an end for designers, and enables them to produce physical products suitable for manufacture. Traditionally, when faced with a complex form, designers have relied on models made from polystyrene foam, clay or cardboard to help them resolve their designs.

While plans, elevations, sections and sketched isometric drawings may have been sufficient to move into three-dimensional modelling, these methods did not provide the required data to move into manufacture. Instead, this role relied on the highly developed craft skills of pattern-makers and panel beaters who interpreted the designers' models and drawings, and as a consequence were effectively 'co-designers' in bringing a design to production. These professions and the design skills they possessed have sadly faded away with the advent of three-dimensional CAD, which enables designers to sculpt, carve and accurately dimension complex forms virtually.

Since its inception, CAD has undoubtedly enhanced the quality of presentation visuals, enabling designers to produce highly beguiling photo-realistic images. The accurate modelling and animations possible have led to the establishment and expansion of specialist design disciplines and firms to sate the need for models, images and technical data. CAD models have

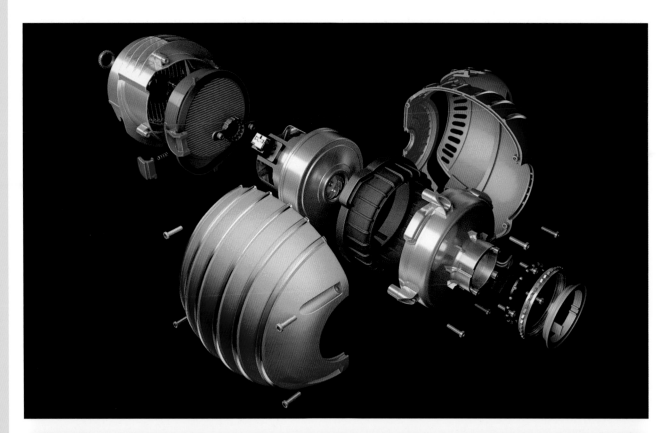

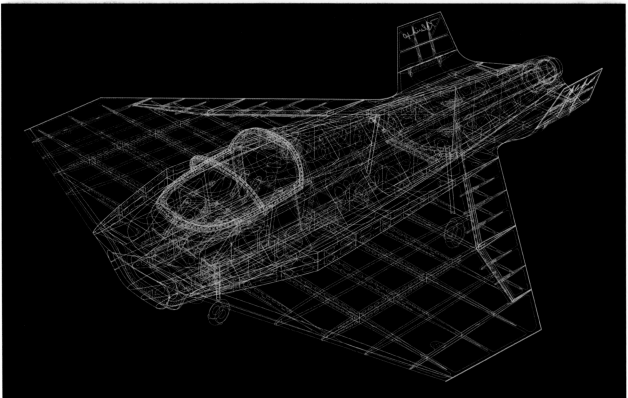

transformed the development process, allowing a designer to visualize his or her designs three-dimensionally without having to produce a full-size physical prototype or build a scale model, which often would take longer, and be more expensive, to produce. CAD is not, however, a replacement for physical modelling as there are still a number of important roles that physical models fulfil. Computer renderings do not capture the experiential or tactile qualities that models can convey, and can often appear to concretize a design in the development stage in the eyes of the design team or client. As the use of computer-generated graphics and special effects has entered mainstream media through film and television, photorealistic renderings have become the common parlance of design, but they lack the interpretive qualities of a hand-generated sketch or the subtlety of sculpting a form by hand.

In design development, CAD plays a key role in helping the designer to resolve issues such as complex arrangements of components or the form of aluminium or steel tools for plastic mouldings or die-castings. CAD also helps to bring presentations to life by making designs seem more real at earlier stages of the design process.

There are two types of CAD modeller: **surface modellers** such as Studio Max, which were developed to satisfy the car design industry's need for freeform design, and the **solid modellers** (also known as volumetric or geometric modellers) that rely on building forms from basic building blocks. Increasingly, software developers are merging the functionality of both systems to create packages suitable for designers and engineers.

Most solid modellers now enable parametric modelling, where parameters are used to define a CAD model's dimensions or attributes. The advantage of parametric modelling is that a parameter may be modified later and the model will update to reflect the modification. This means designers no longer have to completely remodel a design when a change is made, enabling the software to become fully iterative.

Drafting, the technique of communicating technical details through a series of drawing conventions, has almost entirely been replaced by CAD. A product's form, purpose, detailing and specification can be developed collaboratively on screen. However, the conventions of traditional drafting remain the foundation for two-dimensional CAD drafting packages such as Autocad, which are universally used in design and manufacturing, and it is still essential that designers understand the underlying principles of traditional drawing conventions as these can help with sketches and choice of appropriate visuals. Meanwhile, CAD models are often required to be directly outputted to **computer-aided manufacture (CAM)** or rapid prototyping machines for purposes of prototyping or manufacture and therefore need to be highly accurate. Clients also want to be sure that the 3D CAD render they see in a presentation is what they will get once a product is actually produced.

3. Technical drawing

Technical drawing is a means by which a designer can communicate a design to others in a design team, or to those responsible for manufacture/construction, in a complete and unambiguous manner. Various conventions have been developed over the years to support this process, most notably two-dimensional orthographic projections (i.e. plans, elevations and sections) described above and three-dimensional metric projections (i.e. **axonometric** and oblique).

Introduction to three-dimensional visualization

Representing three dimensions on paper is a vital skill for designers, enabling them to communicate their ideas to other people, especially non-designers such as users, managers and marketing personnel. There are several tried and tested drawing systems used to produce a realistic representation of an object such as **perspective drawings**, full-size **elevations** and retouched photographs of models. These methods of drawing are used by designers to communicate different aspects of their designs to each other, to clients and to those responsible for the manufacture/construction of the product design.

In order that a design is manufactured accurately and in accordance with the product's specifications, standard drawing methods and conventions have been developed over the years, so that there can be no misunderstandings between all parties involved in the design process from conception to completion of a project. Some techniques such as **isometric drawings** are based on mathematical systems; others convey a larger degree of realism by applying perspective to the drawing. This section explores a range of drawing techniques utilized during the concept design stage.

Top left
One-point perspective, with one vanishing point towards which all lines, except those normally at right angles to the viewers' sight line, will recede and converge.

Bottom left
A two-point perspective has two vanishing points, placed on the horizon to the left and right of the object.

Below
A three-point perspective has the vertical lines of an object converging towards a third vanishing point directly below or above it.

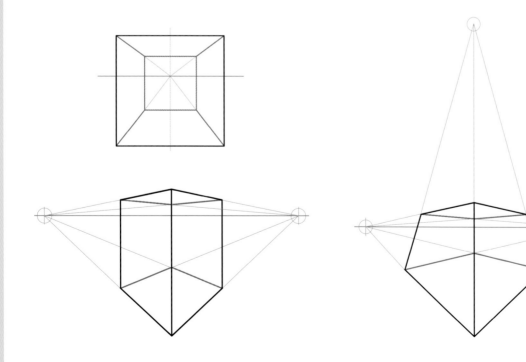

Orthographic drawing

A central problem in drawing for design is how to represent three-dimensional objects on a surface that only has two dimensions. **Orthographic drawing** is one method of drawing used by designers to enable them to represent real or imagined three-dimensional objects on a two-dimensional surface. The other main drawing methods are **oblique** and perspective. The method of drawing chosen by a designer will depend on what he or she wishes to communicate in the drawing.

The multi-view drawing – orthographic projections

This is a related set of orthographic projections that are known as plans and elevations. The plan, or **top view**, shows the view of an object as if taken from above. An elevation may be a front, side or rear view, depending on how you orient yourself to the object or assess the relevant significance of its faces. A section is the view of an object as it would appear if cut through by an intersecting plane. Sections on an orthographic drawing show details it would not be possible to see with the naked eye. Cut solids in a section are shown cross-hatched. And finally, the view of the base of an object, when required to be shown, can be referred to as a **base view** or base plan and is located above the front elevation in a first-angle projection and below the front elevation in a third-angle projection. A single **plan**, elevation or **section** can only reveal partial information about an object, as the third dimension is flattened on to the drawing surface. Together, however, the projections are able to fully describe the object's three-dimensional form.

Drawing conventions

There are two conventions for regulating the relationship between orthographic views: first-angle projection and third-angle projection, each indicated by a **projection symbol**. The difference between the two is in how the different views of an object are positioned on the drawing surface. In the layout of a first-angle projection, the plan is drawn first, then the elevation of the front face positioned immediately above it and the left-end elevation positioned to the right of the front elevation. In the layout of a third-angle projection, the views are arranged so that the front elevation is placed below the plan and the left-end elevation is positioned to the left of the front elevation. In any multi-view drawing, the maximum possible number of views that can be shown of an object is six: plan, front elevation, rear elevation, base plan, left elevation and right elevation. Each orthographic view represents a different orientation and a particular vantage point from which to view an object. Each plays a specific role in the communication of a design.

The method of projection you use will depend on what is most appropriate for the application. For drawing a long, thin product, a third-angle projection would be easier to read because the end elevation is placed to the left and adjacent to the front elevation.

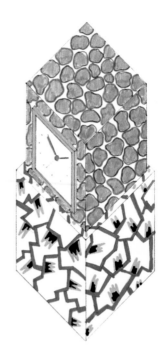

Above top
Axonometric sketch of the Acapulco clock, by George Sowden for the first exhibition by Memphis, 1981.

Above
Oblique projection drawing of the iconic Casablanca sideboard, by Ettore Sottsass for Memphis, 1981 (see p. 39).

Opposite top
Constructing a first-angle projection, as commonly used in the UK and Europe.

Opposite bottom
Constructing a third-angle projection, as commonly used in the United States.

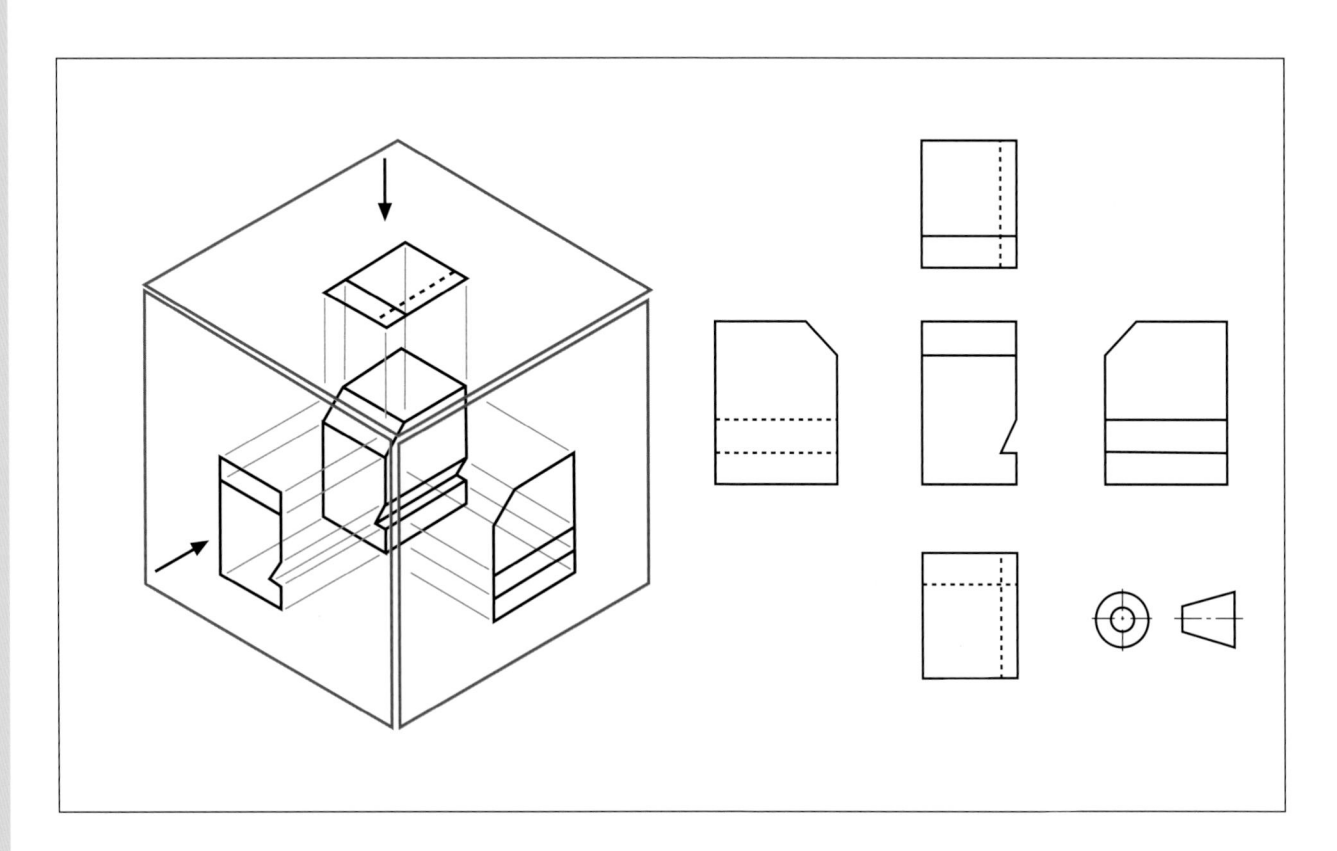

Layout of drawings

The 'A' series of drawing sheets based on the international paper size standard, ISO 216, is normally used for all drawings outside North America. The drawing should be framed within a border. Anything within the border forms part of any contract requirements.

The **title block** should be located within the drawing frame on the lower right-hand corner. The following information should always be included in the title block: designer's name/company name, drawing title, drawing number, date of drawing and scale. All lines should be uniformly black, dense and bold. Lines should be all in pencil or all in black Rotring (or similar) graphic pen. Drawing sheets have two formats: portrait, where the longest side is oriented vertically, and landscape, where the longest side is oriented horizontally. Every drawing should be drawn in proportion, i.e. to a uniform scale.

The scale used should be stated on the drawing as a ratio, e.g. scale 1:2. Do not use descriptions such as full-size or half-size. The scale that you choose for a drawing will depend on the size of your drawing sheet and the size of the object to be depicted. The scale should be large enough to allow easy and clear interpretation of the information. Details that are too small for clear dimensioning in the main representation of an object or building should be shown in a separate view to a larger scale.

Recommended scales to use are:
- For drawings at full size, i.e. actual size: 1:1
- For drawings smaller than full size: 1:2, 1:5, 1:10, 1:20, 1:50, 1:100, 1:200, 1:500, 1:1000
- For drawings larger than full size: 2:1, 5:1, 10:1, 20:1, 50:1

Standard paper sizes

The 'A' sizes are as follows:
A4 = 210mm x 297mm
A3 = 297mm x 420mm
A2 = 420mm x 594mm
A1 = 594mm x 841mm
A0 = 841mm x 1189mm (this nominally represents one square metre and forms the basis of the series)

In the United States paper sizes are as follows:
Letter = 8.5in x 11in (216mm x 279mm)
Legal = 8.5in x 14in (216mm x 356mm)
Junior Legal = 8in x 5in (203mm x 127mm)
Ledger = 17in x 11in (432mm x 279mm)
Tabloid = 11in x 17in (279mm x 432mm)

Guidelines for drawing

In summary, when drawing, visualizing and presenting design concepts you should adhere to the following points:

Visualize early
Don't just visualize as a presentation tool, but as a concept generation device that can convey your concepts clearly and concisely to as wide an audience as possible.

Iterate often
Iterate as much as possible during the initial stages of the design process. This will help you generate ideas in a manner more conducive to evaluating a concept's merits rather than falling for the superficial qualities of a particular visual.

Don't over-visualize
The aim of concept generation is to generate just enough viable concepts as possible. Low-fidelity rapid sketches and models are far more useful at this stage of the design process than more polished techniques as they encourage debate.

Visualize neutrally
When evaluating alternate design options it really helps to keep the quality and style of each visual as similar as possible. By presenting designs in a neutral manner, you can shed a sense of ownership, and the efforts of the entire team can be evaluated on a level playing field.

Be aware of how people interpret visuals
You need to be fully aware of the subtle messages that different forms of visuals carry. For example, a rough pencil sketch has an immediacy that might imply an underdeveloped concept, while a photorealistic computer rendering may imply that a mere concept is, in fact, a finished design that is beyond criticism or change.

INTERVIEW
Nendo

Biography

Nendo are a six-person-strong multidisciplinary design company based in Tokyo and led by founder Oki Sato. They undertake a range of projects from architecture to interior and event design, through to furniture and product design and graphic design. They have worked with major clients, including Camper shoes, Issey Miyake and Kenzo. They were awarded the Elle Decoration International Design Award in 2004. Nendo's motivation, they say, is to give people a small '!' moment in their day-to-day lives. They believe these moments are what make our days interesting and worthwhile. Nendo, therefore, want to reconstitute everyday products, experiences and services by collecting and reshaping them into something that is easier to understand. Ultimately, Nendo state that they would like the people who have encountered their designs to feel these small '!' moments intuitively.

Interview

How do you develop concepts?

In our everyday life, Oki develops a concept (story) first. Then he shares it with our staff and the client via a Manga sketch. After that we decide on all the details (i.e. materials, shape, colour and so on) for the concept. For Nendo, any detail is fine as long as it is linked with the concept.

What techniques do you use in concept development?

There are many aspects that we have to decide, but the story behind the project is the most important for us. There is no set rule for our design. We always say we don't design a product, we design a story. The story is everything around the product.

How do you evaluate your concepts?

We discuss it with the client and our design staff. The most important aspect is, 'Does everything follow the concept?' Usually Oki and another member of Nendo's staff work as a team for a project.

What methods of product visualization do you use?

We mainly use sketches like Japanese Manga. We only use the Manga sketches first to share the concept, then we make 3D renderings and/or models and/or drawings. Then we (or the manufacturer) make the first prototype. And, importantly, we will modify it again and again.

Opposite top left
Cabbage chair, 2008. Nendo were commissioned by fashion designer Issey Miyake to make furniture out of the waste pleated paper that is produced in large amounts during the process of making his pleated fabric garments. Nendo's solution was to transform a roll of pleated paper into this chair, which appears gradually as you peel away its external layers, one at a time.

Opposite top right
Blown, 2009. These fabric lanterns are intended to convey the possibilities of new materials developed within Japanese synthetic fibre technology. The thermoplastic lights glow beautifully when light passes through them, in the style of vernacular *chochin* paper lanterns.

Opposite bottom
Chab table, 2005, draws inspiration from the traditional Japanese *chabudai* low table that can be used in a variety of settings. Nendo's reinterpretation can be a side table when in its high position, and in its low position it's a coffee table. By removing the upper tray it can also be used in bed.

Modelling

Product design is a three-dimensional discipline, and while the immediacy of marker renderings and the visual gloss and ease of CAD offer huge possibilities, it is essential that designers model their concepts physically and test them in the real world.

Design models serve a variety of purposes. They can be used as part of the design development process, enabling designers to visualize their two-dimensional designs three-dimensionally. This allows them to check the functionality, usability, ergonomics, proportion and form of concepts and then develop the concepts further as required. Models also help a designer to convey his or her designs to others in a design team or as a final representation of a design to a client. They can be used to test public reaction to a new design, and evaluate its suitability within a market. They can also be used to test the structural integrity of a design before being implemented, or to test a particular part of a design such as a mechanism.

Design models are almost always produced to scale. This can be either smaller than actual size, i.e. 1:5, 1:10, 1:20, 1:50 or 1:100 for large items such as furniture or interiors; actual size, i.e. 1:1; or larger than actual size, i.e. 2:1; 5:1 for very small products or developing new mechanisms. The scale of a model also depends on the stage of the design development. In the early stages of a design project, smaller-scale models are more commonplace.

There are a variety of methods to develop and present their design ideas using models, but designers usually use four distinct types of models: **sketch model**, **mock-up**, **appearance model** and **test rig**. Many materials are used, most commonly paper, cardboard, foamboard, foam, wood and clay.

Sketch model
A full-size or scale model that aims to capture the embryonic ideas emerging from the design team's initial concept development. These expressive and rapidly produced models will progress in complexity, resolution and finish until the designer or team are confident enough to progress to more time-intensive models.

Mock-up
A life-size physical model constructed from easily fabricated materials such as rigid card, wood and foam to evaluate the physical interaction, scale and proportion of product design concepts during the early stages of the process.

Appearance model
A life-size/actual-size model whose primary purpose is to help evaluate the design's aesthetics and convey detailed finishes, rather than product function.

Test rig
A full-size or scale model that replicates a mechanical action or enables strength, stiffness, comfort or durability to be tested.

CASE STUDY: De La Warr Pavilion Chair

Design partnership Barber Osgerby use models extensively during the design process to create products that pursue a simplicity and functionality that reflects the qualities of the materials used, and combines a hand-built quality with modern manufacturing techniques.

They were commissioned to design a new range of furniture for the public areas of the recently renovated modernist De La Warr Pavilion at Bexhill-On-Sea on the south coast of England. Established & Sons manufactured the resulting chair design in 2005, from cast aluminium inspired by the balustrade and detailing of the original building. The distinctive skid leg of this chair was created in response to the observation that many chairs, particularly dining chairs, are first viewed from the rear.

Far right, top to bottom
Cardboard model; foam and card model to determine proportions; and second prototype in timber showing the distinctive skid leg.

Right
Initial sketch.

Below
Finished product.

CASE STUDY: One Laptop Per Child

Extensive prototyping was required during the design of the innovative One Laptop Per Child, XO Laptop, designed by Yves Béhar and his San Francisco design studio, fuseproject (Nick Cronan, Bret Recor, Josh Morenstein and Giuseppe Della Sala), 2007. The concept designed by Nicholas Negroponte, founder of the One Laptop Per Child organization, was to create the world's first $100 laptop aimed at bringing education and technology to the world's poorest children with a rugged, low-cost, low-power, connected laptop with content and software designed for collaborative, joyful, self-empowered learning.

Top row
Initial sketches.

Second row
Exploded perspective (left) and foam mock-ups.

Bottom row
The finished product, from closed to open.

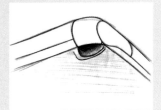
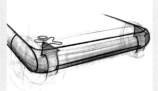

Prototyping

In product design, the word 'prototype' is commonly used as a noun, a verb and an adjective. For example, product designers produce prototypes of their concept ideas; engineers prototype full-scale mock-ups; software engineers write prototype programs. A prototype can be classed along two dimensions. The first dimension is the degree to which a prototype is physical as opposed to analytical. Physical prototypes are a tangible approximation of the intended product, whereas analytical prototypes generally represent the product in an abstract mathematical format. The second dimension is the degree to which a prototype is focused as opposed to comprehensive. A focused prototype tends to concentrate on only one to a few of the product's attributes, whereas a comprehensive prototype is a full-scale, fully operational version of the product. A focused prototype can be produced faster and cheaper than a comprehensive one; these prototypes can usually be grouped under 'looks like' prototypes and 'works like' prototypes.

Prototypes are created to inform the design and decision-making processes. While they have traditionally been perceived as highly developed physical models, contemporary designers now use the term to describe any kind of representation that is created to help designers, users and clients to understand, explore and communicate what qualities a product has, and how a user might engage with it. They can range from the concept sketches described earlier in the chapter through to **storyboards**, scenarios and a variety of models that explore and communicate propositions and context.

Prototyping assists the design and development process by enabling designers to understand existing user experiences and context, explore and evaluate ideas and communicate them to an audience. They are a vital device for resolving a product. They are often fully working and robust enough for trialling with end-users over periods of time, and can play a vital role throughout the whole design process, not just at the concept stage. They enable the design team, users and clients alike to engage with a concept and prompt dialogue between all the stakeholders. Prototypes facilitate informed decision-making, and help ensure a streamlined development process that avoids costly mistakes or delays in bringing a product to market.

The number of prototypes required varies project by project and depends on the scale and the budget available. The need to evaluate a product's form, composition, materiality and production processes can be properly met only through intensive prototyping. The development of the Dyson vacuum cleaner, for example, required thousands of prototypes before innumerable issues were resolved and the concept reached production.

Prototyping tools

There are a number of prototyping tools commonly used by product designers today, ranging from lo-fi DIY techniques through to CAD approaches.

Quick-and-dirty prototyping

'Quick-and-dirty prototypes' are used as a quick way to communicate a concept design idea to other members of the product design team. From this the team can then evaluate, reflect and refine their ideas before progressing further. The benefit of this method is that prototypes can be created quickly and with any materials that may be at hand. The focus of this method is on speed over quality of prototype building.

Paper prototyping

Paper prototypes can be used to quickly visualize, organize and articulate basic design concepts. Product designers can use this method to sketch out functionality and usability aspects of concepts and evaluate them.

Experience prototyping

An **experience prototype** can be a useful tool for detecting unanticipated problems or opportunities as well as evaluating ideas. These are used by product designers to learn what it is like using the product in a given situation.

Role-playing

In role-playing, participants adopt and act out characters or roles to help understand users' personalities, motivations and backgrounds. By enacting the activities surrounding a design problem, within a real or imagined context or scenario, the design team can begin to understand and empathize with actual users. The key stakeholders involved with the design problem are identified and these roles assigned to members of the design development team. A series of improvised scenarios and activities are then acted out and recorded for later interpretation and evaluation in design decisions.

Body storming

In **body storming**, designers imagine what it would be like if a concept existed and act out a scenario as though it exists. It helps you to quickly generate and evaluate behavioural concepts within a defined physical context. In this technique, the design team sets up a scenario and acts out roles, with or without props, focusing on the intuitive responses to the physical enactment.

Empathy tools

Empathy tools can give designers a greater appreciation of what it is like for users with disabilities or special conditions to use products. Tools like clouded glasses and weighted gloves help designers experience better the abilities of different users, seeing the world through their eyes, and gaining a deeper understanding of their issues, needs and desires.

Be your customer

This is a useful method for detecting a client's perceptions of their customers. Start by asking the client to describe or enact their typical customer's experience. This is useful as it allows the client to highlight their understanding of their customers as opposed to actual customers' experiences.

Try it yourself

Try it yourself is a method used in product design and development that allows the design team to sample the product being designed themselves. The rationale is that the design team will gain valuable insights into how the actual users feel when using the product being designed.

Scenario modelling

Scenario modelling can help product designers communicate and evaluate design proposals within their intended context. By devising a scenario carefully with characters, narrative and context, designers can evaluate whether their design ideas will work with their intended users.

Scenario testing

Scenario testing involves the creation of future scenarios using media such as photography, film and video and asking users to provide feedback on them. This is a useful method for communicating and evaluating early concepts to clients.

Storyboards

Storyboards are an effective way to share your concept design with others; they can be particularly valuable in cross-cultural contexts. A good storyboard will tell a rich and convincing story of how particular users will use the product idea that you are proposing. Storyboards can also be a great prompt for discussion in focus groups and interviews. They can be as effective as a rapid prototype for getting high-level feedback.

Storyboards are a great way of demonstrating how a product can alter through time and use. This example by Martí Guixé uses his Galleria H2O Chair, 1998, to show, through his quirky cartoon drawing style, how the chair allows you to adjust the seat height by adding books, growing in height as you grow in knowledge and age.

At 3   At 6   At 13   At 25   At 90

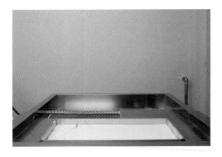

Informance

Informance is an 'informative performance' scenario role-played by the design team that is based on insight and observations collected previously. Informance is an effective method for creating a shared understanding of a design proposal and its implications.

Rapid prototyping

A range of methods that create detailed physical models of products from computer data is known as rapid prototyping. **Stereolithography**, which creates models in plastic, is arguably the most commonly used process; other techniques produce models in paper or metal. Designers produce detailed designs on screen, and then output this technical data for production. Rapid prototyping is often used to check the design of parts before committing to production tooling. However, a number of designers, including Patrick Jouin and Marcel Wanders, have begun to produce one-off and batch-produced products using the technique as a viable manufacturing process.

Diamond Chair, by Nendo, 2008, is produced through powder sintering rapid prototyping (RP). As there is a limit to the size of objects that can be produced by RP machines, the chair is produced in two parts that are then fitted together once both pieces have hardened. The molecular patterned chair takes a week to produce and as such is not designed for mass production, but it can be produced anywhere in the world with an RP machine, as the files can be digitally sent for local bespoke manufacture.

Concept evaluation and selection

While many stages of the design development process benefit from unbounded creativity and divergent thinking, concept selection is the process of narrowing a set of concept alternatives under consideration. Although concept selection is a convergent process, it is frequently iterative and may not produce a dominant concept immediately. Selection and evaluation are iterative processes that must be embedded in the development of new products. Designers are constantly evaluating which direction to take and generating many concepts to choose from.

A large set of concepts will usually be rapidly narrowed down to a more concise and focused set, but these concepts may need to be combined and improved to temporarily enlarge the set of concepts under consideration. Through several iterations a dominant concept finally emerges.

When selecting which idea(s) best satisfy the PDS, it is essential to remember that you may need to generate new concepts, modify existing concepts or undertake further research to proceed. Selection should be a narrowing process, weeding out unsuitable ideas, rather than trying to pick the 'best' idea. By referring back to the PDS and placing yourself in the user's shoes through empathic design methods, you can help avoid selecting on a subjective personal basis.

Once an appropriate number of design concepts have been generated through sketching and modelling, you can refer back to the PDS and choose which concepts fulfil the criteria laid out in the original specification. To avoid subjectivity creeping into the decision-making process, it is best that all members of the design team perform this vital part of the process. If possible, input should also be included from the client and stakeholders, helping to evaluate the designs outlined from a number of perspectives. Explicit evaluation of the product with respect to manufacturing criteria improves the product's manufacturability and helps to match the product with the process capabilities of the manufacturing company.

By adopting structured methods that can become a common language among the design team, from designers, engineers, manufacturers and marketing staff, and beyond the team to users, clients and buyers, the team can reduce ambiguity and confusion, create faster communication and deliver products to market more rapidly.

Common evaluation and selection methods

All designers use some method for choosing a concept. The methods vary in their effectiveness and include the following:

- CAD models – Used to evaluate a design and its perceived use during the different stages of the design process.
- Checklists – Used to help define a product's specification and identify users' needs.
- External decision – Concepts are turned over to the customer or clients to determine the design selected.
- Interviewing prospective or actual users – Used to identify users' needs and test the design against these needs.
- Intuition – The concept is chosen for its 'feel', with the designers relying on tacit knowledge rather than explicit criteria.
- Mock-up evaluation – Used to evaluate product usage with user's participation.
- Multi-voting – Each member of the design development team votes for several concepts. The concept with the most votes is selected.
- Product champion – An influential member of the product development team chooses a concept that determines the design direction.
- Pros and cons – The design development team lists the strengths and weaknesses of each concept and makes a choice as a group.
- Protocol analysis – Used to evaluate a design and understand the users' concept of the product. A verbal and/or video recording of a user undertaking a task is made to gain more understanding of the activity.
- Prototype and test – The design team builds and tests prototypes of each concept to verify a design under 'real' conditions, making a selection based upon test data and set criteria.
- Task analysis – An approach used to define and evaluate the operational procedures of a product.
- Matrix evaluation – Also known as the Pugh method, **matrix evaluation** is a quantitative technique used to rank designs against set criteria.

Conclusion

As we have seen, the manner, style and procedure in which an individual designer or design team develop a design can often be quite distinctive and personal. It is necessary for a designer, therefore, to be able to present his or her development work so that he or she can easily communicate with others within and outside the design team. Documenting the decision-making process enables the creation of a readily understood archive of the rationale behind concept decisions. Such a report is useful for assimilating new team members and for quickly assessing the impact of changes as the product moves through detail design towards the next stage of the design process – manufacture and the marketplace – covered in the following chapter.

4.

From manufacture to market

This chapter outlines and explains the key stages of the design process from detail design to manufacture, and addresses marketing, branding and sales. The way in which a product is made has a big effect on decisions taken by the designer during the detail design phase – after all, it is important that the product can be made. It is vital, therefore, that the correct manufacturing processes are chosen at the detail design stage so that a design does not have to be changed later, which may be detrimental to the budget, schedule and the integrity of the original design.

Detail design

This section covers the key stages of transforming the chosen concept design into a fully detailed design with all the dimensions and specifications necessary to make the product specified on a detailed drawing.

The detail design process

The detail design phase lies between the concept design and manufacturing phases of the design process; it is principally concerned with the process of transforming a product concept into a set of manufacturing drawings and documentation. It should be noted that, as the design process is an iterative one, there are no neat demarcations between the sequential phases and, in reality, many of the activities will overlap or be undertaken in parallel.

The detail design process consists of five basic steps:

Step 1: Product subdivision

The preferred design concept is broken down into a number of smaller units and, as the detail design phase progresses and the product becomes more defined, this subdivision is continued down to component level. The form of subdivision decided at this stage will be mirrored in the structure of the complete manufacturing drawing set. This process enables the designers and design engineers to identify how parts will be sourced and manufactured.

Step 2: Design and selection of components and sub-units

This stage involves the designing, selection and sourcing of the component parts and assemblies that make up the product. New components may have to be designed from scratch, and existing components may be utilized or redesigned if required, in order to successfully produce an integrated design for manufacture.

Step 3: Integration of parts

Following on from the design and selection of components, this stage sees the integration of these parts into the final configuration of the product. The design team will produce definitive whole product layouts that identify the form of each component, and will have commenced work on the general arrangement and major assembly manufacturing drawings.

Step 4: Product prototype testing

This stage involves the final prototyping and testing of the design. While the design team may have already produced large numbers of mock-ups, appearance models and test rigs for development testing, as described in Chapter 3, it is only at this stage that the product in its final form, as intended for production, can be prototyped and tested.

Alpha prototypes are produced to represent the aesthetic design and/or function of the final product, but are not necessarily manufactured using identical processes or materials. This enables the designer to evaluate the design in detail, and avoids costly mistakes when moving towards manufacture. These alpha prototypes are tested and refined through a series of iterative steps before being signed off, when the design engineers can begin to produce what are known as **Beta prototypes**, which evaluate the actual processes or materials intended for manufacture.

The value of prototyping and testing cannot be underestimated, and, as Chapter 3 explained, prototypes enable designers to undertake user testing and market evaluation as well as aid in the preparation of test specification and manufacturing procedures. The aim of this stage is to further define the evolving product and to modify components, parts and drawings in order to address any issues that emerge through the testing process.

Step 5: Completion of manufacturing information set

The final stage is the completion and signing off of the manufacturing data and the approval to commence full-scale manufacture. During the detail design stage, the design team develop the design in increasing detail, ensuring that all changes and drawing modifications are systematically recorded, with each change or 'issue' controlled by the design manager/ team leader. The **information set** will contain final instructions in the form of drawings, diagrams and digital data about the product's form, dimensions, manufacturing processes, tolerances, materials and surface properties of each non-standard part and assembly. It will also contain information regarding the overall arrangement and the sourcing of standard and proprietary parts. The structure of this final information set will reflect the product subdivision of Step 1 and will be uniquely numbered in accordance with national standards, procedures and conventions such as British Standards (BS) and International Standards Organization (ISO).

CASE STUDY: Cobi Chair

This office chair designed was designed by PearsonLloyd in conjunction with Steelcase Design Studio, and was launched in the US in 2008 and the UK in 2010. Designed to encourage movement and support through a variety of postures, it has only one adjustment (seat height), and a mechanism that is weight activated and senses and supports a users own centre of gravity so anyone can get comfortable quickly.

The design process moved through sketches and measured drawings to physical models, before moving into computer-aided design packages where stress analysis software resulted in a refined and structural efficient final product.

Top row
(Left to right) Measured drawings; stress analysis of seat back; and CAD renderings.

Bottom row
Development of arm rest components.

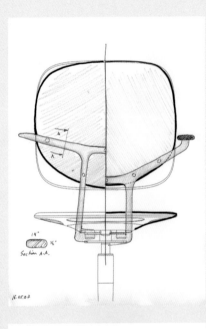

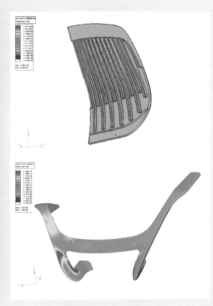

4. Design and manufacture

This section explores and explains the range of materials and the manufacturing processes and techniques commonly associated with, and utilized by, product design.

Working with manufacturers

As a young designer it can be a daunting prospect attempting to see a concept through to manufacture and market. In order to see their products on the shelves, designers need to understand the whole design process and not just focus on abstract 'design concepts'.

The process of designing and manufacturing works most effectively when there are clear channels of communication. Designers need to understand the manufacturing processes of each factory; it is good to ask questions and identify possible design opportunities, while manufacturers need to be open to innovation and allow designers to explore new ways of using their facilities and expertise. By forging working relationships with manufacturers and design engineers, designers can work together to bring products to market. When the inevitable problems crop up, they are best solved collectively as efficiently and quickly as possible.

Integrating design and manufacture

Manufacturing involves the transformation of raw materials from their initial form into finished components that are then assembled into functional products. This is achieved by a variety of processes, each designed to perform a specific function in the process. Designers are faced with a dauntingly wide range of manufacturing methods, materials and assembly processes to choose from, and need to identify potential industrial partners to collaborate with.

In the past, designers were often forced into conflict with engineers due to the practice of handing a design over to be 'engineered'. This outmoded approach resulted in inefficiencies, and contemporary design and manufacturing practice now involves engineers in the design process as early as possible, with designers and engineers sharing data and ideas in what is termed **concurrent design** for manufacture and assembly.

Design for manufacture and assembly, commonly referred to as DFMA, aims to reduce component and assembly costs as well as streamline development cycles, and its ultimate aim is to develop higher-quality products. A feature of a 'good design' for manufacture and assembly is that products and their constituent components use an optimum choice of materials and processes, and meet their required purpose, at minimum cost, and with regard for quality and reliability requirements.

The appropriate selection of materials and manufacturing processes are interdependent, with the final choice of manufacturing process influencing the selection of materials, and vice versa. Selecting the optimum manufacturing processes and materials for a new product depends on the quantity of products to be produced and commercial timescales. As such, it is necessary to distinguish between one-off, batch and mass production requirements when determining appropriate manufacturing approaches.

Significant capital cost items, such as patterns or moulds, can play a role in the cost for each component depending upon their complexity and the production quantities involved, and thus influence manufacturing options. It is essential, therefore, that designers don't merely focus on the form of an object, but consider the appropriateness, viability and economics of manufacture. Designers need to be continually aware of changing production technologies and their effect on the cost aspects of their work, and be able to develop working relationships with colleagues in design engineering. They also need to be aware of the key methods of materials and manufacturing.

Selecting materials

Design can be described as the attempt to achieve a goal such as an ideal product using the available means, materials and techniques. The selection of materials is directly related to a product's PDS, and in particular the product's performance, proposed costs and user requirements.

When choosing materials you need to consider many factors. You need to ask what the product/component has to do, identify the environment it has to work in, while also asking what it should look and feel like. This list of desirable qualities can be matched against the properties of a range of materials. By taking into account the complexity of the forms to be produced and the tolerances (accuracy of manufacturing) required for assembly, you can begin to identify potential materials and processes for a product's manufacture. The Cambridge Materials Selector (CMS) is a widely available software tool for optimal materials selection. CMS enables the identification of the small subset of materials that will perform best in a given design, from the full menu of materials.

Designers are also increasingly aware of the environmental aspects of their work; creating products manufactured using sustainable materials, and enabling products to be dismantled and recycled, is of great social and economic value. Finally, the tactile qualities of a material – its surface texture, translucency, hardness or absorbency – all have an effect on the way a product is perceived and used by consumers and can also determine its value.

Common materials

On the following pages are some of the most commonly used materials.

Ceramics

From simple sun-baked bricks to Wedgwood's Industrial Revolution and a future of innovative material matrixes being developed in laboratories, ceramics offer designers a multitude of creative possibilities. Traditional ceramics applications include tiles, white ware such as toilets and sinks, and pottery. Technical ceramic applications that take advantage of the high thermal conductivity of ceramics include heat sinks for electronic circuitry.

Stoneware

This high-fired clay is usually grey to brown in colour due to the presence of iron and other impurities in the clay. It differs from earthenware in that it has very little moisture absorbency once fired. Stoneware is commonly used for tableware when glazed.

Earthenware

This is a low-temperature fired clay, usually of a red or orange colour. The porous ceramic is similar to terracotta commonly used to make pots industrially, as well as large sculptures and architectural forms.

Porcelain

This wondrous white translucent ceramic is fired at a high temperature to fuse the glaze and clay body together to produce a highly refined material.

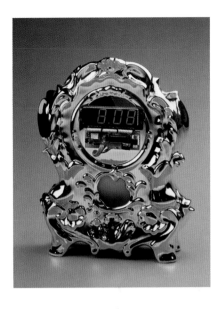

Above
Digi Clock, designed by Maxim Velcovsky for Qubus Design, 2001. This is a wonderful example of how designers can take a traditional form and material and subvert it through technology to create a contemporary design.

Below
Sponge Vase, designed by Marcel Wanders for Moooi, 1997. This was developed using a technique whereby a natural sponge was dipped in a fluid porcelain clay slip, which penetrated the sponge. When dry, it was fired in a kiln, burning the sponge away to leave a perfect porcelain replica.

Composites

Composites is the term used to describe engineered materials made from two or more components. Polymer composites that embed long-strand fibres in a thermosetting resin matrix are highly stiff and strong materials and were one of the great material developments of the twentieth century. The fibres carry the mechanical load, while the matrix provides toughness and protection for the fibres. Composite production is a labour-intensive process, and securing fastenings within, or joining or cutting holes in laminates, dramatically reduces a composite's strength. The resins used in composites are irritants and their vapours potentially toxic.

Honeycomb

These composites consist of a core hexagonal structure named after its visual resemblance to a bee's honeycomb, skinned either side by a sheet. Produced most commonly as sheet material in aluminium and glassfibre, they offer the advantage of stiffness combined with low weight and are often used for architectural panels and lightweight structures.

Glass Reinforced Plastic (GRP)

This consists of a **thermoset** plastic, most commonly polyester resin, reinforced by fine strands of glass. When introduced in the post-war period, the possibilities afforded by the low-cost mouldable material enabled designers such as Charles and Ray Eames and Eero Saarinen to transform the aesthetic, structure and function of furniture design.

The Bugatti Veyron Pur Sand edition, 2004. An example of how designers fetishize certain materials such as exposed carbon fibre and polished aluminium panels, and high-cost, high-tech manufacturing techniques.

Carbon fibre

This consists of woven carbon-fibre yarn, combined with resin to produce a mouldable sheet material. The material has exceptionally high strength-to-weight ratio and is often used in high-performance specifications. Carbon fibre is a highly energy-intensive and expensive material to produce. Recently its popularity has resulted in its distinct surface weave being copied and applied as a graphic to add fake 'technical' visual gravitas to a product, such as in 'hot hatch' cars.

Laminates

This group of materials is defined by its layering of materials together using adhesives. Plywood is a common example of a laminate made up of layers of the same material. The process of lamination enables such materials to be surfaced with coloured polymer sheets such as formica or metal finishes.

Elastomers

An **elastomer** is a polymer – a large molecule composed of repeating structural units – with the property of elasticity, and comes in both natural and synthetic forms.

Natural rubber

This flexible material is formed from the sap of a tapped rubber tree. Once purified and processed, it is used on an industrial scale as an elastomer to produce everything from rubber bands and rubber gloves to mats, dampeners and hoses.

Silicones

These typically non-stick, rubber-like polymer-based materials are used to seal or lubricate products. Silicones are energy-intensive to produce and cannot be recycled.

Ethylene Propylene Diene M-class rubber (EPDM)

This black rubber-like **thermoplastic** elastomer is commonly used for oil seals, gaskets and o-rings due to its resistance to chemicals, weathering and ultraviolet light.

Glass

Glass remains a fantastic, intoxicating, magical medium, as exciting in the twenty-first century as it was in the ancient world. The exploration of the unique properties of glass and how we engage with its extraordinary potential has been the obsession of alchemists, chemists and designers for centuries.

Transparent and invisible, or opaque and coloured, glass can colour space and refract, filter and shape light, offering product designers a range of opportunities uniquely afforded by a material made from mixed sands treated to achieve a state of rigid liquidity.

Soda-lime is the most common type of glass and is used for producing bottles, light bulbs and windows. Borosilicate glass has a higher melting point, and its high resistance to thermal shock means it is used for headlights, laboratory glass and Pyrex® ovenware.

Below
Mistic, vase/candleholder, designed by Arik Levy for Gaia & Gino, 2004.

Opposite
Bobbin Lace Lamp, designed by Nils van Eijk of Studio Van Eijk & Van der Lubbe, 2002. This fibre-optic chandelier provides stunning light without the use of light bulbs.

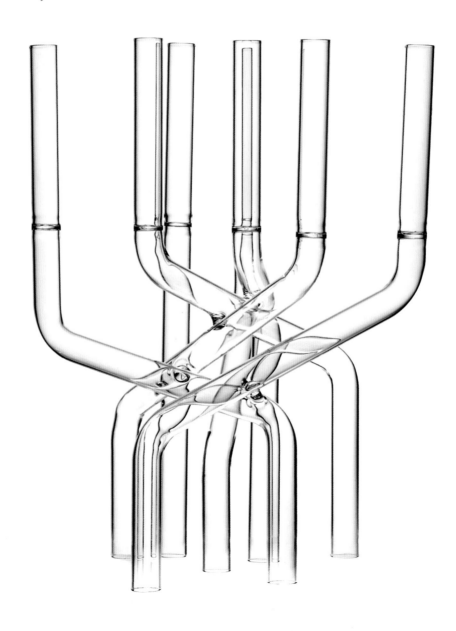

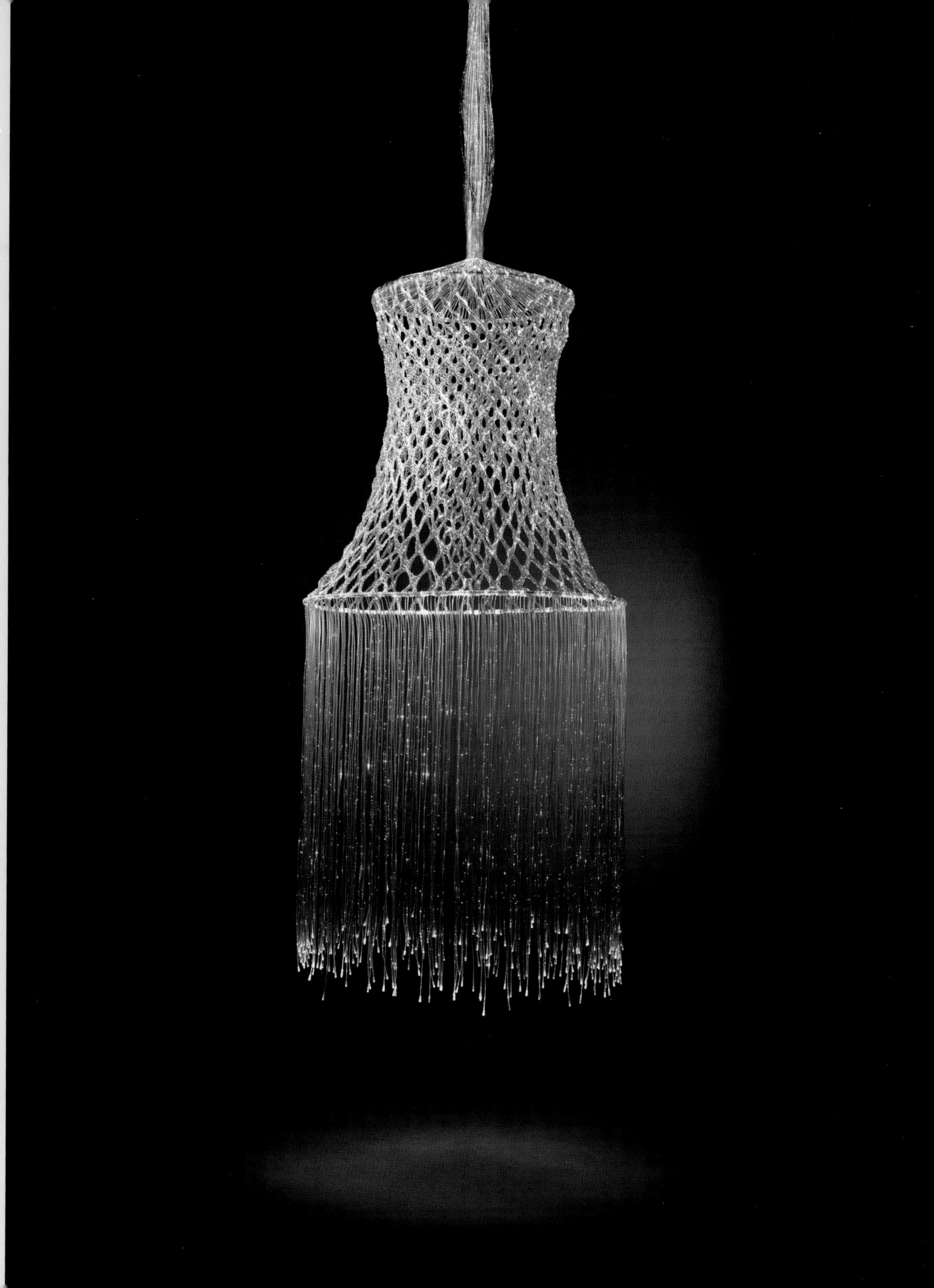

Metal

The discovery, manipulation and use of metal have defined epochs in humankind's history and continue to shape our environment today. From base metals such as copper, which corrode easily, to noble and precious metals that resist corrosion, such as gold and platinum, metals provide a rich resource for designers.

Ferrous alloys (containing iron)

Carbon steel: Carbon steels are alloys containing iron. There are numerous grades, from low-cost cast iron – a hard, brittle metal that rusts easily and is used almost universally from the construction industry to oil rigs – through to high-carbon steels whose hardness lend themselves to making tools. Carbon steels are easy to recycle and are comparatively cheap, with no other material offering the same blend of strength, toughness and easy manufacture.

Stainless steel: A hard, strong, highly rust-resistant and fully recyclable metal with low **ductility** (the mechanical property used to describe the extent to which materials can be deformed without fracturing). The substantially higher costs of stainless steel require designers to specify it responsibly, such as for outdoor applications or where a high-quality finish is required aesthetically.

Below
Ad Hoc, designed by Jean-Marie Massaud for Viccarbe, 2009. The chair is fabricated from brass rods, which give the chair its distinctive net-like form.

Opposite
PlantLock, by Front Yard Company, 2010. This simple solution for green living offers secure on-street parking for bicycles while also creating an attractive environment for the community.

Non-ferrous metals and alloys

Aluminium: An extensively used metal that is strong, light and ductile. Aluminium is the second most commonly used metal after steel, and has begun to replace steel in a number of applications, such as car bodies and aerospace. It requires a great deal of energy to extract, but is easily recycled at low energy cost.

Copper: A **malleable** (deforms under compression), ductile, heat-conductive and electrically conductive metal commonly used in electrical wiring and plumbing. It is easy to recycle and also easy to fabricate and join.

Lead: This poisonous ductile and highly malleable metal is very dense. It can be used as ballast to weigh down objects such as cantilevered lights.

Magnesium: Strong yet light, this metal is often used in alloys for high-performance applications such as high-performance bike frames. A magnesium computer case is 30% lighter than one made from aluminium. Extracting magnesium is energy-intensive, but it is very easy and cost-effective to recycle.

Nickel: This hard, malleable, ductile metal is magnetic and, due to being inert to oxidation, can be used to electroplate other metals. Some people are sensitive to nickel, causing allergic reactions to the small amount of nickel in stainless-steel applications such as watch casings.

Precious metals: From gold to silver and platinum, these materials add value to a consumer product. Gold is the only chemically stable metal, which is why it has historically been seen as the most valuable.

Tin: This malleable, ductile and corrosion-resistant metal is often used as a metallic coating, such as on tin cans.

Titanium: This corrosion-resistant metal has a very high strength-to-weight ratio and is used in high-performance applications such as racing cars. It is very expensive to extract from ore, making it ten times more expensive than aluminium.

Zinc: This is commonly used as a protective coating through a process known as **galvanizing**. It is a hygienic, easy-to-form metal, resistant to alkalis and acids, which lends itself to applications such as bar counter tops.

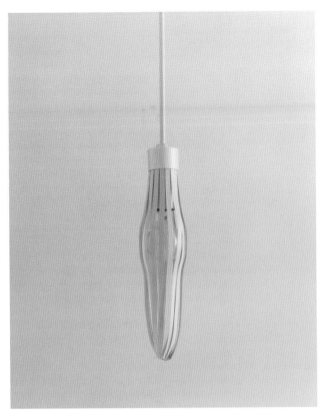

Plastics

Often dismissed as a cheap material due to its ubiquity in contemporary life, and the fact that after its discovery in 1862 it was used to duplicate materials at lower cost, plastics today are more cutting edge. A recent innovation is the introduction of bio-plastics, made from plant starch or polylactic acid. It may even be possible to make polymers from household waste in the near future. At the same time they are increasingly used for high-quality products. There are two types of plastic polymer: thermoplastics, which soften and melt upon heating, and thermosets, which harden when heated.

Thermoplastics

Acrylanitrile Butadiene Styrene (ABS): This polymer has the highest impact-resistance of all polymers and is used in consumer products where the designer needs to specify a durable material with high impact and mechanical strength. It is easily mouldable and, although normally opaque, some grades are now transparent. Some grades are also recyclable.

Acrylic: This transparent material, also known as polymethylmethacrylate (PMMA), is used as an alternative to glass and seen in applications such as lighting, aircraft windows and spectacle lenses, where its rigidity and hardness are necessary. It is recyclable and non-toxic.

Ethylene tetrafluorethane (ETFE): This abrasion-resistant material is most commonly seen in food packaging due to its excellent chemical and thermal properties. It can be made in translucent or opaque forms.

Nylon: One of the first commercially exploited polymers, nylon, also known as polyamide (PA) is a strong yet elastic opaque plastic that is chemical- and water-resistant. Nylon can be drawn into very fine strands, and it is often used as a man-made alternative to silk.

Polycarbonate (PC): A strong, durable and rigid material that can be produced in an opaque or transparent form. It is a high-cost polymer, but its high impact-resistance lends itself to high-performance applications such as mechanical gears, car bumpers and transparent riot shields.

Polyethylene (PE): This flexible material is most commonly used for container lids due to being inert, highly water-resistant and cheap to produce, as well as medical applications to be placed in the human body. It is easily recyclable, although if contaminated it can only be incinerated to produce energy.

Polypropylene (PP): This waxy material is rigid and chemically resistant, and is often used in packaging and rotationally moulded products. It is a low-cost, easily recyclable polymer, light and ductile, but it lacks strength in comparison with more expensive 'technical' polymers.

Ghost Chair, designed by Ralph Nauta and Lonneke Gordjin of the Dutch design studio Drift, 2008. The ethereal chair is made from laser-engraved Perspex.

Polystyrene (PS): This is one of the most commonly used plastics. In solid form it is used in a diverse range of applications such as disposable cutlery, CD cases and electronic housings. When foamed, expanded polystyrene (EPS) is used for insulation, packaging and foam drink cups. EPS is not recycled due to its low density, and is a major pollutant.

Polyvinyl chloride (PVC): Most commonly associated with vinyl upholstery when a plasticizer is added. UPVC (unmodified PVC) is a hard and brittle opaque material. It is a particularly unpleasant polymer that releases a variety of toxic compounds when it degrades, which has led environmentalists to campaign for an end to its production.

Jar Tops, designed by Jorre van Ast for Royal VKB, 2008. This series of readily available lids turn generic jars into reusable storage vessels, and includes a cocoa shaker cap and an oil and vinegar cap.

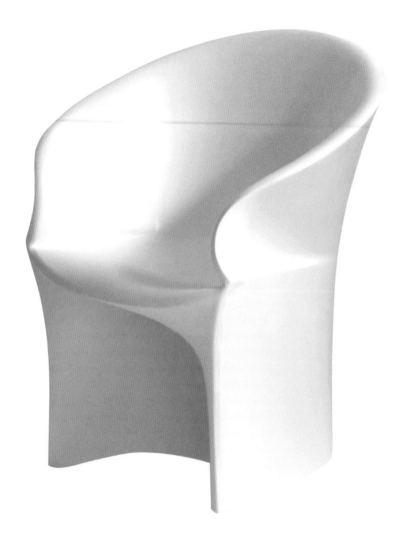

Thermosets

Epoxy: This clear, durable and rigid material is used in adhesives – araldite, surface coatings – or as a resin to impregnate composite fibres such as fibreglass and carbon fibre. It cannot be recycled, but can be broken down and used as a filler to pack out material.

Polyester (PET): Displaying good mechanical properties, polyester is heat-resistant and impervious to water. It is used in a diverse range of applications such as films, textiles and bottles. Plastic PET bottles are lighter and require less energy to produce than equivalent glass bottles. They can be recycled to produce fibres and fleece materials for clothing and carpets.

Polyurethane (PU): This material is an excellent insulator, and can be foamed to produce flexible or rigid cushions and pads. Different grades offer everything from soft and stretchy fabrics such as lycra, to cast applications such as wheels and tyres.

Above
Mermaid, designed by Tokujin Yoshioka for Driade, 2008. The chair is manufactured using rotationally moulded polyethylene.

Opposite top
Tree wall coat hanger, designed by Michael Young and Katrin Olina Petursdottir for Swedese, 2003. It has a cartoon-like profile that is cut out of oak-veneered MDF.

Opposite bottom
Magno Wooden Radio, designed by Singgih S. Kartono, 2009. Hand-crafted in an Indonesian farming village, the radio has an appealing mix of retro and modern styling. Each one is made using an environmentaly sustainable production process, which covers fair social standards for workers.

Wood

Wood comes in an enormous range of species, all with hugely different aesthetics, density and suitability for particular processes. From furniture to floorboards, we rely on wood for modern living. Natural and renewable, it has distinct advantages over less green alternatives than metals and plastics. Innovative uses of wood abound, such as the recent development of bamboo-based products that take structural advantage of the fast-growing plant's tensile strength, which is higher than that of steel. Unfortunately, because our timber demands are growing and we waste so much, our forests are in crisis, and as such designers are increasingly using wood in a more value-added manner.

Engineered wood: Wood manufacturing experienced a revolution in the 1960s with the development of particleboard panels, in which wood was ground down and recomposed into more homogenous and **isotropic** materials such as chipboard and medium-density fibreboard (MDF).

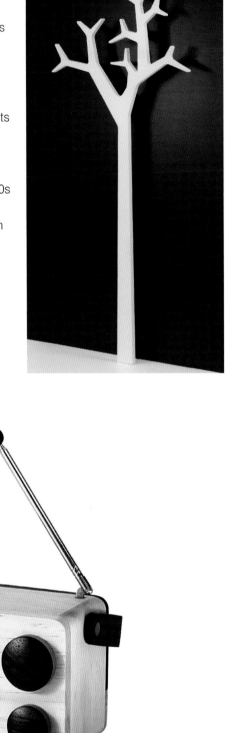

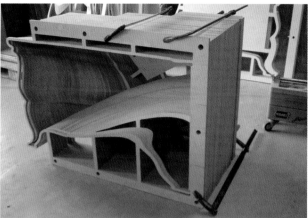

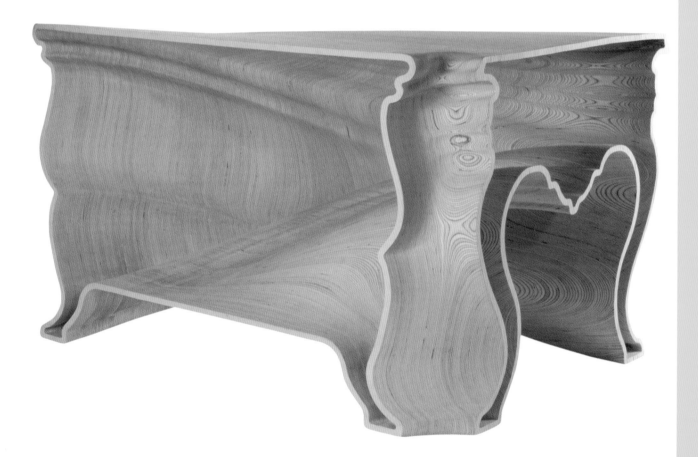

Cinderella, designed by Jeroen Verhoeven of Demakersvan, 2005. The table is produced through an elaborate process of CNC (computer numerically controlled) production. The cutting process results in perfect curves and undercuts, pushing the boundaries of the technology and the forms able to be manufactured out of wood.

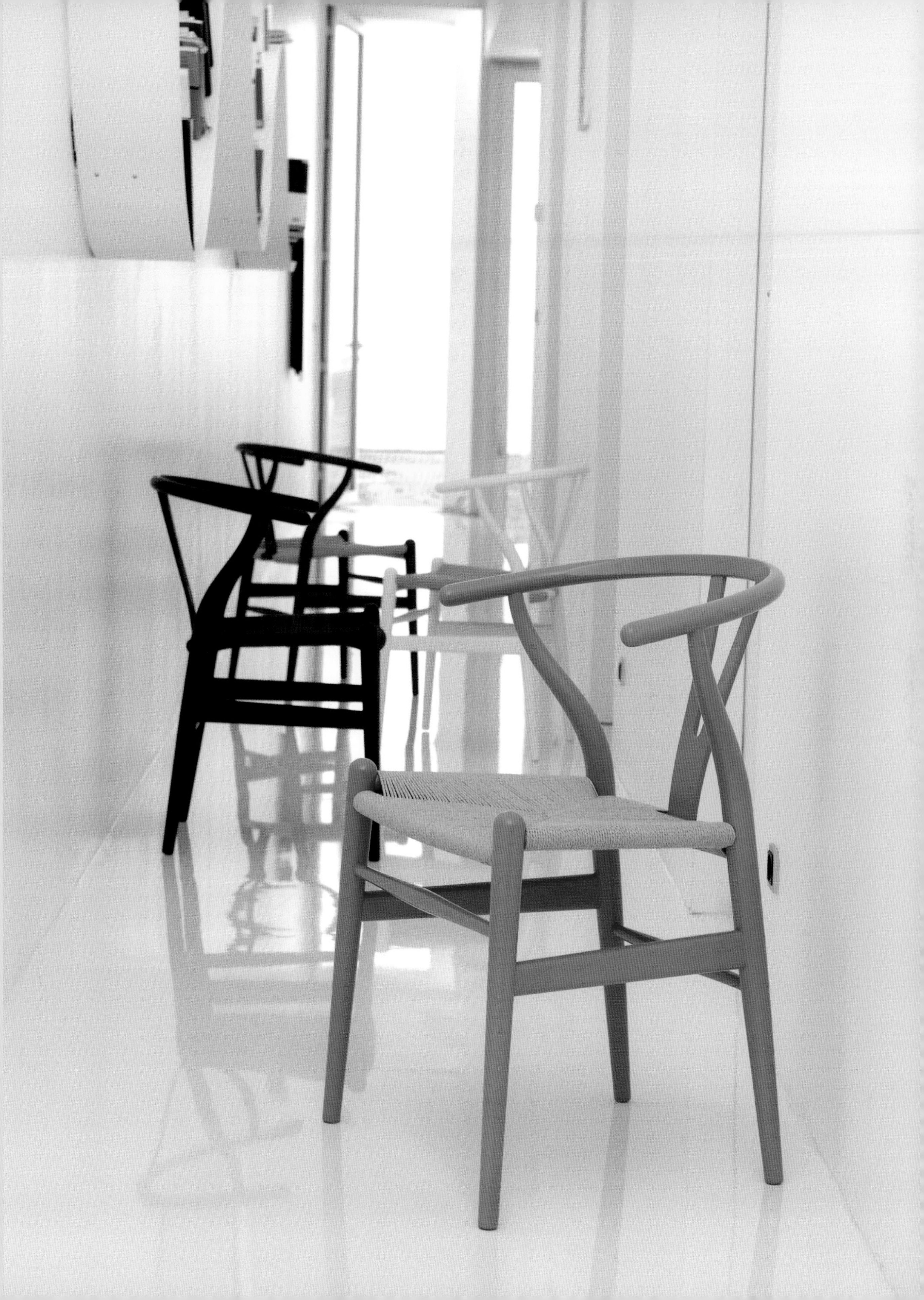

Manufacturing processes

After the creation and signing off of the information set (see p.109), the tooling required to manufacture and design is built and long lead-time components are ordered. It is very common that the tooling required is outsourced to specialist tool-makers. The tooling is subjected to extensive testing and modifications to iron out any glitches and ensure that the tools can effectively produce components and parts that meet the intended aesthetic, functional requirements, quality, volume and dimensional accuracy. It is at this stage that Beta prototypes are produced using parts that represent the actual intended manufacturing processes and components. After extensive user, reliability and performance field-testing, where the general public tests products, the manufacturer will be able to confidently begin producing the product for sale/use.

There are essentially five ways of making things: take something away, add something, cast something, form something, or grow something. Within each way there is an infinite variety. To add to this, there are many techniques to finish the product, such as painting, coating and engraving. Below is an introduction to some of the most common manufacturing processes and techniques.

Cutting

Cutting is the separation of a physical object, or a portion of a physical object, into two portions, through the application of an acutely directed force such as a blade or saw.

Machining

This is the collective term for the numerous processes of cutting or removing material from a solid piece, such as boring, drilling, milling, shaping and turning. These are collectively referred to as **chip forming**. The production of chips of material result from the cutting processes in which power-driven machine tools, such as lathes, milling machines and drill presses, are used with a sharp cutting tool to mechanically cut the material to achieve the desired form.

Machining offers the advantage of being a highly versatile technique to produce a wide variety of complex shapes, in virtually any solid material and to a high degree of accuracy. However, the process can produce a large amount of wastage, especially when having to use stock sizes of material.

Costs	Low tooling costs and low unit costs
Quality	High
Production scale	One-off to medium-volume manufacture
Alternatives	Laser cutting

Previous page
Wishbone Chair, designed by Hans J. Wegner for Carl Hansen & Søn, 1949. Inspired by classical Ming chairs, Wegner created a series of chairs that helped establish Denmark as an international leader of modern design. Considered to be Wegner's most successful design, it has been produced in large volumes for over 50 years.

Drilling: A drill is a tool with a rotating bit (cutting off thin shavings of material or crushing and removing material) used to make holes. Cutting fluid is often pumped to the cutting area to cool the bit, lubricate the cut, and to sluice away the unwanted debris and waste resulting from the process, which is known as swarf.

Boring: This process involves enlarging a hole that has already been drilled (or cast), by means of a cutting tool. Boring is used to achieve greater accuracy of the diameter of a hole, and can be used to cut a tapered hole.

Milling: A milling machine is a machining tool used for the shaping of metal and other solid materials. Like drilling, a rotating cutter rotates about an axis commonly known as a spindle axle; however, a milling machine can perform a wide range of tasks such as planing, drilling, routing and engraving due to its ability to multi-axis cut. Milling machines may be manually operated, mechanically automated, or digitally automated via Computer Numerical Control (CNC).

Shaping: This material removal process involves a single-point cutting tool moving across a stationary block of material to produce a shaped or sculpted surface.

Turning: This process involves rotating a material around an axis on a lathe, and employing a cutting tool to produce 'solids of revolution'. Turning is restricted to producing circular profiles, but can be used for low- or high-volume production runs for a variety of materials and has low tooling costs.

Die cutting

This process involves a formed sharpened block, known as a die-cutting tool, making a predetermined incision when pressure is exerted, cutting or creasing a thin material. Die cutting is ideal for batch production due to its low set-up costs, but if the process is used to produce 3D products then the flat die-cut forms will need expensive hand assembly or secondary processes.

Costs	Low tooling costs and unit costs
Quality	High
Production scale	One-off to high-volume manufacture
Alternatives	Laser cutting, water-jet cutting, punching and blanking

Punching and blanking

This process involves a hardened steel punch cutting through sheet materials, and allows for a variety of profiles to be cut out.

Costs	Low to moderate tooling costs and unit costs
Quality	High, but the cut edges often require finishing
Production scale	One-off to high-volume manufacture
Alternatives	CNC machining, laser cutting, water-jet cutting

Water-jet cutting

This technique employs a tool capable of slicing into metal and other solid materials such as glass and stone using a high-pressure jet of water, enabling very fine details to be cut. It is a cold process that doesn't heat up a material and risk deformation. However, as the cutting jet splays the further it gets from the nozzle, the thicker the material cut, the more the cut edge is deformed. To ensure the back of the material being cut is not damaged from splash-back, it is common practice to use a sacrificial layer of plastic to protect the piece.

Bent, designed by Stefan Diez and Christophe De La Fontaine for Moroso, 2006. These tables are fabricated out of laser-cut perforated aluminium sheets.

Costs	No tooling costs and moderate unit
Quality	Good
Production scale	One-off to medium-volume manufacture
Alternatives	Laser cutting, die cutting, punching and blanking

Laser cutting

This process involves cutting metals or other non-reflective materials using a high-powered computer-controlled laser. The process allows for intricate patterns to be cut and leaves a clean, high-quality finish. While the process has the advantage of not requiring expensive tooling to cut materials, its low speed means that it is best suited for one-off and batch production.

Costs	No tooling costs but medium to high unit costs
Quality	High
Production scale	One-off to high-volume manufacture
Alternatives	CNC machining, punching and blanking, water-jet cutting

Etching

This process uses acid to cut into the unprotected parts of a metal surface to create a design in the material. Photo-etching uses a photo-sensitive coating that is then exposed to light to etch metal.

Costs	Very low tooling costs but moderate to high unit costs
Quality	High
Production scale	One-off to high-volume manufacture
Alternatives	CNC machining and engraving, laser cutting

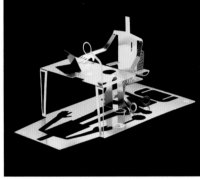

Above
Micro World, designed by Sam Buxton, 2003. This is part of a series of fold-up metal sculpture business cards, where each scene folds from a flat sheet of photo-etched stainless steel just 0.15mm thick. All are packaged flat with folding instructions for buyers to complete the sculpture.

Left
Garland Light, designed by Tord Boontje for Habitat, 2002, and Artecnica, 2004. Made from a continuous etched metal strand that is wrapped around a light bulb, the charming floral forms of this shade have led to the popular rediscovery and use of decorative motifs in recent years.

Joining

Joining is the mechanical, structural or chemical bonding of different components to form a larger object.

Mechanical fixings

A variety of removable or permanent fastenings are often used in assembly, such as rivets, pins, screws, staples, collars and snap-fits.

Costs	No tooling costs but may require jigs and labour
Quality	Low- to high-strength fixings available
Production scale	One-off to high-volume manufacture
Alternatives	Adhesive bonding, welding, joinery (wood)

Adhesive bonding

This is the process of joining two or more parts by using an adhesive. A form of mechanical fixing such as a clamp or bracket to prevent misalignment is often used to ensure a secure bond. Most commonly used in bonding plastics, this method has begun to be used to bond metals.

Costs	No tooling costs but may require jigs and additional mechanical fixings
Quality	High-strength bond
Production scale	One-off to medium-volume manufacture
Alternatives	Mechanical fixing, welding

Soldering and brazing

This process involves adhering metal components together using a metallic soldering or brazing alloy that melts below the temperature of the metals being joined to avoid thermal distortion of the components. The metallic soldering or brazing alloy is essentially a type of 'glue'. The difference between them is that the melting point for soldering is much lower.

Costs	No tooling costs but may require jigs; high unit costs
Quality	High-strength bond
Production scale	One-off to high-volume manufacture
Alternatives	Welding

Welding

This is the process of joining metal parts by applying heat and/or pressure. The process results in a joint as strong or stronger than the parts themselves. The two basic categories are **fusion welding** (where the temperature of the metal is brought to its melting point and joined, with or without filler material) and **solid state welding** (where the metal is joined at a temperature below the melting point of the material, without the addition of a filler material). The most common example is friction welding, where two rods or pipes are rubbed together, with the heat generated causing the two parts to weld together.

Costs	No tooling costs but may require jigs; low unit costs
Quality	High quality
Production scale	One-off to high-volume manufacture
Alternatives	Mechanical fixing, adhesive bonding

Joinery

This is the term used to describe woodworking techniques to join wooden parts with glue or without, known as dry joints. These can be constructed by hand or machine-made. They offer a variety of structural and aesthetic qualities suitable for a wide range of applications, from furniture and cabinet-making to the construction industry.

Costs	No tooling costs but may require jigs; unit costs can be moderate to high depending upon the complexity
Quality	High-strength bond
Production scale	One-off to medium-volume manufacture
Alternatives	Mechanical fixing, welding

Weaving

This describes the passing of strips or strands of material over and under each other to form an intertwined structure. Traditional woven furniture was made from bamboo, rattan and willow, but modern techniques enable a far wider range of materials to be woven together, from paper and plastic to wood and metal. Woven structures rely on mere friction (rather than the adhesives used in laminating) to create rigidity; by being more flexible they can easily be deformed and moulded, enabling designers to produce complex forms impossible to develop through lamination. Hand-weaving is a relatively slow process that requires skilled labour, while machine weaving is a high-speed process.

Costs	No tooling costs
Quality	Dependent on which material is used
Production scale	One-off to high-volume manufacture
Alternatives	Upholstery for flexible applications or laminated wood or composites for rigid applications

Below
Apollo, designed by Ross Lovegrove for Driade, 1997. This modern chaise lounge chair is made from rattan.

Opposite top
Togo, designed by Michel Ducaroy for Ligne Roset, launched in 1973. This was the first sofa to be manufactured without a frame, and simply made of multiple-density foam with generously quilted covers that are fully removable and available in a wide range of colours and textiles.

Opposite bottom
Pools & Pouf!, designed by Robert Stadler, 2004. These upholstered seating components in black leather with tufted details are like a traditional Chesterfield sofa. They deliberately blur the boundaries between functional furniture and design as art.

Upholstery

This is the process of bringing hard and soft components and materials together to create finished furniture. Typical chairs consist of structural wooden frames, foam padding and a textile cover. This traditional approach has been complemented by design innovations, such as creating seating without a frame – for example, the first all-foam sofa, the Ligne Roset Togo, which reinvents the traditional Chesterfield.

Costs	No tooling costs but unit costs depend on complexity, and material selection and can be costly
Quality	Skilled upholsterers can achieve very high standards of quality
Production scale	One-off to high-volume manufacture
Alternatives	None

Casting

Casting involves pouring a liquid material into a mould, which contains a hollow cavity of the desired shape. The liquid is allowed to solidify and the solidified part, known as the cast, is then ejected or broken out of the mould.

In manufacturing, the terms **tools** or **moulds** refers to a cavity in which a part is formed. Tools can be made from a variety of materials depending on the material to be cast. High-volume tools can be manufactured from exceptionally hard and brittle tool steel, while shorter-run parts can be produced from less durable wooden, plastic or aluminium 'soft' tooling.

Injection moulding

The process of injection moulding, in which granules of raw material are conditioned by heat and pressure to reach a fluid state and then injected into a steel mould, is frequently employed for the common polymers polystyrene, high-density polyethylene, polypropylene and acrylanitrile butadiene styrene (ABS). A common technique for making multiple-colour or component thermoplastic objects, such as toothbrushes, is multiple-shot moulding. This typically involves the injection moulding of the first part, before inserting this into another mould in which a subsequent part is moulded onto it. Injection moulding also enables decoration such as graphics to be added during the moulding process through the use of printed foils being placed into a mould prior to the plastic being injected. Injection moulding is a highly versatile process, enabling the production of complex forms very precisely. However, it involves considerable investment and is only really appropriate for high-volume production.

Costs	Very high tooling costs but very low unit costs
Quality	Very high-quality surface finish
Production scale	Only suitable for high-volume production runs
Alternatives	Rotational moulding

Blow moulding

This enables the production of hollow forms. Plastic is melted down before being forced into a mould by compressed air, pushing the plastic out to match the mould. Once the plastic has cooled and hardened, the mould is opened up to release the finished part. Blow moulding demands high production volumes to be financially viable due to the high cost of making the moulds required. However, it does allow manufacturers to make simple hollow forms exceptionally fast and with a very low unit price.

Costs	Moderate tooling costs and low unit costs
Quality	High, enabling uniform wall thickness and a high-quality surface finish
Production scale	Only suitable for high-volume production runs
Alternatives	Injection moulding, rotational moulding

Opposite

Algue, designed by Ronan & Erwan Bouroullec for Vitra, 2004. The brothers have created injection-moulded interior design components and decorative elements here. Reminiscent of plants, the plastic elements can be linked together to form vine-like structures, from light curtains to thick, opaque partitions.

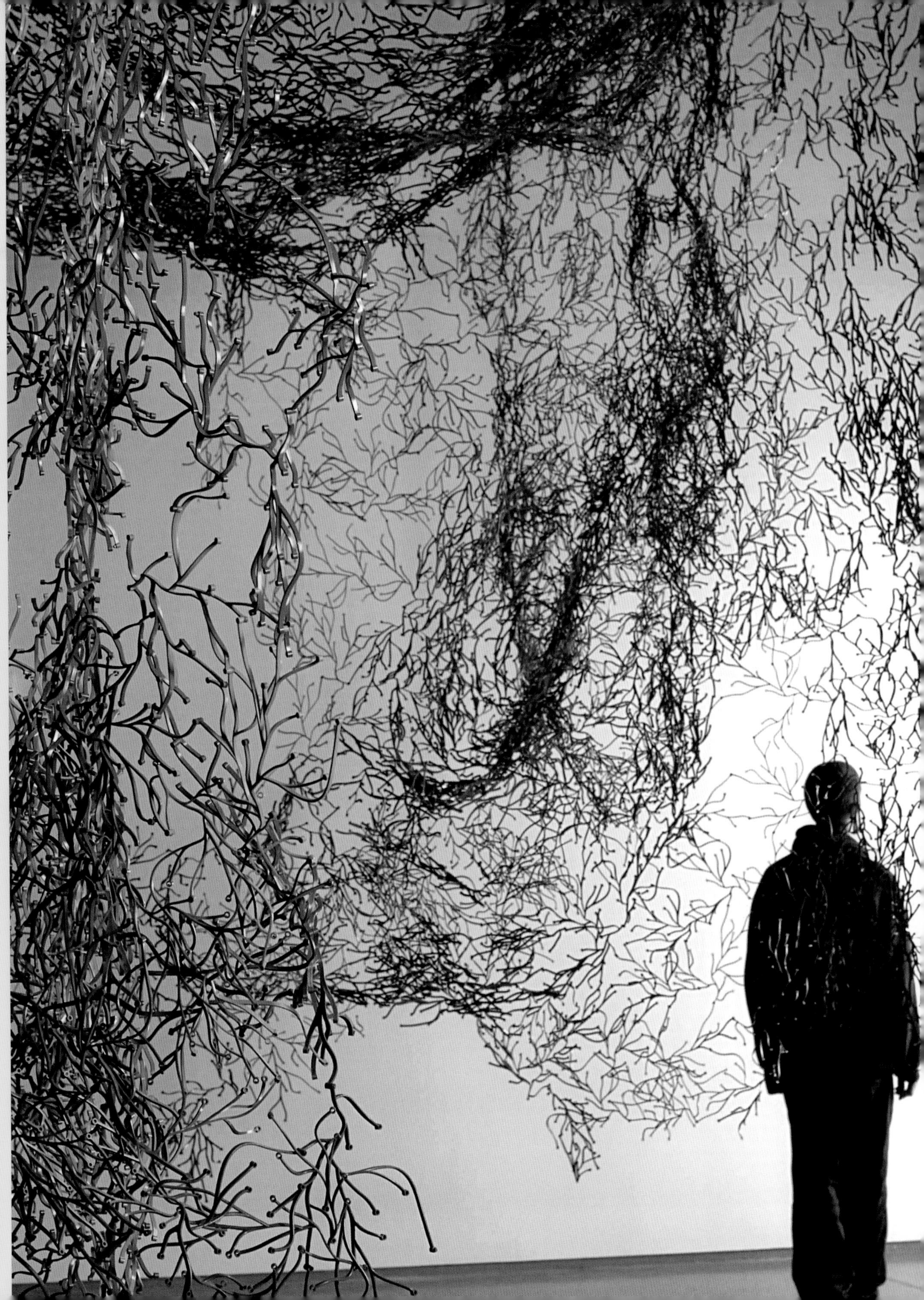

Dip moulding

This is one of the oldest techniques for forming shapes, and simply involves dipping a shape into a melted material. Best known for producing rubber gloves and balloons, it is highly cost-effective for short production runs.

Costs	Very low tooling costs and low to moderate unit costs
Quality	Good, with no flash or split lines caused by two-part moulds used by other methods
Production scale	One-off to high-volume manufacture
Alternatives	Injection moulding of sleeves and covers

Reaction injection moulding (RIM)

This is a similar process to injection moulding, but rather than using thermoplastics, thermosetting polymers are used, which are cured within the mould. Typical applications are foam mouldings for furniture and soft toys.

Costs	Low to moderate tooling costs
Quality	High-quality mouldings
Production scale	One-off to high-volume manufacture
Alternatives	Injection moulding

Glassblowing

This centuries-old process involves inflating molten glass with the aid of a blowpipe or tube. Hand-blowing can be used to produce a large variety of forms for one-off, batch or medium-volume production, but the unit costs can be expensive due to the high cost of skilled labour. Industrial glassblowing and blow moulding offers the potential for low unit costs, but has very high tooling costs and the designer is limited to specifying comparatively simple forms only.

Costs	Low for studio glassblowing; high tooling costs but low unit costs for industrial mechanized production
Quality	High perceived value and quality
Production scale	One-off to high-volume manufacture
Alternatives	Blow moulding if plastic is an acceptable alternative

Glassblowing is a technique that involves inflating molten glass into a bubble with the aid of the blowpipe and then manipulating the form using tools to create the desired design.

Rotational moulding

Ideal for producing hollow shapes in low volume, this simple process enables designers to create large components cost-effectively. The process involves loading a hollow mould with plastic pellets or liquid, heating the mould externally and rotating it to distribute the plastic evenly on the internal surface of the mould. Rotational moulding is a comparatively low-cost process due to its simple tooling requirements and is ideal for runs of up to 10,000 units, but is not suitable for producing small, precise products or components. Cycle times are long, and fewer parts can be produced than with processes such as injection moulding.

Costs	Moderate tooling costs, with low to medium unit cost, but processes have long cycle time of, on average 30 minutes, which adds cost if volumes are high
Quality	Good surface finish; dimensional tolerances are subject to cooling deformation
Production scale	Low to medium-volume manufacture
Alternatives	Blow moulding, thermoforming

Above
Outgang XP, designed by Alex Milton and Will Titley, 2008. This multifunctional design, enabling the chair to be rotated into three different seating positions, provides maximum versatility from the one piece. Its faceted ergonomic form takes full advantage of the structural and manufacturing possibilities that rotational moulding provides.

Below
Rotationalmouldedshoe, designed by Marloes ten Bhömer, 2009. This innovative couture design was specifically created, using polyurethane rubber and stainless steel, for the 'After Hours' installation in the Krannert Art Museum in Illinois, USA.

Die-casting

A high-volume, high-tooling cost, metal-forming process in which molten metal is forced into a mould or cavity under pressure. The process is ideal for complex shapes and produces an excellent surface finish and dimensionally accurate part.

Costs	High tooling costs but low unit costs
Quality	Very high-quality surface finish
Production scale	High-volume manufacture
Alternatives	Sand casting, machining

Compression moulding

This process involves a measured amount of ceramic, thermoset plastic or elastomer being placed in a heated mould and compressed into the desired shape, before being left to harden and removed. Excess material, known as 'flash', can occur at the parting line, which will require trimming. First used in plastic manufacturing in the 1920s to produce Bakelite, the process is ideal for producing largely flat and simple parts that require large, thick-walled sections such as wellington boots.

Costs	Moderate tooling costs and low unit costs
Quality	High-quality surface finish, with high-strength components able to be produced
Production scale	Medium to high-volume manufacture
Alternatives	Injection moulding

Slip casting

This traditional method of producing ceramics involves pouring clay slurry (a thick suspension of clay solids in a liquid) into a plaster mould; as the water from the slurry is absorbed by the mould, the clay begins to gather on the surface of the mould. Once the desired thickness has been reached the excess slurry is poured out. The clay part is then removed from the slip-casting mould, dried and fired in a kiln. The advantage of this low-cost technique is that it enables decoration to be integrated into complex forms easily.

Costs	Low tooling costs, but moderate to high unit costs
Quality	The surface finish is dependent on the quality of the mould, the ceramic glaze and the skill of the worker
Production scale	Low-volume manufacture
Alternatives	Traditional clay-throwing on a wheel

Forging

This is the traditional process of deforming metal between dies or with hammers using impact or pressure. Blacksmiths use this approach of manipulating metal to make products.

Costs	Moderate to high tooling costs and moderate unit costs
Quality	Forged metals displayed an excellent structure
Production scale	One-off to high-volume manufacture
Alternatives	Casting, machining

Opposite

Chair_One, designed by Konstantin Grcic for Magis, 2004. An example of aluminium die-casting, the chair is constructed like a football with a number of flat planes assembled at angles to each other, creating the distinctive three-dimensional form that is then mounted on a cast-concrete base.

Spinning

The manufacture of hollow rounded metal shapes is often achieved by forcing a spinning metal blank against a pattern. The process offers limited control over wall thicknesses and often requires surface finishing to achieve the desired quality.

Costs	Low tooling costs and moderate unit costs
Quality	The finish is dependent on the skill of the operator and the speed of spinning
Production scale	One-off to medium-volume manufacture
Alternatives	Deep drawing

Investment casting

This process, also known as lost-wax casting, enables the production of high-quality parts with complex shapes. An expendable wax pattern is created and then coated in a ceramic to form a mould. The mould is then heated to remove the wax, leaving a hollow mould into which molten metal is poured. Upon cooling, the ceramic mould is broken away to leave a high-quality part. Investment casting enables complex shapes to be produced without requiring any post-process machining, and it is possible to reduce the weight of large castings by forming a hollow core.

Costs	Low-cost wax tooling and moderate to high unit costs
Quality	Excellent
Production scale	Low to high-volume manufacture
Alternatives	Die casting, sand casting

The iconic Rolls Royce Flying Lady mascot, 1913 to present, is constructed using investment casting.

Sand casting

This traditional low-cost technique enables the production of cast metal by forming a sand mould using a wooden pattern and pouring molten metal into the cavity. The metal is allowed to cool and the casting is separated from the mould. The process produces porous components and can be highly labour-intensive, as parts may require a lot of finishing.

Costs	Low tooling costs, moderate unit costs
Quality	Poor surface finish
Production scale	One-off to medium-volume manufacture
Alternatives	Die casting

Pewter Stool, designed and made by Max Lamb, 2006. Cast into crude sand formations on a sandy beach, it takes shape as the incoming tide cools the molten metal.

Forming

Forming covers a set of manufacturing processes that involve the manipulation of sheets, tubes and rods into predetermined forms.

Bending

This is the application of hand-controlled or CNC formers to fold flat metal sheets, tubes or rods into three-dimensional forms.

Costs	Standard tooling required, no cost; specialized tooling can incur significant costs; unit costs are low
Quality	High
Production scale	One-off to high-volume manufacture
Alternatives	None

Panel beating

This process requires highly skilled craftspeople to stretch and compress sheet metal to create almost any shape using a variety of tools and techniques.

Costs	Low to moderate tooling costs; high unit costs
Quality	Handmade process can produce a high-quality finish
Production scale	One-off to low-volume manufacture
Alternatives	Stamping

Stamping

This high-volume process enables sheet metal to be formed into complex shapes between two matched steel tools. The technique is used to produce a wide range of products from large-scale car bodies to mobile phone cases.

Costs	High tooling costs; low to moderate unit costs
Quality	High
Production scale	High-volume manufacture only due to tooling costs
Alternatives	Panel beating

Below
Leaf Lamp, designed by Yves Béhar with fuseproject for Herman Miller, 2006. The lamp is stamped using a tool before being bent to form the final shape. It uses LED (light emitting diode) lighting, giving the user a variety of options such as intensity and colour and enabling them to set a mood or a location. The LEDs use less than 12 watts of power and use 40% less energy than the compact fluorescent lights used in conventional angle-poise lights.

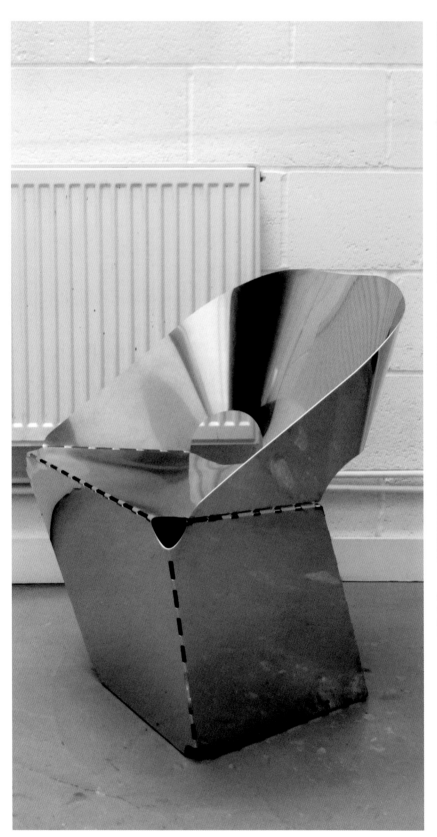

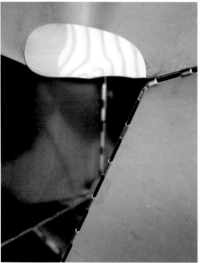

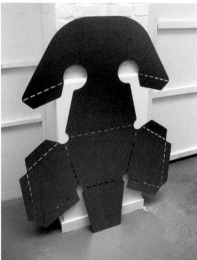

Sheet Steel chair, designed and produced by Max Lamb, 2008. First, it is formed from a single sheet of steel (above), then bent along the punched holes for assembly (top and left).

Thermoforming

This process involves heating a sheet of thermoplastic until it is soft and pliable, enabling it to be stretched over or into a single-sided mould until cooled. The most common method is **vacuum forming**, where air is sucked out of a chamber to force the draped thermoplastic to mould around the pattern. The process requires the moulded sheet to be trimmed. Any form must not involve vertical sides but instead feature draft angles (tapered forms) that enable the pattern to be removed. Thermoforming tooling costs are comparatively low and the process is suitable for low- and high-production volume runs.

Costs	Low to moderate tooling costs and unit costs
Quality	Depends on material and pressure applied
Production scale	One-off to high-volume manufacture
Alternatives	Injection moulding, composite laminating

Plywood forming

This process, commonly used in furniture, involves forming and bending plywood sheets made up from layers of veneered wood glued together by applying pressure through vacuum and patterns to produce laminated sheets. Bending plywood can only be done in a single direction but can be achieved through handmade jigs that help control the location and motion of a tool, as well as industrial tools such as presses. Thin plywood can also be pressed in a similar manner to plastic forming, although it is difficult to achieve deep impressions and forms.

Costs	Depends on complexity
Quality	Depends on grain variation of material
Production scale	One-off prototyping to mass manufacture
Alternatives	None

Steam bending

This process steams wood to soften it sufficiently so that it can be bent into tight bends. It combines traditional handmade craft skills with industrial techniques. It was first pioneered as an industrial process by Danish furniture manufacturer Thonet in the 1850s.

Costs	Low tooling costs; moderate to high unit costs
Quality	Good
Production scale	One-off to high-volume manufacture
Alternatives	CNC machining, wood laminating

Above
Pigeon Light, designed by Ed Carpenter for Thorsten Van Elten, 2001. An urban souvenir, it is a successful example of using a low-cost vacuum formed component to produce a commercially viable product. The playful and iconic light features a clothes peg foot, which enables the pigeon to perch on a wall fixing or clip itself to its own cable to be self-standing.

Opposite
Gubi Chair, designed by Boris Berlin & Poul Christiansen of Komplot Design, 2006. This is the first industrial product based on an innovative technique of moulding three-dimensional veneer. The organically shaped shell provides a friendly and comfortable form, while offering the unique possibility of reducing its thickness and consumption of natural resources by half.

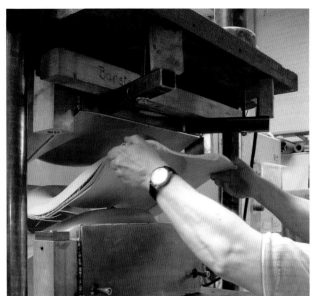

Superforming

The pace of technological change and adaptation of processes into new materials can be seen in the recent innovation of superforming. This process enables thermoforming processes to be applied to aluminium alloy sheets to produce complex forms within a single component.

Biomega MN bike, designed by Marc Newson, 1999. It makes use of superforming to create a bonded aluminium frame.

Costs	Low to moderate tooling costs; moderate to high unit costs
Quality	Good surface finish and dimensional tolerancing
Production scale	Low to medium-volume manufacture
Alternatives	Stamping, thermoforming

Glass slumping

This forming process involves heating a sheet of glass sufficiently to soften it enough to slump into or over a mould. Slumping is a slow process, commonly used to produce bowls and plates. This requires a skilled technician, and often needs extensive trial and error to arrive at the desired result.

Costs	Low tooling costs; but high unit costs due to slow speed of production
Quality	Dependent on skill of operator
Production scale	One-off to medium-volume manufacture
Alternatives	None

CASE STUDY: the VENUS chair

4.

Tokujin Yoshioka's VENUS chair, 2008, is made by growing natural crystals on a substrate frame of sponge-like polyester elastomer that is submerged in a tank of water saturated with minerals, the production process being half controlled by Yoshioka and half left up to nature.

Below
(Left to right) The chair in the aquarium, and details showing the chair and minerals in water.

Bottom
Finished chair as presented at the exhibition 'Second Nature', directed by Tokujin Yoshioka at 21_21 Design Sight in Japan.

Growing

Technological developments are provoking the biggest change in the nature of mass production since the Industrial Revolution, with processes like rapid prototyping enabling the production of parts without tooling.

Rapid prototyping (RP)

This is the process of constructing objects by taking virtual designs from CAD software and transforming them into data that can be laid down layer by layer using liquid, powder or sheet material. Originally used to prototype parts, today designers are actively exploring the possibility of manufacturing production-quality high-cost parts in small numbers.

Costs	No tooling costs but high unit costs due to slow speed of production
Quality	High quality is possible depending on process chosen
Production scale	One-off to low-volume manufacture
Alternatives	CNC machining

Fused Deposition Modelling (FDM): This is a process that extrudes a molten metal or polymer to create layers of material generated from CAD files. The cross-sectional layers are built up one at a time to complete the finished part.

Stereolithography (SLA): This is an additive fabrication process that uses a vat of photo-sensitive liquid resin that is cured in layers by a laser to build parts. SLA requires designers to add support structures to the CAD data to enable the creation of forms that would deform due to gravity. SLA offers unlimited geometric freedom, but is slower than many other rapid prototyping processes.

Selective Laser Sintering (SLS): This is an additive technique that uses a high-powered laser to fuse small particles of ceramic, metal or plastic into a mass. The process allows highly detailed, lightweight and high-strength components to be produced, but as with other RP processes SLS manufacturing has high unit costs.

Opposite
Chair from the Solid collection, designed by Patrick Jouin for Materialise, 2004. Manufactured using the rapid-prototyping technique of stereolithography, the structural form is reminiscent of blades of grass or ribbons waving in the wind to create this unique design.

Finishing

Many manufactured parts may be subjected to additional processes to enhance their appearance, performance or corrosion-resistance. Finishes can be additive – such as plating, galvanizing, painting or applying adhesive labels – or subtractive, such as etching, engraving, polishing and sanding.

Plating

This process involves covering a conductive surface with a metal, with common applications including chrome-plated car bumpers and plating base materials for jewellery and decorative items.

Costs	No tooling costs; high unit costs
Quality	Dependent on coating material
Production scale	One-off to high-volume manufacture
Alternatives	Galvanizing, spray painting

Spray painting

This common process involves applying a layer of paint, ink or varnish by using a spray gun to atomize paint particles and spraying them though the air onto a surface.

Costs	No tooling costs; unit costs dependent on scale and complexity
Quality	Dependent on skills of operator
Production scale	One-off to high-volume manufacture
Alternatives	Powder coating

Powder coating

This process involves coating metal parts with a fine thermoplastic powder that is heated until it melts and forms a protective durable layer over the part.

Costs	No tooling costs; low unit costs
Quality	Glossy and uniform high-quality surface finish
Production scale	One-off to high-volume manufacture
Alternatives	Galvanizing, spray painting, dip moulding if used as a coating

Subtractive processes

This set of processes includes polishing, sanding and grinding components to achieve the desired surface finish.

Costs	No tooling costs; unit costs are dependent on the surface finish required
Quality	High-quality finishes are achievable
Production scale	One-off to high-volume manufacture
Alternatives	Spray painting or powder coating to finish a material, the various subtractive processes if different finishes are required

Anti-theft Bike/Car Device, designed by Dominic Wilcox, 2008. These stickers are designed to deter thieves from attempting to steal a vehicle by making it appear old, damaged and worthless.

INTERVIEW
Raw-Edges Design Studio

Biography

Raw-Edges Design Studio is an ongoing collaboration between Yael Mer and Shay Alkalay. Together, Mer and Alkalay share a common goal to create objects that have never been seen before. Mer's main focus is in transforming two-dimensional sheet materials into curvaceous functional forms, whereas Alkalay is fascinated by how things move, function and react. Since graduating from the Royal College of Art in 2006, they have received a number of awards, including the British Council Talented Award, iF Gold Award, Dutch Design Award, Wallpaper* Design Award 2009 and the Elle Decoration International Design Award for best furniture of 2008–09. Their work has been shown in major exhibitions worldwide including New York, Paris, Basel and Milan, and their designs can be found within the permanent collections of the Museum of Modern Art, New York and the Design Museum, London.

Interview

What are the difficulties of bringing a product to market?

Keeping the core idea fresh, clear and direct without compromising too much due to functionality, production constraints and market needs. Unfortunately, it does not happen every day, but when you get a good idea, somehow all these factors complete each other quite smoothly.

How do you decide which materials and manufacturing methods to use?

The usage of materials and manufacturing methods is fundamental in our design work. From the first stage we experiment with the actual material and it is very rare that we finish the sketching stage without knowing how to make it and from what material. We feel very comfortable with turning simple and common materials into something new by twisting ordinary processes into unconventional methods. The way we treat materials and methods leads to new design ideas. For example, in the Tailored Wood series, we used veneer not as a surface covering but as a structural mould that held the shape before the polyurethane casting.

How do you define the markets for your products?

We are driven by the ideas that we have and we hope to find someone out there who will appreciate them. We actually don't have target markets as such, and we don't direct our designs towards specific customers. Maybe our market is in fact people who find our designs interesting and inspiring.

How does your designed product reach the market?

Through exhibitions, retailers and shops, publications and press and, of course, through design blogs and websites.

Opposite top left
Plastic Nostalgic, 2008. This cabinet is a carefully crafted beech wood design redolent of the Fisher Price plastic toys of childhood memories.

Opposite top right
Tailored Wood, 2008. Making this stool involves a technique commonly used in the clothing industry to furniture design, to create a pattern that is filled with foam. The pattern itself becomes both the defining surface and the mould. In a sense it is a reversal of upholstery in which normally a skin is applied over the stuffing.

Opposite bottom
Collection of innovative designs, 2006–10, ranging from batch-produced limited editions to commercially produced products for companies such as Established & Sons.

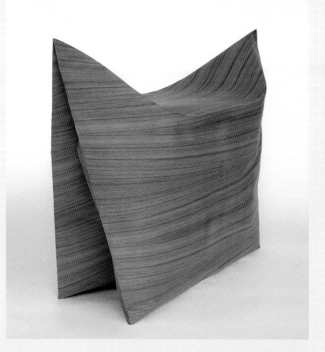

Marketing and selling

This section discusses the branding, marketing and selling of designers and the products they produce – from working with brand DNA and market research, to the role of packaging and retail design.

Branding

The products we use and consume say a great deal about our individual tastes and personalities. A brand is an amalgam of product design, logos, slogans, advertising, marketing, packaging and consumer recognition. Designers need to ensure that their designs inspire an emotional resonance in consumers, encouraging them to develop a relationship with a brand or product line that evolves over a lifetime of purchasing.

Consumers are drawn to brands because they embody values they are attracted to, such as authenticity or exclusivity. Brands create mythologies about their past, such as Coca-Cola® promoting that it is 'the real thing'. The purchase of up-market 'designer' goods positions the buyer in a social hierarchy through conspicuous consumption.

While brands are created by designers and marketing executives, they are living, evolving entities that are constantly subjected to alteration by consumers, for example, in the phenomenon of 'IKEA hacking', where an IKEA product becomes the basis for the consumer's own product, the rationale being that the product is cheaper than the raw materials.

Pimp My Billy: Billy Wilder, by Ding3000, 2005. Thirty-five million units have been sold world-wide, making it the world's biggest seller when it comes to shelves. The design enables buyers to customize each shelf, inspiring a DIY design craze known as 'IKEA hacking'.

Glossary of branding and marketing terms

- Brand values – The essential guiding principles and rules of a brand.
- Brand image – The look, feel and impression generated by a brand's logo, products, retail environments, advertising, marketing and customer service.
- Brandscape – The visual environment and marketplace that products and brands exist within.
- Brand DNA – The design language, visual codes and signifiers that embody a brand.
- Brand guidelines – The documents produced by companies to assure the consistent tone and use of brand values and identity.
- Brand manager – The person responsible for actively managing the brand image.

Consuming design

A visitor to a contemporary department store cannot avoid being dazzled by the plethora of products on sale, with each type of product coming in an enormous variety of styles. Equally bemusing is the advertising mythology surrounding them. For example, customers are led to believe that buying a Dualit toaster will not only mean better toast, but also a better life. Few really believe that nirvana comes with a new toaster or shaver, but the advertisers continue to succeed in persuading us that these are essential lifestyle purchases.

In contemporary society it could be argued that our possessions represent what we are. Lifestyle magazines reinforce this belief. Over and above any operational usefulness products may have, all goods act as part of an elaborate display, reinforcing identity and sending messages to others 'like us'. More important than the possession of an item are the details – the minutiae of appearance, the well-developed visual styles – that carry the messages of the taste cultures or dress codes.

Trying to identify and classify these styles is a highly challenging task for a designer, but the successful commercial brands and 'household name' have, without exception, developed an identifiable 'house style' or 'brand' consisting of aesthetic codes and data that make up the brand's design 'DNA'. These carefully nurtured and constantly evolving visual languages enable designers to communicate their ideology, with their portfolio of products resembling physical manifestos for each taste culture.

Below left
Bling Bling, by Frank Tjepkema for Chi Ha Paura, 2002. This medallion critiques our consumer obsession with brands, and how shopping has become our new religion in a secular age.

Below
Mods ride their scooters along the seafront at Hastings, East Sussex, 1964. Arguably the first subculture to openly consume design, their way of life was expressed through a carefully coded set of clothes and products such as bespoke suits, parkas and scooters.

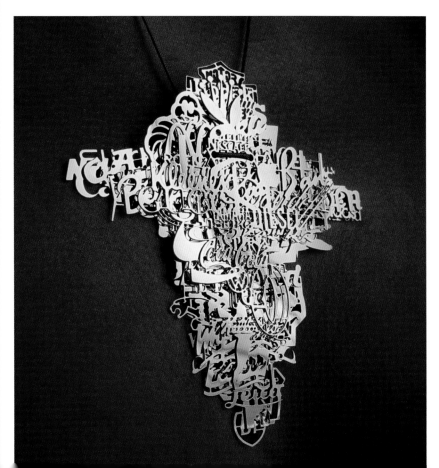

Porsche has carefully evolved their brand over 60 years. Comparing the product line-up from 1956 and 2010, one can see clearly how a brand's visual language can be developed, stretched and applied to a variety of models within a product range.

Design as brand

Any design is capable of absorbing meanings and values from other sources, even if these are not intrinsic to the design itself. Design branding is an approach to design that demands that the entire design, not just the logo or features, should be regarded as the brand's identity. Successful design branding is about increasing the symbolic power of a design by making it work harder, more actively, to communicate the right values, rather than leaving it to time and chance. A prime example of this is Porsche, which has developed a visual language that is applicable to accessories such as sunglasses as well as the iconic sports cars it produces.

A brand's identity should not be set in stone. Brands are living entities, and brand managements should be ready to embrace new visions, new structures, new shapes and new textures in response to changing consumer attitudes and changing technology – while always staying true to the brand's core values. At the heart of successful product design should be a strong idea to communicate the proposition driven by the brand's personality, through an evolving and dynamic visual language.

Designer as brand

The first designer who achieved superstardom was American industrial designer Raymond Loewy (see Chapter 1), who was responsible for the first major redesign of the Coca-Cola® bottle and the Avanti car. Featured on the cover of *Time* magazine in 1949 with the slogan 'he streamlines the sales curve', Loewy was the first designer to realize that consumers perceive products to possess personalities and identities, and that the personality of a product could be the personality of the designer.

Designers were not slow to follow in his footsteps, and the phenomenon of the celebrity designer reached its zenith during the 1980s when Philippe Starck (see Chapter 1), the enfant terrible of French design, became a household name, capable of turning his creative eye and signature to a dazzling range of products such as the Juicy Salif lemon squeezer and Bubble Club sofa. His commercial bankability was such that he could even convince leading manufacturers to develop a sub-brand featuring the creative input and signature of his young daughter, Ara.

The cult of personality is such that the design industry, fuelled by the design media, has elevated designers to such heights that it is possible to lose sight of the need to produce actual products, not just objects that demonstrate our designer awareness, taste and wealth. Our obsession with designer labels and celebrity design has produced many commercial casualties. Young and emerging designers need to refocus their efforts and develop sustainable careers rather than risk deluding themselves that it's all about becoming the next big thing.

Designers are often keen to promote themselves as a brand in itself, creating a cult of personality. New York-based designer Karim Rashid has carefully constructed a media identity where his products and personality are one and the same.

Design as brand language

It is critical to be aware of the 'design language' employed in the sector you are working in and the brand values within that sector. A brand value must be high in both resonance and contribution. In other words, it must enjoy a high level of recognition in the target market, and also actively contribute to a product's meaning.

Alongside brand values, there are signifiers and identifiers – high in resonance and able to signify membership of a particular category or identify a particular brand, but low or lacking in active contribution beyond these basic levels. At the lowest level of brand language are generics and passengers: visual elements that may not be remembered and that signify and contribute nothing; they are simply there and might just as well not be there.

Treat a brand's DNA with respect, but do not necessarily treat it as a fixed and sacrosanct design element. Once you have understood its value there may be better ways of communicating this more strongly. The key is to build on the DNA, not blindly preserve it, as this can result in a brand losing relevance and resonance in the market over time. Brand values do not exist in isolation but rather in relationship with other elements, and with the brand's identity in a broader competitive context. This context is in a constant state of flux, as is the way the product is decoded by the consumer.

TIME

THE WEEKLY NEWSMAGAZINE

Artzybasheff

DESIGNER RAYMOND LOEWY
He streamlines the sales curve.

EDITION
ETTORE SOTTSASS

ISSEY MIYAKE

Packaging

Packaging is a thriving sector of design today, from graphic designers creating eye-catching boxes to structural packaging designers specializing in the bottle and container. The role of packaging is not restricted to merely protecting the contents of a package, but also includes helping sell a product at the point of purchase and promoting a product's attributes and benefits.

Many products are meaningless without their packaging, as generic products, foods or materials require a branded package to differentiate their contents. The retail environment plays a vital role in creating a branded experience that builds upon the message being conveyed by the product and its packaging.

Acting upon consumers' conscious and subconscious wants, needs and desires, the retail environment can become a highly crafted brandscape that has as dramatic an effect on consumers' perceptions of a brand as the quality and nature of the products themselves.

CASE STUDY: Apple's visual language

Apple has established itself as a leader in product design in terms of its visual language, as much as its technology. From beige to candy to minimalist and beyond, its story has evolved from the 1980s to today.

Beige stage

The original 1984 Apple Macintosh, with its minimal detailing and integrated screen, was the result of Apple founder Steve Jobs declaring that the then market leader in computing, IBM, had it all wrong, selling personal computers as data-processing machines, not as tools for the individual.

The Macintosh, with its all-in-one beige box designed by Hartmur Esslinger of Frog Design, rejected the 'black box' business aesthetic of IBM and instead conceived a user-friendly product that would be small enough to fit within the home and present an image that was more helpful friend than technological foe. The Mac was famously launched on television in a spectacular advertisement, created by leading film director Ridley Scott, that aimed to show an individual 'breaking the mould'. This set the tone for Apple's non-conformist, highly sophisticated and enduring design language, which encompasses product, brand and company.

Left
Original Macintosh, 1984.

Candy stage

Steve Jobs left Apple in the late 1980s and the company floundered during the 1990s, losing market share until its very survival was threatened. In 1996 Jobs returned, determined to return Apple to its former creative and commercial glory. His first act was to recognize that Esslinger's beige aesthetic and visual language was no longer appropriate. He promoted Jonathan Ive, a young designer within the company, to create a new Mac that could reclaim Apple's heritage of user-friendliness in both form and interface.

The result was the iconic iMac, launched in 1997. Featuring a highly distinctive, highly playful and toy-like translucent 'bondi' blue and frosted white casing, it was an instant marketing and commercial hit that led to a range of copycat designs from companies producing everything from kettles to staplers. However, Apple sensed that they then needed to adopt a more restrained aesthetic for their maturing customers and launched a new stage of their evolution in 2001.

Left
Original iMac, 1998.

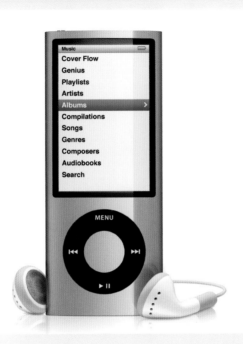

Minimalist stage

Apple was among the first manufacturers to see that product and content were set to merge. The iPod MP3 player, and accompanying iTunes software, revolutionized the way people downloaded and listened to music. This iconic, lightweight, pocket-sized design has evolved into the designer 'must have' iPhone, a device that reflects contemporary society's obsession with product convergence, combining a phone, portable web browser, MP3 player and application portal. The iPod's original form revolutionized how people perceived products, turning technology into jewellery. While the touch wheel interface enabled users to quickly and intuitively scroll through an entire music collection, the shuffle mode allowed for a personal jukebox experience.

The minimalist purity of the iPod, and of Apple's contemporaneous laptops and desktop computers, presented a cold 'masculine' aesthetic that spoke of maturity, rational technology and an obsessive attention to detail that radiated a confidence to and from its owner. The iPod's colour and material palette of white, aluminium and chrome sought to signify a futuristic aesthetic that draws upon post-war design. The iPod closely resembles Dieter Rams' 1958 T3 pocket radio for Braun. Rams is famous for saying that 'Good design is like an English butler', and given Apple's continued focus on user-friendliness, it is appropriate that Ive draws inspiration from his design hero while seeking to develop the next stage in the evolution of Apple's visual language.

Above
T3 Pocket Radio, by Dieter Rams for Braun, 1958.

Above left
iPod nano, 2009.

Left
iMac 27-inch LED 16:9 widescreen computer, 2009.

Marketing

Traditionally, research focused on the early stages of the design process to develop a PDS, but it is now broadly recognized by the industry that research can play an important role throughout a product's life cycle. While a designer's intuition will always remain vital to the design process, sustained and rigorous research can often lead to surprising, counter-intuitive results, identifying new possibilities and helping designers to avoid derivative design directions.

The innovative research techniques described in Chapter 2 are ideal for all stages of the research process and provide viable methods for consulting 'real people' about a product design. There are also specific techniques that can prove highly useful during the marketing stage.

Market research techniques

Here are the key points for researching category and brand values within a focus group:

Drawing from memory
Give test consumers blank paper and have them draw particular branded products from memory. Then discuss with the group what each of them has drawn and why.

Camouflage
Modify a series of existing designs, each with different elements removed. Use your focus group to discuss the saliency of differing visual elements. The disappearance of some elements may cause the perception of a brand to alter.

Name swapping
Swap the names and logos on different designs from the same market, then discuss if and why the resulting designs are 'wrong' for the brands.

Image and mood boards
Prepare a series of image and mood boards portraying a range of potential directions. It is important to go beyond the obvious, and keep the boards credible in the context of the brand.

Perceptual mapping
By doing these exercises you will be in a position to create a perceptual map where the use of an XY axis enables you to arrange the category visually using comparator terms such as cost, quality and impact.

Trend forecasting

Product designers need to continually strive to understand what their current and target customers want, how they use a product, and to forecast what the customer will desire next season and beyond. The gestation time to bring a product to market is such that the global conditions impacting on its success can alter from conception to product launch. With stock-market crashes, socio-cultural trends and fashion moving so fast, expert research into future trends is becoming ever more important to the design industry and process. Trend forecasters and futurologists (specialists who postulate possible futures by evaluating past and present trends) are commonly working in timescales of eighteen months in advance, in rapid turnover fields such as textiles, to ten years or more in areas such as car design.

A note of caution is perhaps required here: although market and trend analysis is a very useful tool, designers and companies should not put all their eggs in one basket. Some innovative products are very hard to market research as they ask people to project beyond their experience, where they find it difficult to provide revealing answers to situations or products they have never encountered or even imagined.

The marketing mix

Once market research has been undertaken, there are a number of ways you can help bring a product to market. A common technique to analyse these is the 'Seven Ps of Marketing'. In order to ensure that your product or products are aligned with your business strategy, you should explore each of the following components to help you achieve a successful blend of marketing:

Product: You need to ensure that you can identify and communicate what features and benefits your product has over its competitors. This is commonly described as your Unique Selling Proposition (USP).

Place: Where is your product sold to customers and how is it transported and distributed?

Price: How much can you charge for your product in the market based on its development, manufacturing and marketing costs and its perceived value to customers and users?

Promotion: How will you make your potential customers and users aware of your product and what it offers?

People: You, your staff and those that represent you and your product. You should remember that good customer service builds customer loyalty.

Process: Can the methods and techniques that you use to design and produce your product have a role in helping build your brand?

Physical environment: Every environment you work within, and those your product/s are sited within, from your workplace to your showroom or retail environment, can make a positive or negative impression on your customers, suppliers and staff.

Once you have explored these possibilities in detail, you will be ready to write a marketing plan. This will outline your intentions and the means you will use to achieve all your business objectives. You should list all the tasks, deadlines and individuals responsible, and determine the costs associated with achieving these tasks. By regularly monitoring and reviewing your progress against your detailed plan you can ensure the business develops as planned, changes of direction are discussed and made if required and, importantly, ensure that you stay firmly within budget.

Conclusion

In conclusion, developing a product and bringing it to market requires a complex series of interconnected activities that place considerable creative, managerial and administrative demands upon the designer. Contemporary design practice sees designers tackling the entire life cycle of a product, from manufacturing to packaging to point of sale to point of use. Consumers are even getting in on the act and designing their own products through interactive websites such as Nike ID.

Mastering these design phases can take a lifetime, but the process is continually creative and fascinating, and involves addressing a number of issues impacting on design today, from product disposal, recycling and afterlife to producing designs that move beyond mere function and incite emotional desire and engagement.

5.

This chapter explores and explains some of the more significant issues – green, ethical, inclusive and emotional – that surround modern product design practice. It provides valuable tips on how to ensure a product's impact on the environment is minimized and identifies methodologies that can help lead to successful inclusive designed products. Guidelines are also given to help you act in a professional and ethical way as a product designer.

Green issues

This section examines the issue of 'green' or 'sustainable' design and discusses the impact of the emergence of environmentalism on product design and manufacture, from pioneers such as Vance Packard and Victor Papanek to the sustainable designs of today. It outlines the product design life cycle, examining products through their design, assembly and manufacture through to their disassembly, disposal and recycling. Issues such as material selection, component recovery, product longevity, energy consumption and the efficiency of recycling are illustrated through contemporary examples.

Green design

The manufacture and use of the vast array of consumer products on the market today produce much of the pollution, deforestation and global warming that impact on our environment. Designers often focus exclusively on the form and function of their creations, and take insufficient interest in the fabrication and manufacture of their designs.

The desire to produce ever more complex products has resulted in a trend towards energy-intensive manufacturing processes. A prime example of this can be seen in the evolution in sheet-metal cutting from energy-efficient guillotine cutting, through plasma cutting, to today's widespread use of energy-intensive laser cutting. With the energy consumption of the manufacturing sector growing steadily and the need to lower carbon dioxide emissions to reduce global warming, it is essential that product designers try to address this issue, and carefully consider the environmental impact of their design.

Designers need to realize that their responsibilities don't end with the design of a product. They need to consider a product's use, from its birth to its death, and what happens once it has come to the end of its useful life. Environmental issues are complex and designers can feel overwhelmed by what they need to consider while designing new products. The methods and case studies outlined in this section aim to help you create sustainable products that are environmentally sound, good for people, profits and the planet.

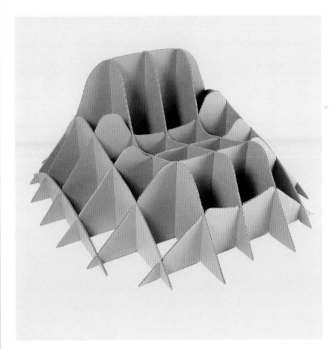 

Green pioneers

In 1960, cultural critic Vance Packard published *The Waste Makers*, promoted as an exposé of 'the systematic attempt of business to make us wasteful, debt-ridden, permanently discontented individuals'. Packard identified a phenomenon known as **planned obsolescence**. He revealed that designers and manufacturers had developed a technique to encourage the consumption of new products by introducing new styles and functions that made consumers' existing products feel less desirable and ready for replacement despite the fact that they still functioned adequately. Packard quoted leading American industrial designer George Nelson, who wrote: 'Design...is an attempt to make a contribution through change. When no contribution is made or can be made, the only process available for giving the illusion of change is "styling".'

With consumers increasingly aware of these techniques, designer and critic Victor Papanek confronted the design profession head-on with his classic book, *Design for the Real World*, published in 1971. He demanded that designers face their global, social and environmental responsibilities and wrote that 'design has become the most powerful tool with which man shapes his tools and environments and, by extension, society and himself'. His message continues to have resonance with today's 'green' movement, and is the foundation for many sustainable design methods.

Above
Terra!, by Nucleo, 2004, uses a recycled cardboard frame, which is filled with earth and turfed over to create a living seat in the landscape. The armchair as a frame (left) and in-situ (right).

Sustainable design

'Green design' has recently been replaced as a term with 'sustainable design', which reflects the need for a more systematic approach to the environmental problems facing us today. Sustainable design is the design of systems that can be sustained indefinitely, and sustainable product design can be defined as the design of objects that aid the sustainability of the systems in which they operate.

These definitions highlight the fact that sustainable design needs to be considered in a holistic, systematic manner. Design does not exist in isolation, and as a result, when creating sustainable products you will often have to look beyond merely the design of physical objects and consider looking at other aspects of the system in which the objects operate.

The success of a business is normally measured on what is commonly referred to as the 'bottom line', or financial profit or loss. When measuring the sustainability of a product, service or business you should consider not just the financial factors but also the environmental and social ones. The success of sustainable design is therefore measured on what is known as the **triple bottom line**. Sustainability requires that you should consider your products systematically, and avoid making a loss in any of the three identified areas: environmental, financial and social sustainability.

TransNeomatic, designed by Fernando and Humberto Campana for Artecnica, 2007. Made from recycled tyres and woven wicker fibre by Vietnamese artisans, keeping alive traditional techniques.

Environmental sustainability

Issues such as global warming, resource depletion and waste disposal are strongly affected by product design, and urgently need addressing. The following guidelines will help ensure environmental sustainability:

- Materials should exist in a 'closed loop system', where all materials inputted are recycled without the need for additional material, ensuring complete recyclability.
- All energy should ideally come from renewable sources.
- No harmful substances should be emitted to the environment at any stage in the product's life.
- Products should be as efficient as possible and use fewer resources and energy than the product they replace.

Financial sustainability

A financially sustainable product, and the system it operates within, should have the following characteristics:

- Generates long-term revenue by constantly meeting customer needs.
- Does not rely on finite resources.
- Maximizes profitability by minimizing consumption of resources.
- Does not threaten the financial well-being of its customers.
- Does not have any significant liabilities.

Sustainable product design can result in solutions that have long-term financial viability and consistently generate financial profit and wealth. Contrary to popular belief, it is possible to avoid social or environmental damage while generating holistic profit.

Social sustainability

Social sustainability is about maintaining and enhancing the quality of life of all stakeholders of a product. Designers need to ensure their products:

- Protect the mental well-being of all stakeholders.
- Protect the physical health of all stakeholders.
- Encourage community.
- Treat all stakeholders fairly.
- Provide all stakeholders with products that deliver essential services.

Kyoto Box, designed by Jon Bohmer, 2009. Capturing solar energy to heat up the air in the box, it boils and bakes food and water to provide an eco-friendly solution to cooking.

Sustainable design models

The following design models can be used to create more sustainable products, and can be considered as a checklist throughout the design process:

Biodegradable materials

Recycling is not always the most effective method of disposing of materials, and it is possible for many renewable materials to be composted. The benefits of composting biodegradable materials are dependent on effective systems being in place to ensure that the materials are treated correctly. If these systems are not in place then biodegradable materials can contaminate plastics recycling, and adversely impact on a product's sustainability.

Designers have taken advantage of biodegradable materials in a variety of products. The Rothko Chair designed by Alberto Lievore, for example, is made from Maderon (a moulded bio-material made from pulverized almond shell mixed with natural and synthetic resins), while Tom Dixon has produced a wholly organic range of biodegradable tableware, where the fibres and resin are produced from natural sources and not petrochemicals. Perhaps the most striking recent example of promoting the use of these materials is Jurgen Bey's Gardening bench for Droog Design, which proposes using garden leaves to create seating that lasts a season and then turns to compost within the garden.

Clarify core functions

When designing a product it is essential to remember what the true purpose of the product is. Consumers may accept losing some secondary functionality in order to achieve other benefits, but will not tolerate a product that does not meet its core functions. Products must deliver what they promise and additional features are bonuses that must not impact on the core functions.

Below left
Rothko Chair, designed by Alberto Lievore for Indartu, 1996. It is manufactured from discarded ground nut shells and resin.

Below
All Occasion Veneerware®, by bambu LLC, 2004. This range of products is made from certified organic bamboo.

Opposite top
Gardening bench, designed by Jurgen Bey for Droog Design, 1999. The container extrudes a garden bench from park waste, such as hay, leaves and tree bark. Any length of bench is possible, and after a season or two of use, it returns to nature in the form of compost.

Design for disassembly

What happens to a product at the end of its life is a designer's responsibility. Products should be designed so that they can be easily disassembled into their constituent parts for appropriate treatment at a product's end of life. Such an approach will also ensure that a product is easier to assemble during its manufacture, which saves cost and improves efficiency.

Durability

Designers should reject the conventional approach of planned obsolescence and instead increase the durability of their products. Stokke designed their classic Tripp Trapp chair to grow with the child. This means that the same chair can be used for children from 0 to 15 years, greatly increasing the effective use or utility of the chair.

Above
Tripp Trapp, by Stokke, 1972. The chair grows with the child, creating an eternal product that can be handed down from one generation to the next.

Efficiency

The Aeron Chair by Don Chadwick and Bill Stumpf for Herman Miller is a highly successful case study of an efficient piece of product design. The iconic chair is easily assembled and disassembled, allowing for maintenance in situ and for recycling at the end of its life. Designed to be more durable than most office chairs, it also eliminates traditional foam-and-textile upholstery with a breathable membrane. Not only does this keep the sitter's body at ambient temperature, but it can also reduce air-conditioning costs within an office environment.

Energy

Products use large amounts of energy in their production, and electrical products use frighteningly large amounts of energy during their operation. As such, designers should attempt to ensure their products use considerably less energy and materials during their design, manufacture and use than equivalent products did previously. Innovative thinking in this field has resulted in products such as the wind-up radio designed for the third world, and imaginative designs such as Martí Guixé's Flamp light (1998), which creates a nightlight that uses no electricity at all (see below).

Flamp light instructions:

We recommend you place your Flamp beside a conventional lamp.

Light is on.

Turn off: You have 20 minutes before you are in dark. Enjoy the shadow!

Eternal

Creating objects that last a lifetime, and get better with age, challenges the planned obsolescence model of much design and manufacture. Traditionally this approach has been employed in high-end luxury products such as Savile Row suits, but increasingly designers and engineers are looking to create more durable products. For example, low-energy bulbs don't just consume less energy but also last dramatically longer than traditional bulbs. Designers should attempt to create future classics that are eternally desirable, such as the iconic Ferrari 250 GTO, which is as much rolling sculpture as classic racing car.

Identify materials

Efficient end-of-life treatment of materials relies on users and waste-disposal services knowing the type of material and preferred method of treatment. Many materials are difficult or impossible to distinguish from others without clear identification. Products should be designed to be disassembled easily, ensuring that surface finishes such as paint and graphical decoration do not irreversibly contaminate materials.

Components should be clearly labelled with recycling data to help consumers and recyclers to identify the type of materials and enable segregation, which is especially important for plastic recycling. Recyclers need to ensure that materials are not contaminated with lower-grade materials; when plastics are mixed together they turn into a brown sludge, which is why most recycled plastics are turned into black dustbin liners.

Opposite top
Aeron Chair, from Herman Miller, 1994. This iconic office chair has been designed to be easily disassembled at the end of its life for recycling.

Opposite bottom
Flamp, designed by Martí Guixé for Galeria H20, Barcelona, 1997. Resembling a traditional electrical light, it is in fact a ceramic form painted in a fluorescent colour to absorb light, and when placed in a dark room emits light for up to 20 minutes.

Left
Bin Bag Bear, by Yael Mer & Shay Alkalay of Raw-Edges Design Studio, 2006. This fun product encourages recycling and responsible waste disposal through its childlike design.

Life cycle assessment

If the products you design aim to minimize or avoid altogether any environmental impact, then you need to consider the impact of the product throughout its entire life cycle. This means that you need to consider how every product you create is produced, manufactured, transported, packaged, used and disposed of. When designing new products it is useful to storyboard the life story of the product to help identify the possible impacts and events that may occur. This can be useful because the reality of many products' lives does not follow the exact route planned during the design phase, and so alternative eventualities should be considered.

The next step is to establish exactly what the environmental impacts of the product are or will be, and what they are caused by. By doing this you can identify where the greatest need for improvement lies and so focus your design efforts effectively. Full life-cycle analysis can be extremely time-consuming and complicated, and is consequently often not viable in the high-speed commercial product design and development process. However, a number of simplified software systems exist that allow products and designs to be assessed and compared quickly and easily.

Cradle to cradle design models the production of products on nature's processes, with materials viewed as nutrients circulating in healthy, safe metabolisms. It suggests that the design industry must protect and enrich ecosystems and nature's biological metabolism. Such a holistic economic, industrial and social framework helps enable designers to create products that are not just efficient but essentially waste-free.

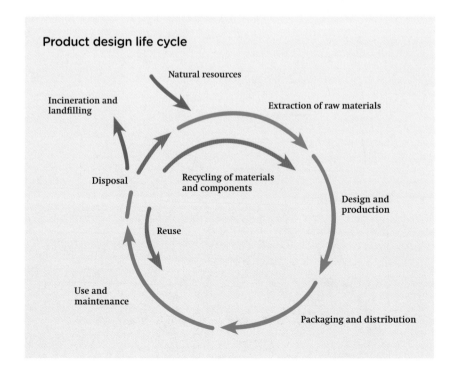

Product design life cycle

Natural resources

Incineration and landfilling

Extraction of raw materials

Disposal

Recycling of materials and components

Design and production

Reuse

Use and maintenance

Packaging and distribution

Local resources

Acting local to think global, Trannon make all their furniture from British hardwood grown less than 50 miles (80.5km) from their factory. By using only the thinnings (narrow wood that is cleared to make way for bigger trees and that is usually wasted), they demonstrate their stewardship sourcing of materials.

Multifunctional

Creating products that can do more than one thing avoids the environmental impact of having to produce two products. It is often possible for a designer to combine several products into one unit. For example, a mobile phone is not merely a communication device, but incorporates the functionality of an alarm clock, personal organizer, camera, hand-held gaming machine and more.

Modular

Designers can create products as a set of modules that can be fitted together to provide a combination of functions. Such an approach enables customized products to be created from a set of standard modules, and for products to be easily repaired or upgraded.

Organic

By using organic and renewable materials, designers can challenge the primacy of man-made materials. Julia Lohmann's Ruminant Bloom lights, made from preserved sheep stomachs, creates an utterly new aesthetic, while Tom Dixon's bamboo chair for Finnish manufacturer Artek demonstrates how grown materials can have as high a performance as metals or synthetics, as bamboo has a slightly higher tensile strength than steel.

Bamboo bike, designed by Ross Lovegrove in 2000 for Biomega, 2009. Bicycling is a very energy efficient form of transportation and this handmade bamboo-framed bicycle combines sustainable materials with mobility.

Recyclable materials

If a product is to be recycled once it reaches the end of its life then it must be fabricated and manufactured from materials that can be recycled. You must consider current technologies and infrastructures when deciding which materials to use. Many materials claim to be recyclable, but are not unless the systems exist to ensure that the materials will be. If the proper infrastructures are not in place, the process can be energy-intensive and less effective than incinerating the materials to produce electricity. The Louis 20 chair by Philippe Starck, for example, is made from only aluminium and polypropylene, both over 99% pure, and is held together with only five screws, making it very recyclable.

Recycled materials

Unfortunately, although a large proportion of designs are manufactured from materials that are theoretically recyclable, very few actually are. This is partly due to a lack of an adequate infrastructure, but also to the lack of demand for such materials. Designers should always try to specify recyclable materials where possible, but also aim to create products that can be systematically recycled by the manufacturer. A number of products promote these materials; the RCP2 Chair by Jane Atfield readily employs the aesthetic of its constituent recycled material – in this case, HDPE sheet, while Piet Hein Eek's Scrapwood Cupboard is manufactured from beautifully crafted scraps of recycled wood.

Below left
Louis 20, designed by Philippe Starck for Vitra, 1992. Recycled plastic was used to form the chair's main body.

Below
Scrapwood Cupboard Classic, designed by Piet Hein Eek, 1990. This poetic recycling of old wood shows how designers can question conventional notions of beauty and what constitutes waste.

Opposite
Tide, designed by Stuart Haygarth, 2005. This chandelier is assembled from washed ashore beachcombed everyday objects.

Reduce material variety
When designing products you should attempt to standardize the materials used to simplify and assist in the recycling process.

Renewable materials
It is possible to produce materials from renewable sources such as wood, starch and sugar cane as a substitute for plastics.

Reuse
Sadly, many products are irresponsibly designed to be viewed as disposable or have artificially limited life cycles of use. Frequently, these rejected products are actually in excellent condition when consumers discard them. You should consider ways of reusing these products, salvaging components and products, and reimagining them to create new products.

Simplification
Many products are extremely and unnecessarily complex. Designers should seek to simplify the product from the outset of the design process. A good example of such an approach is Industrial Facility's 2nd Phone for Muji, which has the sole function of enabling a user to answer the phone and talk, with every other function deemed unnecessary.

2nd Phone, designed by Industrial Facility for Muji, 2003. Here the design simplifies the phone to an unadorned brick-like form devoid of screens and extraneous function buttons. All you can do is make a call, no more and no less.

Upgrade and repair

The notion that a product can evolve and adapt to the changing needs of consumers can be seen to work efficiently in the design of mobile phones; their casings can be removed and changed, enabling people to stay in fashion and style while retaining the internal components. Personal computers have been designed to enable the easy upgrading of RAM, hard disks and graphics cards, through easily accessed ports and slots, and allow users to perform DIY upgrades.

Weight reduction

Designers should attempt to reduce the weight of products by using less quantity of material and lighter-weight materials, which helps lower transportation costs and environmental impact. Avoiding excess material, Jasper Morrison's Ply Chair is an example of minimalism and the elegant paring back of material usage.

Ply Chair, designed by Jasper Morrison for Vitra, 1988. This is a great example of how one can pare back excess, simplify forms and reduce waste to create a minimal design.

INTERVIEW
Max Lamb

Biography

Max Lamb's rugged and bold designs are laboriously created through his direct manipulation of tools, materials and processes. A graduate of the Royal College of Art, London, the topography and industrial heritage of his native Cornwall are a major source of inspiration for his work. Lamb is perhaps best known for his Pewter Stool, where he cast pewter into crude sand formations on a Cornish beach. He has also experimented with lost-wax and sophisticated electro-deposition methods for his Copper stools, and extruded biodegradable materials for his Starch stools.

Interview

Do you adopt an ethical approach in your design practice?

I live by strong moral principles and these naturally translate to my design work. I practise what I preach, as it were, and believe all designers should. I only design and make objects that I would be happy to live with myself and I am probably my strictest critic. So finding sincere justification for the projects I make can be a tough job. My work typically takes a long time to realize and often involves arduous physical processes; thus the decision to proceed with an idea is not made lightly.

Have you developed a greener approach to product design?

My approach to design and creation evolves continuously. I began my career with a 'green' approach to design, but it has changed a lot. I'd say it began with a bright lime green approach; one that is obviously green and wants to shout about it. This is a very common approach to 'green' design and one that we must be wary of. As with personal differences in ethics, the concept of what is green can be very different to actual knowledge of what is and, more importantly, is not green. Consumer demand for 'green' products is definitely moving in the right direction,

but manufacturers know this and have the ability to exploit consumer desires by labelling their products as green. Going green is now a huge marketing tool so beware of false advertising. It is also important to note that going green is not an excuse to consume more. My furniture is very personal; people only buy it if they respond emotionally, so they're unlikely to throw it away. Lifespan and the relationship between an item and its user can be more important than so-called ecological or 'green' materials. It's the culture of disposal that I think we need to address. The materials and processes I use are very durable – you can be very rough with them!

Can a designer balance commercial pressures and beliefs?

In theory yes, but in practice more often than not the answer is no. A designer has to be very strong both morally and ethically if they are to resist commercial pressures. But every circumstance is very different and every designer's ability and willingness to resist also differs. I have been very fortunate in that most of the interest in my work has come directly from the customer, allowing me to satisfy their needs directly without the influence (and

commercial pressures) from retailers and manufacturers. Thus the cost of my work to the end-user is inherent to its value, rather than being driven by typical retail mark-ups, percentages and profit margins.

Do you design for all or a select few?

So far I have only really designed for a select few – the few people who have selected me! I could design for all, but not all come to me asking me to design something for them. I really enjoy the personalized approach to designing furniture and other objects – to design a chair for a known person rather than unknown people.

Opposite top left
Electroformed Copper Stool, 2007, a typical one-off unique piece.

Opposite top right
Ladycross Sandstone Chair, 2007, was carved from a solid block of stone, hand picked from a quarry in Ladycross, England.

Opposite bottom
Pewter Stool, 2006, cast into the sand on a beach. This one-off design was subsequently modified and put into mass production by Habitat.

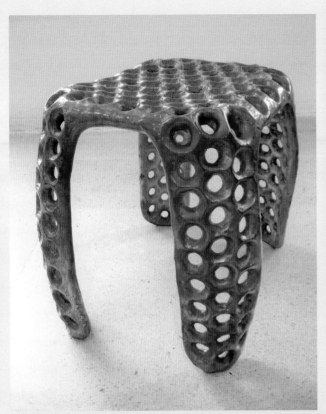

Ethical issues

This section looks at the increasingly contentious field of design ethics. From the birth of the discipline, designers have had to attempt to satisfy all the stakeholders in the design process. Greater self-awareness and external factors such as globalization have led to ethical issues increasingly impacting on design, manufacture and consumption.

Design ethics

The design industry is continually evolving, responding to and shaping technology, society and the economy. Designers help determine how people perceive a product, how they live and what they wish to buy. Playing such an important role, designers have an immense responsibility to society. The green design responsibilities and universal design concerns discussed at length elsewhere within this chapter are part of a much broader system of moral values and obligations that face product designers today.

Consumers increasingly wish to buy products and services that are made ethically, without any exploitation of people, animals or the environment. Consumers are now favouring ethical designs and looking for fair trade, cruelty-free, organic, recycled, reused, or locally produced products. Through such 'positive buying', consumers are forcing companies to alter their practices, actively supporting progressive companies while boycotting companies and brands that produce unethical products.

The rise in ethical consumerism and green brands that identify themselves as ethical has led to a rise in ethic-based decisions in the marketplace. Individual consumers and consumer groups are increasingly taking pride in uncovering information about business practices. Designers have responded to this growing awareness by adopting more ethical standards and practices.

Design is fundamentally a problem-solving process, and the world today has so many problems it is clear that designers need to initiate solutions rather than merely respond to them. Ethical design aims to contribute to the betterment of all and to ensure abundance, diversity and health to future generations.

While many products are necessary and desirable, they all fulfil a role. This role may be as a prop for an experience, a tool to accomplish a specific task, or a loved heirloom. Given the environmental and social impact of mass production, designers are increasingly asking whether we need to automatically go through the default process of creating new products when another more sustainable, local and humane manner of fulfilling that role may be possible. An example of the move away from tangible physical products and towards a new model of service design based on user experience is the growth of car-sharing clubs, with people asking themselves if they really need to own a car when they merely wish to use one.

Above

War Bowl, by Dominic Wilcox, 2004. This is made by melting plastic toy soldiers to create a bowl that works beyond the level of mere function and texture, and which provocatively asks questions of its viewer.

Left

World Trade Center, September 11, 2001, from Buildings of Disaster (1998–2009), designed by Constantin and Laurene Boym. In our media-saturated time, world disasters stand as people's measure of history, and the sites of tragic events often become involuntary tourist destinations. This project is a thoughtful response to our collective need for introspection, remembrance and closure.

Design responsibilities

Product design has been a key driver for fuelling consumerism and economic growth since the Industrial Revolution. Designers employed in industry are tasked with ensuring they produce profitable products and 'good' design. Private profit-making, however, is often at odds with public good. Product designers have a dual responsibility, balancing the needs of their business, employers and corporate clients on the one hand, while on the other acting as social advocates for the people who will purchase their products. To ensure a satisfactory balance is struck, you could ask yourself whether a design is useful, well made, and produced in a sustainable manner.

Designers can shape their careers through the clients and commissions they choose. Some designers have shifted their activities away from business and towards social activism and critique and self-generated projects – working at a small scale in order to have the latitude to explore new creative models and practices.

Designers have an ethical and professional responsibility to produce products that are safe to use. In the unfortunate situation that a product fails, consumers will often seek to prove legal liability. **Product liability** refers to the legal action by which an injured party seeks to recover damages from personal injury or property loss from the producer or seller of a product. In product liability law, the seller is liable for negligence in the manufacture or sale of any product that may reasonably be expected to be capable of inflicting substantial harm if it is defective.

Negligence in design is usually based on one of three factors:
• That the manufacturer's design has created a concealed danger.
• That the manufacturer has failed to provide needed safety devices as part of the design of the product.
• That the design called for materials of inadequate strength or failed to comply with accepted standards.

In order to minimize the likelihood of producing a product that is unsafe for use, designers should always strictly adhere to industry and government standards, extensively test and modify designs to remove any potential causes of failure, and document all design, testing and manufacturing quality activities. When preparing a design for market they must ensure that warning labels and instruction manuals are fully comprehensible and, above all, create a means of incorporating legal development and responsibilities into the design decision-making process.

Top
Roadkill Rug, designed by Studio Oooms 2008. Simultaneously attracting and repulsing the viewer, on the one hand it's a warm, soft, cuddly carpet, and on the other it's a repulsive image of a car-flattened, bloody fox.

Above
Flood Light, designed by Julie Mathias and Michael Cross of Wokmedia, 2006. Electric light bulbs and coils of brightly coloured wire are plunged under water. The resultant design defies taboos about mixing electricity and water, encouraging the viewer to question their notions of safety by flirting with danger.

Opposite
Gun Lamp, designed by Philippe Starck for Flos, 2005. Proposing that design is as much about storytelling as function Starck suggests that even adults need fairy tales to dispel their fears, and that they perhaps need to play war to evoke a peaceful night's sleep.

Beyond the profession

While there is strong agreement within the design industry about what constitutes professional behaviour towards clients and fellow designers, there is far less consensus about the obligations that designers have towards society as a whole, and their role in addressing the complex issues of today.

Creating products is a complicated process, and designers need to be aware of the larger contexts surrounding their work. In today's global economy, even a simple product's raw material may come from one part of the world, with manufacturing occurring on another continent, and final sales being carried out in another. This globalization can have a significant impact on local cultures and lead to economic imbalances that can impact adversely on environmental practices, human rights and labour conditions, particularly in developing countries.

In order to address these issues, you will need to work alongside experts in many other disciplines, such as anthropologists, biologists, economists, politicians and sociologists, to name just a few. Design is a powerful tool for shaping the world and defining how we live in it, and as such you can bring creative skills and critical thinking to these collaborations.

Top and opposite
Rat Wallpaper, by design collective Front, 2004. Here, traditional aesthetic sensibilities are challenged as rats gnaw through rolls of wallpaper to create repetitive patterns of holes that reveal the old wallpaper beneath the surface.

Above
Cuckoo Clock, designed by Michael Sans, 2006. Taxidermy meets product.

Ethical guidelines for product designers

- Would you use the product you are designing yourself?
- Would you like everyone to have one?
- What would that mean in practice?
- Can your design be easily misused?
- Can and should you even try to prevent that misuse?
- Do you think it creates a better world?
- Does your design improve people's lives?
- How does it improve people's lives?
- Why does it improve people's lives?
- What is ethical in terms of sustainable design?
- Are you solving the problem or merely contributing less to it?
- Are you promoting environmentally sound design or just paying lip service to it through 'greenwashing'?
- Are your goals bound by cultural imperatives?
- What cultural issues are you addressing and why?
- Should you change them?
- Should you make your design solution local (works for specific cultures) or global (works in as many cultures as possible)?
- Who is 'all' and is it appropriate for this market?
- Does the need of the many outweigh the need of the one or vice versa?

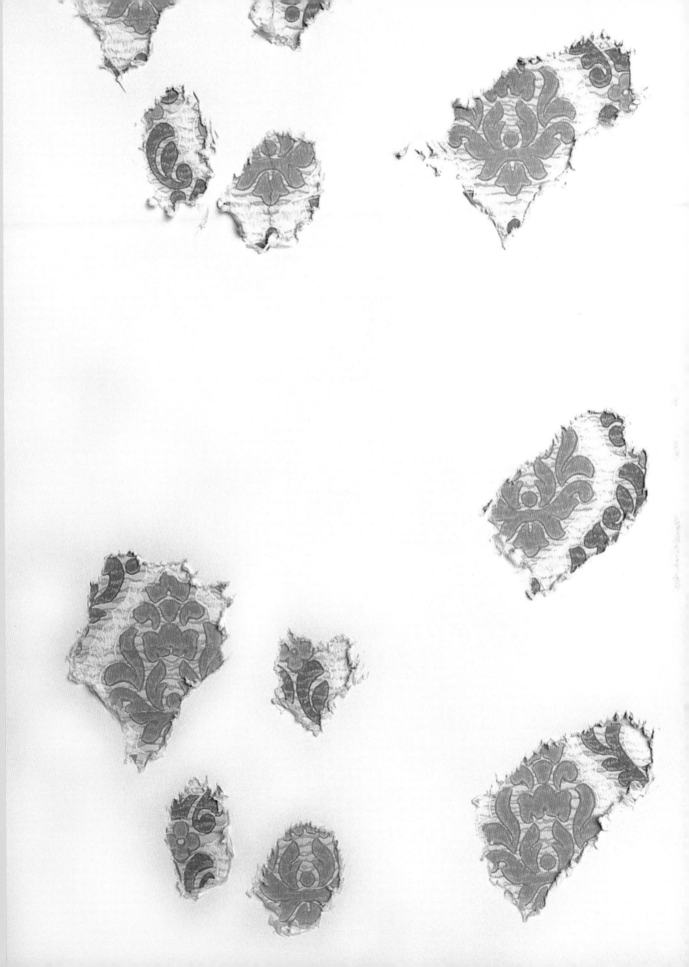

Inclusive design

This section outlines the social and commercial rationale for ensuring that designers create products and services that address the widest possible audience, irrespective of ability, age or social background. It will discuss the demographic changes occurring in Western society and identify key criteria and user-centred methodologies that need to be considered when 'designing for all'.

What is inclusive design?

'Inclusive design', also known as 'universal design' and 'design for all', is an approach to design that aims to ensure that products are usable by, and accessible to, as many members of society as reasonably possible, without the need for special adaption or specialized design. All products exclude some users, often inadvertently, and it aims to highlight and reduce such exclusion.

Inclusive design forces designers to question their own practice. All designers strive to create products that satisfy the needs and desires of their intended users, but are they always aware of what the actual rather than perceived needs are? Designers know that intuitive, easy-to-operate products are satisfying to use, but why do they persist in producing designs that place unnecessarily high physical demands on users or exclude some altogether? Are designers fully aware that each decision they take during the design process can adversely affect large numbers of people, from older people and the disabled to economically vulnerable groups and those affected by changing technologies and work practices? Design that includes marginalized social groups is not just socially desirable but a genuine commercial opportunity, and a responsibility that designers should embrace.

Within the European Union there are currently more than 130 million over-50-year-olds, and by 2020 one in every two adults in Europe will be over the age of 50. This demographic shift is having a profound impact on how designers are developing new products, and the methods required to develop them. Over the last decade society has begun to treat older people and the disabled differently, moving away from the outdated perspective of viewing them as special cases, and embracing a new social equality agenda that aims to integrate them into the mainstream of everyday life through a more inclusive approach to the design of buildings, products and services. By addressing the needs of those excluded from using products, designers can produce better designs that improve how a broad range of users experience their product designs, increase their potential customer base, and ensure a more equal and cohesive society.

Designers need to be aware that inclusive design is an integrated approach to design that extends to all stages of the design process, and is not simply a stage that can be bolted on. By embedding it within the design process, designers will be able to produce better-designed mainstream products that are pleasurable, desirable and satisfying to use. Many companies and designers, while agreeing with its basic principles, pay lip service to the practice, assuming that if a product is deemed easy to use that they are adequately covering their social responsibilities, or naively believing that it is always possible to design a product that addresses the needs of an entire population.

To avoid such pitfalls and promote an inclusive design agenda, designers need to develop an awareness of the needs of users with different capabilities and how to accommodate them into the design cycle. The Center for Universal Design, a leading American design research centre, published a set of principles in 1997 drawn up by a working group of architects, product designers, engineers and environmental design researchers. These seven principles of universal design can be applied to evaluate existing designs, guide the design process and educate both designers and consumers.

Definitions for designing usable products

Equitable use
The design is useful and marketable to people with diverse abilities.

Flexibility in use
The design accommodates a wide range of individual preferences and abilities.

Simple and intuitive use
Use of the design is easy to understand, regardless of the user's experience, knowledge, language skills or current concentration level.

Perceptible information
The design communicates necessary information effectively to the user, regardless of ambient conditions or the user's sensory abilities.

Tolerance for error
The design minimizes hazards and the adverse consequences of accidental or unintended actions.

Low physical effort
The design can be used efficiently and comfortably and with a minimum of fatigue.

Size and space for approach and use
Appropriate size and space is provided for approach, reach, manipulation and use regardless of user's body size, posture or mobility.

(Copyright © 1997 NC State University, The Center for Universal Design.)

How do we design inclusively?

Faced with the challenge of using design as a tool for delivering on social, cultural and political expectations of equality and inclusivity, leading design researchers in the field, such as the Helen Hamlyn Research Centre at the Royal College of Art in London, have created a series of techniques that enable designers to create products that support people to live independent and fulfilling lives for as long as possible.

The following techniques aim to provide you with the knowledge and tools to maximize inclusivity and minimize design exclusion.

Capability assessment

Cabability assessment enables designers to evaluate products by comparing the capability levels required to use them. How users interact with or use a product can be broken down into a series of tasks and activities where demands are made on users, which are then measured against each other to form a comparison. These user capabilities are commonly grouped into three categories:

- sensory – vision and hearing
- cognitive – thinking and communication
- motor – locomotion, reach and stretch and dexterity.

By using these crude yet effective scales, with low demand to the left and high demand to the right, designers can evaluate different products and concepts against each of the three categories, and focus on reducing capability demands in order to produce products that can be used by a larger percentage of the population.

Capability simulators

Capability simulators are physical or software devices that designers can use to reduce their ability to interact with a product. Basic simulators can be created using gloves or sports braces to reproduce the loss of dexterity or movement, while spectacles can be smeared with grease to simulate the loss of a user's vision.

Such quick and cheap devices enable designers to empathize with potential or an actual user's capability losses, and can be used throughout the design process to help designers simulate the physical and cognitive issues that their design needs to address. However, no capability simulation device can ever truly reproduce what it is like to live with a particular capability reduction on an everyday basis, and as such they should never be considered as a replacement for involving real users in developing, designing and evaluating a product.

Ergonomics

Ergonomics is the study of human anatomical, anthropometric, physiological and biomechanical characteristics as they relate to physical activity and usability. Designers commonly use such data and testing to evaluate the physical design of controls and displays, seating postures and health and safety. Ergonomics also addresses the psychological aspects of how people interact with products, such as user perception, cognition, memory, reasoning and emotion. Designers need to consider such aspects in order to identify characteristics that should inform the design process.

Although product designers have considered the comfort and scale of products on an intuitive level since the discipline's emergence, and architects such as Le Corbusier had attempted to develop aesthetic design styles based on the proportions of the human body with his *Le Modular* man, the widespread use of ergonomics was not established until the 1960s. Henry Dreyfuss, the founding member of the Industrial Designers Society of America and famous for his streamlined designs, published his seminal book *The Measure of Man* in 1960, establishing the industry-wide application of such data.

Humanscale 1/2/3, female selector, by Niels Diffrient, Alvin R. Tilley and Joan Bardagjy, 1974. This invaluable tool for designers incorporates an extensive amount of human anthropometric data, which enables designers to create ergonomically appropriate products.

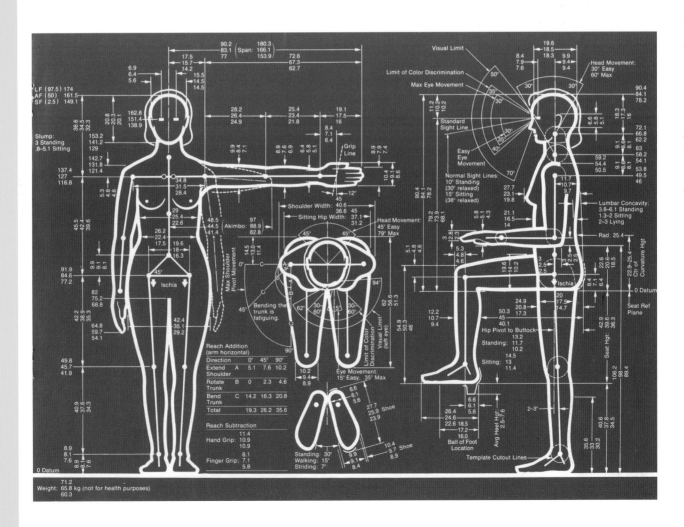

Exclusion audit

An **exclusion audit** is a technique used to evaluate different products by comparing the proportion of the population that will be unable to use them. Exclusion audits provide more detailed statistical data than simple capability assessments, and often require the assistance of specialist consultants. Exclusion audits use objective scales to measure the level of capability that a product requires in order to use it. For example, such an audit when applied to a new portable television design would evaluate a series of tasks: opening its box, plugging it in, tuning it, turning it on, changing channels and moving it around.

Once the appropriate demand level has been identified, data from international and national surveys can provide the number of people that will be excluded and, in conjunction with other techniques, provide a framework for specifying and designing products and the interactions required to operate and understand them.

Inclusive user involvement

Designing 'with' rather than 'for' users is an approach that yields success at all stages of the design process. To ensure a truly inclusive design agenda it is vital to realize that members of the design team are often not representative users, and as such it is important to involve an appropriate mix of people to input into the design process. This mix may vary from stage to stage.

As in all user-centred design methods, the focus of inclusive design research is to ask, observe and participate. Involving large numbers of users undoubtedly improves accuracy and the possibility of uncovering unperceived issues, but is often impossible due to time or financial constraints. As such, it is common practice to try to gain useful feedback from a number of diverse representative users to reduce biases in the sample users' responses and observations. The following list can help to structure such research:

Broad user mix – this involves users from a range of market segments, which can help understand general user requirements.

Boundary users – this involves users on the limit of being able to use the product, which can help identify opportunities for design improvement.

Extreme users – those with a severe loss of capability can inspire creativity during concept development.

Mixed-experience users – those with different levels of experience with similar products can help understand the impact of experience on use.

Community groups – again, those sharing experience of interacting with similar products can provide a broad understanding of product use.

CASE STUDY: OXO Good Grips

All too often, commercial or time pressures mean that inclusive design and ergonomic principles are compromised or not given adequate priority until too late in the design process, but the commercial benefits of adopting a fully integrated inclusive approach are significant. A prime example is Good Grips kitchen utensils for people whose capabilities are limited by arthritis. Working with users, OXO International moved beyond merely functional agendas and the traditional assistive model of designing for a specific disability, by focusing on meeting actual users' needs and experiences.

These award-winning products, created by New York-based Smart Design, from 1999 to present, offer a distinct stylish aesthetic and desirability that enables the ergonomically designed products to cross over to a mainstream consumer audience, thus bringing the benefits of ergonomic inclusive design to all. The financial benefits to the company of such an approach were manifested in the company growing at an annual rate of over 30% since the Good Grips range's introduction, and a number of major companies have since adopted similar design strategies.

Clockwise from top left
OXO Good Grips Salad Spinner with pump mechanism and brake, which also doubles as a salad bowl; Y-Peeler; and the Pour & Store Watering Can, with soft-grip handle and rotating spout that tucks away for storage.

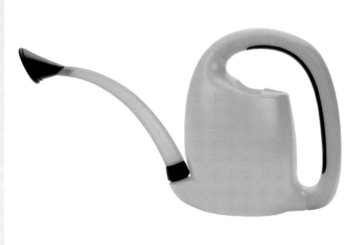

Emotional design

This section explores the idea that the look, feel and pleasure-giving properties of a product are just as important as function in product design. It draws on the 'emotional design' work of luminaries including Donald Norman and Pat Jordan, and explores the visceral, behavioural, aesthetic and tactile qualities which make up a 'pleasurable' product.

> 'More and more people buy objects for intellectual and spiritual nourishment. People do not buy my coffee makers, kettles and lemon squeezers because they need to make coffee, to boil water, or to squeeze lemons, but for other reasons.'
> Alberto Alessi, designer and manufacturer

Beyond usability

The functionalism promoted during the Modernist era of design is being supplemented by the more complex pleasures of emotional design, with designers now producing products that aim to strike a certain emotional chord. Consumers have come to expect that new products are intuitive and easy to use, and as such are no longer pleasantly surprised when a product is usable, but are unpleasantly surprised by any difficulties in use. Consumers no longer simply expect the products they buy to be functional and usable, but now actively seek products that elicit emotional feelings of connection, pleasure and status. This can be achieved through the way a product looks, the feel of its materials, the tactile or 'haptic' response of controls, or more abstract feelings, such as reflected status and brand values.

Designing emotions

Emotions play a crucial role in how people understand their environment, and how they engage with objects. Aesthetically pleasing products often appear to users questioned in focus groups to be more effective, by virtue of their sensual appeal. This is due to the affinity people feel for a product that appeals to them, and how they form an emotional bond with particular products, brands and styles. Norman defines three types of design perception:

Visceral design

Visceral design refers primarily to that initial impact a product and its appearance has when you first catch a glimpse of it on the shelf, on the road or on television. Successful examples of this approach include the Jaguar E-Type, Malcolm Sayer's classic 1960s design, whose mathematically calculated streamlined and provocatively phallic form tapped into the psyche of a generation. More recent examples include Ross Lovegrove's water bottle for Ty Nant (see p. 198), where the product successfully captures the aesthetic of flowing spring water, and persuades consumers to buy a freely available substance, and believe its taste, smell and appearance is worthy of their desire.

Behavioural design

Behavioural design is about a product's look and feel. It refers to the total experience of using a product; the physical feel and pleasure people can derive from it and the functional effectiveness and usability. Designers are now creating products that adopt traditional 'simple' interfaces, such as the pull cord used to switch on Muji's Wall-Mounted CD Player by Naoto Fukasawa, or producing critical products that question our social relationships with products, challenging or altering our behaviour, and representing the complexity of contemporary life.

Reflective design

Reflection is concerned with how a person feels about a product after use, and the social and cultural image it portrays to others. Norman proposes that Philippe Starck's iconic Juicy Salif lemon squeezer for Alessi is a highly successful 'item of seduction' that rejects the utility of function, and instead focuses on being a successful conversation piece and sculptural design. The lemon squeezer's aesthetic is redolent of classic 1950s science fiction, and its stance resembles that of a spider's. The technique of creating objects that resemble animals is known as zoomorphic design, and is a commonly used approach in emotional design.

How to create emotional products

While some designers intuitively bring visceral, behavioural and reflective design together into a harmonious whole to produce successful emotional product design, there are a number of scenario modelling methods that can help designers to create more satisfying and pleasurable products and experiences:

- Product as person – The designer pretends that a product is a person. By imagining this personality in a series of contexts, the designer can deduce how the product would talk, behave and dress, and gain an unconventional insight into the emotional demands of the selected product.
- Design as magic – The designer describes how a product works by pretending it is magic. This enables the designer to ignore technical constraints and focus on what it could do unconstrained by conventional practice.

Pleasurable products

In parallel to creating emotional products, another possible framework for taking a structured approach to product design and marketing can be identified. Four types of human motivation or 'pleasures' can help success in the marketplace and are dependent on connecting with users in one or more of these ways – physio-pleasure, psycho-pleasure, socio-pleasure and ideo-pleasure.

Physio-pleasure

This is derived from the senses of touch, smell and taste to create sensual delight, such as the smooth feel of an Apple iPod in the hand, the smell of a new car or freshly made espresso, and the taste of Belgian chocolate.

Psycho-pleasure

This includes issues relating to the cognitive demands of using a product and the emotional reactions engendered through the experience of using it. Pleasure also comes from the extent to which the product makes the task more pleasurable, such as the interface of an ATM cash machine that is quick and simple to use, or the enjoyable ritual of playing a vinyl record on a Wurlitzer jukebox rather than downloading and playing an MP3 file.

Opposite top left
Ty Nant water bottle, designed by Ross Lovegrove for Ty Nant, 1999–2001. The visceral qualities of water are captured in this bottle design.

Opposite top centre
Wall-Mounted CD Player, designed by Naoto Fukasawa for Muji, 1999. Its simple pull cord on-off switch is an example of behavioural design.

Opposite top right
Juicy Salif, designed by Philippe Starck for Alessi, 1990. An example of reflective design, where the sculptural quality is the prominent design feature.

Opposite bottom
Do Break Vase, by Frank Tjepkema in collaboration with Peter van der Jagt for Droog Design, 2000. An example of extreme behavioural design. The ceramic vase is lined with rubber, and rather than smashing into pieces when thrown in anger, it physically records such events to create a lifetime relationship with the vase.

Below
Toyota Prius, 1999 to present, was the first commercially successful hybrid electric car. It is an ideo-pleasure product that appeals to consumers' philosophical and environmental tastes and values.

Socio-pleasure

This relates to the relationship and status people derive from a product, and the pleasure gained from interacting with other people through a product. This may be a 'talking point' product like a special ornament or 'artwork', or the product may be the focus of a social gathering such as a vending machine or coffee machine.

This pleasure can also come from a product that represents a social grouping, for example, a particular style of scooter that gives you a social identity, such as the Mod subculture of Vespa riders. Products can facilitate social interaction in a number of ways, with email, the internet and mobile phones enabling communication between people.

Ideo-pleasure

This describes the pleasure derived from entities such as books, art and music, and is the most abstract pleasure. Products that are aesthetically pleasing can be a source of ideo-pleasure through appealing to the consumer's tastes. Values could be philosophical or relate to a particular issue such as the environmental movement. For example, the Toyota Prius is a self-consciously 'green' choice due to its hybrid drive, and embodies the growing green movement despite its questionable **cradle to grave** statistics.

Conclusion

Product design is a rapidly evolving discipline, and you need to be constantly aware of the ethical, environmental, social, cultural, political and technological issues impacting on your work. Innovations in technology and software are blurring the boundaries of what is commonly understood as 'product' design. Mobile phones, such as the iPhone, are less defined by the physical hardware that you hold in your hands than by the virtual world of the interface and the social spaces of Facebook and YouTube. These developments were unimagined a mere decade ago, and illustrate the need to identify, research and propose new design strategies that don't merely respond to change but proactively help to redefine our world.

Designing products for this more complex world requires you to consider products holistically and adopt a deeper, more emotionally engaged and ethical approach to future physical, virtual and 'meta' product design development. By educating yourself in the emerging issues facing design today, you will ensure that you are trained for the design industry of the future.

6.

This chapter explains the educational training and experience undertaken by student product designers internationally. It outlines what you will study, the nature of student projects and how to prepare for the culmination of your studies – your degree show. It provides practical advice and guidelines on how to write a CV, create a portfolio and perform well in interview, and looks at career opportunities both in product design and related fields.

Studying product design

Courses in product design explore the ever-changing ways of making connections between objects and people. When choosing a college or university you should consider each course's curriculum, employability of graduates, reputation, location, facilities, staff–student ratio and above all, philosophy. Courses come in all shapes and sizes and you need to decide what is right for you: a studio-based course focusing on conceptual individuality, or a technical university-based course focused on producing design for a specialist sector.

On your course you will be taught the broad process of how to make and talk product design that enables you to develop and appropriately define the boundaries of your own personal approach. Tutors value innovative and thoughtful exploration and development of concepts through drawn, physical and virtual sketching in combination with a hands-on engagement with people, materials, technologies, markets and methods of fabrication. Facilities at colleges and universities usually include drawing studios and individual offices, computer labs for two-dimensional and three-dimensional CAD, and workshops for producing three-dimensional prototypes.

Leading universities and colleges provide dedicated personal desks and studio space. Also encouraging peer group collaboration and a dynamic and creative studio culture, the design studio is set up to work as the student's home from home.

What you study

Undergraduate courses are usually three or four years in duration. In Europe they are often preceded by a foundation year where students are exposed to a broad art and design education before selecting their chosen discipline.

During the early years of study, students usually undertake a series of fundamental three-dimensional design problems structured around innovation and making techniques that explore and develop research, drawing, innovation, prototyping, fabrication, manufacturing and communication techniques. Collaborative workshops, industrial visits, lectures, drawing classes and computer-aided design studies are commonly used to support these projects.

Having developed key skills and an understanding of the discipline, students then progress to more in-depth projects intended to develop their understanding of form, interaction and material through the exploration of new techniques and start to develop their personal product design direction or specialism.

During the final year of undergraduate study, students consolidate and refine their design practice and techniques, developing an individual design agenda, philosophy and style that they demonstrate through a self-directed major project. They communicate an awareness of the commercial potential of their work and the wide-ranging career possibilities for the future.

The workshop is a vital facility during studies and provides the student with the opportunity to develop their products through the manufacturing of prototypes, test rigs and models.

Design projects

During your studies you will move from basic tutor-set briefs through to externally set projects such as live examples with companies or design competitions, and on to more detailed and comprehensive self-generated product design projects, leading to your final degree show.

As major projects are often the first time students get the chance to generate their own briefs, this freedom can result in self-indulgent pet projects, superficial novelty generation or unrealistic expectations. Dreaming up new ideas is not that difficult, but coming up with good ideas is. How we discriminate between the merely novel and the genuinely good lies in the fit: how it fits to technology and if it is fit for society.

To explore notions of 'fitness for purpose', you have to think about processes of innovation and engage with the challenge of being more systematic, more rational, more explicit and more critical. Every design project needs to show its relationship to precedents, historical and contemporary examples. Your ideas are not merely ideas dreamt up from nowhere. Despite the pretence that we start from zero, we all stand, in fact, on the shoulders of giants. It is essential that you display a good understanding and acknowledgment of the sources you draw upon. It is also essential that you test your concepts, using a variety of established and proven techniques while also forging innovative approaches to the design process.

Your design project must build a design language that is fit for purpose, and not just be about an enclosed and narrow self-expression. As Charles Eames pointed out, self-expression has no place in design!

- Who is this design for? It may be a group of users, or a business.
- Look for projects that are socially appropriate and that, where possible, have real value to a distinct and specified group of users.
- Try to display an understanding of technical and material processes.
- Faced with a set of rigorous criteria, evaluating your design work from an aesthetic, social, technical, cultural, philosophical, functional and marketing context, your emergent tentative ideas will move from fragile concepts to robust viable products fit for the marketplace.
- A project can address any number of issues, but ultimately could be proposing something new and innovative. Try to make it useful, usable and delightful or innovative in some way.
- It may comment on the state of, or trends in, our society and thus help to make people think about the nature of our society and whether design solutions can help effect positive change within it.
- It may solve an identified problem with an existing product, or it may be about fulfilling an identified consumer need/market opportunity or a brand's commercial need.

Ideally, all approaches should result in a design project that makes life better in some way for someone, and can be assessed against a set of agreed criteria.

While studying design, students will be involved in critiques of their project work through discussion, collaboration and evaluation.

Presentations may be held at regular intervals, e.g. at key points during project work, at project reviews and end-of-year assessments. These may be formal or informal, showing work in progress within small groups of students, and may be accompanied by visual aids, performance and/or installations. Formal presentations are known within the design world as 'critiques' (more commonly abbreviated to 'crits'), which constitute a formal appraisal and discussion of completed work. All students attend these events and gain a comparative view of their work in relation to that of their peers. Crits involve dialogue between student and tutor, and may be held individually or in a group setting. They are a vital means of assessing a student's work.

The assessment schemes used to evaluate student work vary between different universities and colleges, and your specific course handbook will explain what level of achievement the grades you gain represent. Projects are commonly assessed by teams of staff and moderated by discussion, before being confirmed by an external examiner, who has been invited from industry or academia to ensure that the assessment and quality procedures meet the required standards.

You may also be expected to undertake peer and self-evaluation and assessment of fellow students. This process improves your critical analysis and helps develop a sense of responsibility and control over the subject matter. When you are giving feedback to your colleagues, you should always aim to balance positive comments with negative ones, and focus on whether they have achieved what they set out to and met their assessment criteria (often referred to as learning outcomes). In order that feedback is valuable, and enhances your personal and peer group learning, it must be specific, descriptive and non-judgmental. It should also be directed towards the individual and linked with his or her personal goals and aspirations.

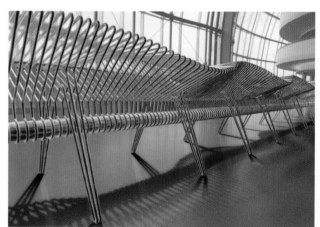

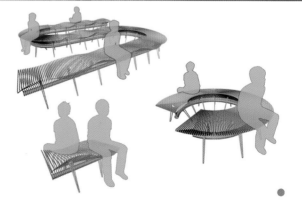

The degree show

Your degree show is the culmination of your studies. This gives you and your colleagues the opportunity to showcase the original, innovative and inspiring work that you have produced during your studies. In today's internet age, it is essential that you have a website to promote your degree show. The website should list the names of all the students exhibiting, feature visitor information including the venue, dates and opening times, have a map with directions for parking, and include a clear webpage heading to ensure that search engines such as Google will list your site.

Your tutors should have a mailing list of companies that need to be invited, and you should produce posters and flyers that you can send to design companies and local press. Remember to use the website address on all promotional material and make sure you ask other relevant websites to link to it.

Make sure that your display is hung with real care and attention to detail. To present a professional show, you should ensure consistency and make sure signage and exhibition labels use the same fonts and layouts. You should all have business cards with your name, email address and phone number on them. Ideally this will have an image of your work on it to remind the visitor what they saw in the show, as this will be a once-in-a-lifetime opportunity to launch yourself into the world of design.

Opposite
Final year student projects can address many issues, as evidenced by this small selection of project designs.

Below
The degree show is an opportunity for students to present their products, skills and abilities to potential employers.

Many influential designers, companies, collectors, retailers and galleries visit degree shows as talent spotters and you should always have someone to meet and greet visitors on arrival to the exhibition. You should consider wearing name badges so visitors can identify who they want to talk to, and you and your colleagues should have a basic knowledge about each other's work on display and be confident enough to present somebody else's work if they are not there, as you will probably be invigilating the show in shifts.

You may wish to produce a catalogue for the show featuring work from all the exhibitors. While this can be a costly option, it does provide a lasting document that visitors will hold onto long after the show has ended. You can charge a small fee to cover some of your design and print costs if your tutor feels this is appropriate. A comments or visitors book is a useful way of collecting feedback, and contact details can be used for post-show mailouts providing consent has been given.

Many colleges and universities aim to further promote their design courses and graduates by exhibiting on a bigger stage at prominent and prestigious graduate art and design shows, which bring the strongest graduates together under one roof, such as New Designers and Free Range in London. You may also be lucky enough to exhibit at a major trade show such as the famous, and highly influential, Milan Design Week Satellite Show. Exhibiting at these events enables you to show your work to the general public and, most importantly, potential employers, giving you the best opportunity to promote your work, and possibly winning one of the prestigious prizes awarded by panels of sponsors and industry observers at such events.

Detail from a degree show. If a number of students have produced products for a similar context then it can often be appropriate to exhibit them together.

Design rights

In a world where 10% of products in worldwide circulation are fakes, it is essential that designers can formally protect their intellectual property, and commercially exploit and capitalize their innovative ideas. This section outlines the issues surrounding intellectual property rights, copyright and more general legislation involved in product design.

Intellectual property

Intellectual property is the area of the law that protects designers' innovative work, enabling them to commercially exploit their work and stop other designers, companies or individuals from misappropriating them. Designers, manufacturers and companies are highly vulnerable to having all, or aspects of their ideas, work or technology copied. This can result in serious operational or financial problems, so they need to protect themselves by establishing legally that they hold the exclusive rights to a particular design.

Once legal protection has been granted to the 'rights holding' designer, he or she can exercise this to prevent third parties from copying, manufacturing or adopting features of the relevant designs or technology. If designers fail to obtain protection they leave themselves open to unauthorized acts of plagiarism, and will be unable to prevent their ideas being used. They will also be unable to claim any payment for such actions.

Protecting your designs

In order to protect your work, and avoid suffering at the hands of copycats, you should start by identifying what aspects of your design/s are unique or innovative, as these are all important details that could give your designs and products the protection they need. If you feel that you need to seek legal protection, consult a legal advisor specializing in intellectual property and design law. Government bodies such as the United States Patent and Trademark Office offer support in making applications, and trade associations and organizations also offer valuable advice, such as Anti Copying in Design (ACID). ACID has assisted many businesses in their defence of their designs against copycat products, and offers excellent pre-emptive protective advice to young designers entering business.

When a designer is considering talking to a company or manufacturer about a new design, he or she should strongly consider the use of a **non-disclosure agreement (NDA)**. NDAs are commonly signed when two individuals or companies are considering doing business together and need to be exposed to each other's commercially sensitive information for the purpose of evaluating the potential business relationship. These legally binding contracts outline confidential materials or knowledge the designer and other party wish to share with one another for certain purposes, but wish to restrict access to, with the parties agreeing not to disclose information covered by the agreement. NDAs create a confidential relationship between the parties to protect any such information or a trade secret, and protect a designer's intellectual property.

Intellectual property law is made up of many elements of legal protection, and a designer who owns the intellectual property of their work will be concerned with any number of them. What follows is a basic introduction to the key routes of protecting design ideas and work.

Registered design rights

A registered design provides protection for the appearance of the whole or part of a product resulting from the features of, in particular, the lines, contours, colours, shape, texture or materials of the product or its ornamentation. The benefits of registering a design are considerable, establishing the priority of a design over others, and giving a legal monopoly right for the outward appearance of a design. Once a design has been legally registered it can be bought, sold, hired or licensed like any other commodity, and the designer is consequently free to negotiate his or her own price.

Legal experts will always suggest that you apply to the patent office as soon as possible, ensuring nobody else registers the same or similar design before you do. However, you may want to wait until you know whether your product or service is profitable before you incur the expense of registration.

Unregistered design rights

Uniquely in the European Union, designers are granted limited protection against the copying of the shape and configuration of a design for a maximum of three years (ten years in the UK). However, it is almost always cheaper and quicker to enforce rights in a registered design than in an unregistered design, and designers do not benefit from monopoly rights.

Copyright

Copyright is a form of intellectual property that gives the creator of an original work 'exclusive rights' for a certain time period in relation to that work, including its publication, distribution and adaptation, after which time the work is said to enter the public domain. It protects the form or expression of a work rather than the idea underlying it – for example, manufactured products, surface decoration applied to manufactured products, drawings, manuals and text and other product documentation, as well as the artistic aspects of product packaging. Copyright does not merely cover the aesthetics of an object but can also be applied to sounds such as Microsoft's distinctive jingles, tastes such as Coca-Cola®, and smells such as Chanel No. 5 perfume.

The intent of copyright is to allow 'authors', such as designers, to have control of and profit from their works, thus encouraging them to create new works and to aid the flow of ideas and learning. Copyright comes into being automatically when the relevant work is created, and as such does not need to be formally registered.

Trademark

Trademarks, identified by the symbols ™ and ®, are words, logos, devices or other distinctive features that can be graphically represented. They are used by companies to clearly and legally distinguish its products from competitors. Designers and/or companies that legally register such trademarks protect them indefinitely, subject to paying renewal fees.

Patent

Patents cover creations such as unique mechanical devices, mechanisms and processes, and protect inventions. When applying for patents at the patent office, the applicant must demonstrate that the relevant invention is new and capable of commercial application. Patents must be applied for in each legal territory (country or group of countries) where exploitation is intended to take place.

Patent applications take a considerable effort to verify, with the designer and patent officer having to conduct detailed searches to discover if a design has already been patented or if it infringes on existing work. Once a patent has been applied for it is covered for a year from the effective filing date, and enables the designer to apply the term 'patent pending' to the product.

It is worth pointing out that if a designer/inventor publishes or markets a product without the benefit of a patent they will be deemed to have placed their ideas in the public domain and will not enjoy any intellectual property protection. When determining whether an invention can be awarded a patent, you should search for existing patents to validate their discoveries using online patent office databases. This is a crucial step, and one that will help to provide the best possible patent protection for your inventions, enable you to gain insight into competitors' designs and avoid future conflict if you risk infringing on previous patents.

In conclusion, designers and companies need to evaluate what forms of intellectual property protection are possible and required for every new product design developed, manufactured and brought to market. For example, when BMW launches a new car, it will ensure that it exploits a range of protection of its design rights. The car's carefully evolved appearance and brand aesthetic will be protected by design registration; its manuals will be protected by copyright; the 'BMW' brand will be a registered trademark, and BMW will use patent protection to cover numerous mechanical features.

INTERVIEW
Tim Brown, IDEO

Biography

Tim Brown is the CEO and president of IDEO. An industrial designer by training, his own work has earned him numerous design awards and has been exhibited at the Museum of Modern Art in New York, Axis Gallery in Tokyo, and the Design Museum in London. Tim has a special interest in the convergence of technology and the arts, as well as the ways in which design can be used to promote the well-being of people living in emerging economies. Tim writes extensively, with articles in the likes of *Harvard Business Review* and a book, *Change by Design*, on how design thinking can transform organizations.

Interview

What has changed in product design since you graduated?

Everything has changed in the broader perception we have as product designers of what it is we are doing. No matter how simple a product is, it's part of a system; we're designing the system and not the product, whether we like it or not.

What advice would you give to today's graduates?

I would say figure out how to be collaborative and interdisciplinary, but not in a bland, compromising way. Actively collaborate with other disciplines, whether it is business or engineering or social sciences or whatever it might be. You have to take an active interest in those disciplines. It's not about figuring out where to compromise; it's figuring out where to contribute. I think it's hard to get many experiences of that at college because colleges are not set up that way. It's one of the great things about work placements – they are a great opportunity to do it. Figure out how to get those collaborative experiences as early as possible. As designers we can help bring collaborations together because of the tools we have. The way

we visualize things, the way we describe things, the way we tell stories – we can be catalysts for collaboration. Learning that skill as a product design student, I think, is incredibly precious.

What does it take to be a successful product designer?

I think these days it takes a willingness to think about systems and a willingness to look at a problem in a multi-faceted way. You need to ask questions not only about form and function in a traditional sense, but about the overall system the product is part of and how that can be optimized or improved. You might need to consider closed-loop supply chains or the impact on society or the impact on the business that you're designing for. For me the other important characteristic of a product designer these days is the ability to ask the question, not simply answer it.

How do you define 'success'?

I suppose you could think of it in two ways: the first definition of success is impact and then the definition of impact is good impact, whatever that is. When I think about our goals for IDEO, it's to have an impact in the world through what we do, but

preferably to have a beneficial impact. That goes back to this notion of asking the right questions. I think it's relatively easy as a product designer to have an impact, but relatively hard to have a beneficial impact, particularly when you take a broader systems view. The other thing that's difficult about the idea of impact is that it occurs over time, so you don't know whether you've done a good job as a product designer when you've finished your product...So there's a level of patience and a certain sort of long view that I think you need to have as a product designer.

Developing your design skills

Product design courses combine a number of theoretical and practical activities within the curriculum. These include research, concept development, technical and manufacturing knowledge, creativity, presentation and communication skills. Alongside the academic and technical knowledge developed during your studies, you should also gain other valuable skills.

Over the years designers have proved remarkably adept at constantly evolving their practice and skill-sets to adapt to the changing needs of industry. This process has accelerated as we move away from an age of mass production to one of mass customization, where manufacturers tailor production to satisfy individual tastes. Designers are now set the task of stimulating and meeting ever more sophisticated and complex consumer demands, and the skills traditionally perceived to guarantee success are arguably in danger of becoming outdated.

Given the impact that design can have on profit margins, it is unsurprising that industry has become increasingly vocal in demanding that academia produces design students who have the following attributes and skills.

Personal attributes
- An inquisitive nature and an ability to demonstrate intellectual curiosity.
- Self-motivation and drive.
- Empathy with clients/consumers.
- Creative spark.
- An 'eye' for good design.
- Curiosity and passion for design.
- Consider the skills developed through your other activities, such as volunteering, family responsibilities, sport and membership of societies.

Design skills
- Strong research, visual and manipulative skills.
- Ability to be realistic in their ideas.
- Good communication skills – visual, verbal and written.
- Basic drawing skills – freehand, measured and technical.
- Core software skills – two-dimensional packages such as Photoshop and Illustrator, and three-dimensional packages such as Solidworks, Rhino and 3D Studio.
- Knowledge of research, management and marketing methods and techniques.
- Organizational skills.

Workplace skills
- Ability to articulate ideas.
- Ability to take criticism.
- Team-working skills.
- Ability to work to deadlines.

'To apply for a research role in our design studio, you'd need skills such as electronic prototyping, CAD for circuit boards and RP machines, carpentry and other making skills, and software prototyping. You need to be able to work in a group of people from different backgrounds, have presentation and communication skills, and an enthusiasm for writing and talking about your practice.'

Tobie Kerridge, product design researcher

Professionalism

The role of a product designer carries a set of professional responsibilities; these have been codified by a number of trade associations and organizations that attempt to promote the profession and regulate and control their members' design practice for the benefit of industry and the public. The Chartered Society of Designers is the largest international professional body for designers. The Society exists to promote concern for the sound principles of design in all areas in which design considerations apply, to further design practice and to encourage the study of design techniques for the benefit of the community.

Guidelines for professional practice

Professional bodies such as the Chartered Society of Designers and Industrial Designers Society of America commonly adhere to the following principles:

- Designers should conduct their business competently and act at all times with integrity and honesty.
- Designers should not seek to supplant another designer already engaged on a project.
- Designers should treat all knowledge and information relating to their client's or employer's business as confidential and should not divulge such information to any third parties without the consent of the relevant client or employer.
- Designers should not knowingly work simultaneously for clients or employers who are in direct competition with each other without their full knowledge.
- Designers should not knowingly copy the work of another designer.

Engaging with industry

A vital element of product design education is its role in preparing you for a career in industry. Many universities and colleges employ tutors who are active designers with their own design consultancies and practices, bringing their extensive experience to the classroom. They can help to bridge the gap between industry and education through activities such as study trips to design companies and factories, setting up live projects set by industry, and helping students find placements within the design industry.

Placements

There are few better ways to obtain hands-on professional experience than through a placement, also known as an internship. You should start considering your first job early in your college career, and at the very least try finding holiday jobs with a company that interests you. Many colleges offer students the possibility of a sustained period of work experience as an optional or compulsory part of their course. These placements are a fantastic way of gaining experience, and offer an insight into the different career paths available to product design graduates. They provide an opportunity to learn about a company or industry sector, develop a network of professional contacts, and may even lead to a full-time position.

Finding a placement can be as challenging as finding a regular job. You need to target companies you are interested in working with and prepare a CV, cover letter and portfolio along the lines described below. You never know who might have an important professional contact, and it's always worth asking friends and family as well as tutors and alumni if they have any possible leads you can explore.

Most placements are paid, but some companies offer unpaid work experience or merely pay expenses. While this can appear to be unfair, such companies will often point out that they are providing valuable professional training, experience, networking opportunities and often result in a job offer if the student performs well.

'Work placements help you gain experience without getting paid. It's a good way to gain invaluable experience as long as you make the right choice of placement. Work hard, gain contacts, be reliable, produce good sketching and conceptual ideas, don't be afraid to get your hands dirty, and work long hours – a mixture of these will pay off!'
Matt Jones, Director

Preparing a CV

Once you have completed, or better still before you end, your education or training in product design you will need to turn your attention to preparing your Curriculum Vitae (CV) and personal design portfolio. Both of these items should contain a clear, compelling and impressive collection of work that shows off your design skills, critical thinking and practical capabilities.

A good CV should promote your design skills, knowledge and experiences that you will bring to the job. There are no hard and fast rules, but most CVs are made up of the following sections (not necessarily in this order):

- personal details
- education
- work experience
- specific skills (such as languages or CAD skills)
- interests and activities
- referees

Remember that an employer will read your CV with one thought in mind: 'Why should I hire this product design graduate?' Don't be tempted to include information that isn't relevant to that employer. If you want a design job and you have good CAD skills, include them. If you studied life drawing at night school, leave it out, unless you are applying for a job as a painter.

It is also important to get the length right. Ideally it should not be over two pages – but even so, busy employers may not even make it to the second page of a CV if there's nothing relevant on the first page. So cover the most relevant thing you have to offer (perhaps your degree or work experience) early in your CV.

Finally, a note on presentation: the information in your CV should be consistent and presented in clear, distinct sections. Check and double-check for spelling and grammatical errors (don't rely on a computer spell-checker). Use good-quality white or off-white paper and present each page on a different sheet of paper, not double-sided. See page 218 for a sample CV.

How to write a cover letter

Cover letters are a vital method of introducing yourself to a company. When writing a cover letter you need to ensure that you have thoroughly researched the company you are approaching and, if applying for an advertised position, that you have analysed the job description. Try to demonstrate that your skills are a match for those required for the role, and mention your qualifications and portfolio as a means to showcase your talents and experience. See page 219 for a sample cover letter.

Curriculum Vitae

Francis Woodman
[address]

Personal Profile
I am an innovative, multi-disciplined Product Designer with good experience in Graphics, Fashion, Web, Branding and Marketing, with a specialist background in Product Design research. Possessing well-developed communication and interpersonal skills, along with a high degree of technical competence with a commitment to quality I have a proven ability to understand client requirements and deliver effective creative solutions to brands and design. I am outgoing with excellent, strong and effective organizational and communication skills.

Your opening statement
Use this opening short paragraph to convince a potential employer that you are the right person for the job and express your interests and ambitions.

Education

MA	Product Design	Northumbria University, 2010
BA (Hons)	Design and Marketing 2:1	Glasgow University, 2008
A-Levels	English Lit, Politics, Business Studies IT [Grades A – C]	Bradford Grammar School, 2003
9 GCSE's	[Grades A – C]	Bradford Girls High School, 2001
Extra Curricular	Photography	Leeds F.E. College, 2000

Your key qualifications
List these in reverse-chronological order so that the most relevant and higher qualifications are read first.

Work Experience

Service Designer
Design Innovation Lab, London [February 2008 to present]
[list Main Duties]:

Freelance Graphic / Web Designer
Newcastle and London [2006 to present]
Clients include: Saints, UES, Jenni Photography and Inamoco
[list Main Duties]:

Assistant Designer
Boxfresh, London [December 2005 to April 2006] (placement)
[list Main Duties]:

Professional experience
Also featuring the most recent first, list each company you have worked for as well as job title, length of employment and the main key duties. Decide whether any student summer jobs have relevant skills of if they are best omitted.

Key Skills
Software Proficiency | Adobe Photoshop/Adobe Illustrator/Adobe InDesign/QuarkXpress/ Macromedia Dreamweaver/Microsoft Word, Excel, PowerPoint, Publisher and Access.
Research and Analysis | Ability to seek information from a broad range of sources to evaluate and apply as necessary. Creative instinct for customer desire.
Market Awareness | Ability to research and analyse current trends in the marketplace through applying knowledge of branding and culture to better understand a product or company.
Website Design | Ability to design and create functioning websites through macromedia studio.
Visualization | Ability to visually translate design ideas into colour illustrations and present them in strong communicative layouts. Creating flat drawings and specification sheets.
Prototyping | Ability to produce quality 3D prototypes through a variety of means including machining, rapid prototyping, and hand finishing techniques.

What other skills do you have?
What other projects have you been involved in or courses have you completed that have given you particular relevant experiences or skills? Be specific and use examples where you can.

Personal Qualities
Design | Thorough and meticulous, fast and able to work under pressure, capable of diversity, not just my own styles, ability to stick to the creative brief and other guidelines.
Personal | Friendly, inquisitive, hardworking, funny, eager and passionate.
Interests | Interested in all facets of design, fashion, advertising, art, photography, technology, music, movies and retro gaming. Produced and presented own local community radio show (2000–1).

References available on request

What else do you have to offer?
Transferable skills such as organization, motivation or teamwork may be evident in your hobbies and personal activities. Choose those with relevance.

6. Cover Letter

Francis Woodman
[address]

21 April 2010

Dear [name]

Vacancy for Product Designer

Please find attached my application for the position of product designer recently advertised on the B daily bulletin. I see this role as an excellent opportunity to use and further my range of abilities in an exciting and dynamic environment. I feel I have the necessary skills and experience, as well as the motivation to fulfil the potential that you are looking for in this role. My background is varied and I can lend my skills to many styles and feel that my designs both in print and digital would suit JUMP well.

I currently work at the Design Innovation Lab as a Service Designer. One of the main duties of this role was to develop a brand identity for the Design Innovation Lab, which led to launching the MDI range of products. Within this role, I have designed all promotional materials for the MDI and taken them through to print. This position is part design, part marketing and for the latter, I created an integrated campaign both internally and externally to recruit industry sponsorship. This involved creating and designing press ads, exhibition stands, viral marketing, online and offline marketing materials, product literature from concept to design, organizing and running photo shoots. Using our internal reprographics agency to develop the work for print, I created the design template, worked closely with them, successfully managing timelines and budgets. My current role also involves liaising with industry, developing a B2B relationship and attracting Industry to work with us on collaborative projects and provide sponsorship. This included a B2B campaign led by a launch event to bring industry together to raise awareness of the Design Innovation Lab, a follow-up promotional campaign included a targeted brochure, web content and e-communications to industry. I feel this has allowed me to develop confident communication skills to audiences of all levels.

I originally come from a design and marketing background. From this I developed an interest in graphic and web design, which led to a freelance role working for an array of clients. I undertook the service design role at the Design Innovation Lab as it allowed me to utilize my original design skills, and served as platform for the three constants in my life; brand, communication and design.

I am intelligent, have an enthusiastic, outgoing personality with a good sense of humour and a track record of success. I am flexible, able to work well under pressure and meet deadlines, as well as being committed to my responsibilities.

I would welcome the opportunity to discuss this role further with you and show you what I have to offer. Please don't hesitate to contact me should you require any further information and thank you for your time.

Many thanks,

Francis Woodman

Name of potential employer
Write to a particular person – even if you are 'cold-calling', try to research who you should address the letter to.

Why are you writing?
Begin by stating the purpose of your letter. What specific position are you applying for? How did you hear about the job? Did someone refer you?

Why should they hire you?
Creatively summarize what qualifies you for the position, your educational achievements, previous experience and skills, and how they directly relate to the position for which you are applying. Explain why you are interested in the position and why you are the best candidate for the job. Give specific examples of projects that you have worked on that demonstrate your abilities and how they match the job specification and duties of the position. Demonstrate that you have researched the company and know about them and the nature of their work.

Initiate the next step
Refer the reader to the items you have enclosed (CV, portfolio, references). If you are writing a speculative enquiry letter, say something along the lines of, 'I will contact you the week of the [date] of [month] to discuss the opportunities within your company.' If you are applying for a specific job, simply thank the reader for their time and consideration and say that you look forward to hearing from them.

Designing your portfolio

Having a great design portfolio is a must. Your design portfolio is one of the most important things you will create during your studies and is what you will mainly be judged on. It must, therefore, be well presented and include about five or six of your strongest and most impressive pieces of design work. Think about the kind of work the company you are applying to does and try to tailor your portfolio towards that. For example, if the company specializes in sports equipment and branding then try to include work of this nature in your portfolio.

Be prepared to talk about your product design work, what inspired you, why you approached the project in the way you did, even your choices of materials, colours and imagery. Show the company some of your sketches and development work. Many companies will want to see your early development work more than the finished piece as it shows your design process and how you think and work through design projects.

Before taking your portfolio along to job interviews, make sure you show it to a few people such as your design tutors, friends and other design students and talk them through it. Get them to ask you questions about your design work and practise and rehearse your responses with suitable answers. This will get you used to talking people through your portfolio, making you better prepared for that all-important interview.

A strong design portfolio opens doors, showcases your talents to prospective employers and is a physical representation of your design ability, process, personal approach, passion and skills.

The following step-by-step guide will help you create a personal portfolio you can be proud of:

Who are you?

Determine what you want your portfolio to say about you, who it is aimed at, and what they wish to see evidenced in it.

Creative resumé

Choose a variety of examples that highlight your very best work. Demonstrate your skills and talents by choosing only projects that you can confidently discuss. Ensure that your portfolio presents a balanced body of work, including a variety of projects that demonstrate the breadth and depth of your work.

Show your creativity

Remember that you wish to work in a creative industry. There is nothing worse for an employer than spending a day looking at a load of portfolios all presented in the same unthinking way. Show how far your creativity can stretch by creating a portfolio that is personal, while ensuring it appeals to as many people as possible.

Less is more

You should edit all your previous work to create a concise resumé of your work. You should not try to impress a potential employer with a portfolio crammed full of everything you have ever done. Their time is precious, and you should respect this. Simplify your presentation and try to think from the employer's point of view.

Only show your strongest work

People don't need an excuse to reject your work; one bad piece of work in your portfolio can prevent you getting a job, so don't add any filler pieces just to pad it out. Learning to critique your own work is something that comes with practice. You need to be objective when choosing what pieces to keep in, and it often helps to seek out the opinions of peers and colleagues.

Stand out from the crowd

Employers look at portfolios all the time so yours needs to stand out. Many portfolios follow the same format so you need to make sure yours makes an impact. To truly stand out in an extremely competitive field, your work needs to show a thoughtful approach from initial concept through to presentation, indicating that you can reflect upon your work and refine it to a highly polished state.

Display your personality

Let the potential employer or client get a feel for the way you like to work so they can see if it fits in with their own approach. Just as your clothes can give a first impression, so too does the way in which you present your portfolio.

Show your ambition

Your portfolio should show that you can take creative initiative, resolve a wide range of problems, and complete projects from start to finish. Show that you can work with limited supervision, generate ideas and motivate yourself and others.

Use your presentation skills

Show your full range of presentation abilities, including sketching, rendering, model-making, finished products, photography and three-dimensional modelling.

Target your intended audience

Tailor your portfolio to the industry sector you wish to work within, and demonstrate your commitment to work in this field. You should rearrange your work based on the specific nature of each job application, position and duties. Your portfolio should be able to evolve over your career, being updated as you develop your skills, ideas and abilities.

Process

Demonstrate your mastery of the design process by including examples of work from research to concept and execution.

Have a web presence

Create a web presence that enables potential employers to view your work digitally. By uploading examples of your work on to your own website, preferably with your first and last name as the domain address, you increase your visibility in the marketplace. There are also a number of online portfolio websites that you can register with to promote your work, such as www.coroflot.com.

Digital

Create a DVD or CD with your digital portfolio that you can mail with a cover letter or leave behind after an interview. Remember to label both the sleeve and CD with an appropriately designed label that includes your name, address, telephone number and email address. Ensure that your disk isn't corrupted or carrying a virus, as this is a surefire way not to get a job!

Keep it up to date

Design moves quickly and you need to show that you can keep up with the current trends while retaining the individuality that will make you stand out from the crowd.

To stand out in an extremely competitive field, you need to show commitment, ability and the passion that employers are looking for from designers. If you critically review and select your work to create a considered and creative portfolio then you will be ready to apply for that first design job.

'When I graduated, I presented my portfolio to potential employers through a CV, cover letter with images, and a smart business card with a website link. I exhibited at my degree show, before showing at a design store in SoHo and at the Funeria gallery in California. You need to show you have multi-disciplinary design skills and thinking, communication skills, business skills, confidence, time management, self-promotion and future thinking to find a job.'
Eleanor Davies, designer

CASE STUDY: Tom Harper

After undertaking an internship with leading design manufacturer Established & Sons, recent Edinburgh College of Art Product Design graduate, Tom Harper, chose to explore the potential opportunities of redesigning apparently mundane domestic cleaning products such as brooms, brushes, mops and buckets for his final year self-selected design project, 2009.

Tom's design interests concern everyday experiences, interactions and environments. His project and portfolio clearly demonstrated his personal design agenda and how he aims to exploit subtle behavioural insights and observations and apply them to the context of designing understated yet luxurious products through extensive visual and physical testing, evaluation and refinement.

Top row

Sketchbooks reveal a designer's ability to produce a diverse range of concepts (left); extensive sketch modelling demonstrates that you can think in 3D and refine design solutions (right).

Bottom row

Paper test models (left); the final design collection of cleaning products (right) conveys a broad portfolio of design skills.

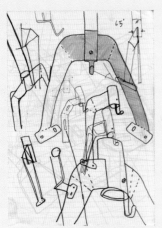
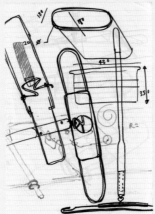
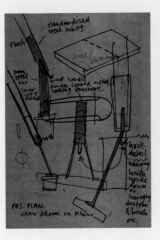

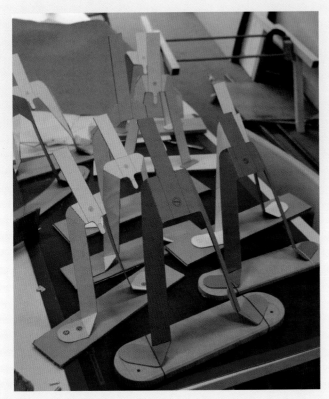

Getting a job

After the excitement of the degree show and graduation, the reality of getting your first job can be a daunting prospect. Only a very few lucky graduates are plucked from their college shows and set to work immediately. Most graduates take a number of months to find employment, and often have to start at the bottom, work hard and make slow progress until reaching their goals. Your first job may not be the job of your dreams, but it will hopefully teach you basic skills and responsibilities and provide a stepping-stone to your next job and a successful long-term career in product design.

The following tips should help you find your first job:

- Identify which designers, consultancies, companies and industrial sectors you would like to work for, and which industry sectors, countries or cities you would like to live in. Ask yourself why you have made these decisions and what skills you wish to develop.
- Research the designers and companies you have identified through looking at books, magazines and websites, and talking to alumni, tutors and designers working in the area.
- Assemble a strong portfolio and CV, and write a good cover letter that introduces you and your work to the firm or designer by following the guidelines above to create a package for sending to potential employers.
- Call, fax or email the company or designer to get the contact name of the person responsible for hiring staff and label your package for their attention. Send this to them even if they are not currently recruiting.
- Follow up your letter by contacting the company by phone, fax or email. Ensure that you talk to the person you sent the package to. Confirm they have received your package and ask them if there are any questions about it and if they would like to see more work or meet you for an interview. If you are lucky enough to be asked for an interview, then try to give yourself time to check out the location during your visit. If you are travelling a long way, see if you can arrange a number of interviews for the same time. If the company is not interested you can send them occasional updates of work, but don't pester.
- You should continue sending out speculative letters and applying for jobs until you are invited for an interview. The process of getting your foot in the door can be an arduous one, but you must remain committed, as your persistence will pay off eventually.

'It is never easy to find the right job, but 'design' is such a huge and diverse discipline that my key piece of advice would be to really know what you want to do and what drives you. Always try to find a position that has room for growth and diversity.'
Katy Buchan, product champion

Tips for interviews

Interviews can be a stressful occasion. You are meeting new people, selling yourself and your skills, and often being asked probing questions to ascertain what you know or don't know about design. Here are some interview tips to help you prepare for the event:

- Ask family or friends to stage a mock interview to help you prepare.
- Dress appropriately.
- Arrive early.
- Hand over your business card.
- Shake hands firmly.
- Tailor your portfolio to meet the expectations and aspirations of the company.
- Have at least six questions ready to ask; if you have fewer you'll find they will all have been answered in the course of the interview.
- Take a pad and pen and take it out at the beginning of the interview. This shows you are organized, committed and serious about the position and helps capture the feedback you will be receiving during the interview.
- Talk about your work before you show it in your portfolio, but don't talk too much. You should try to engage the interviewer/s with you.
- Bring sketches, samples and mock-ups. Companies are as interested in how you got to the final solution as the solution itself.
- Have a copy of your CV at the back of the portfolio and offer it even if you have already sent them a copy previously.
- Don't talk about holidays or how much you'll be earning unless the interviewer/s bring up the subject.
- Tell them you really want the job, as believe it or not, lots of people forget to say this.
- Ask for the interviewers' business cards.
- When you get back home, send an email thanking the company for the interview.
- Look over your notes and if you don't get the job, at least you'll have a good idea of where you can improve next time.

Career opportunities

Product design graduates have a wide range of career opportunities that exploit their knowledge and experience of the product design process. They may become a member of a freelance design consultancy, join a manufacturing company as a specialist within a product design development team, or decide to set up their own practice as a designer or designer-maker.

Transferable skills also enable graduates to work in diverse fields such as computer-aided design, marketing, retail, multi-media or management. The best courses often have strong links with industry to ensure that graduates are aware of the full range of possibilities and have access to them.

Product design students have a range of prospects, such as:

- Designer within a team working within a product design consultancy with scope to work on designs for a range of consumer products.
- Own design business, with longer-term aim to act as consultant.
- In-house designer for a product manufacturer.
- Designer-maker, self-production using own or shared workshop.
- Interior product design specifier for interior or architectural firm.
- Other type of freelance or in-house designer, e.g. graphic, web, CAD.

The product design industry covers a number of different sectors such as:

- Consumer electronics – From computers to televisions to iPods.
- Digital media – CAD visualization for manufacture and media.
- Exhibitions – From trade shows to museum installations.
- Furniture – From one-off pieces of 'design-art' to mass production.
- Lighting – From domestic luminaires to lighting landscapes.
- Packaging – Structural packaging and point of sale.
- Research – User-centred design to design forecasting.
- Sports equipment – From trainers to skateboards.
- Toys – From educational learning products to film tie-ins.
- Transportation – From cars to public transport.

The range of skills developed on product design courses is wide and are adaptable across a wider range of organizations and roles such as:

- Design engineer – Designs, tests and develops vehicles and/or components from concept stage through to production.
- Industrial buyer – Purchases the highest quantity of goods and services at the most competitive rate in order to meet specific user needs.
- Agency account executive – Makes potential customers aware of a product and its advantages to them; includes market research, marketing and packaging. Communication skills are vital.
- Marketing executive – Understands and meets the needs of the consumer in order to market a successful product.
- Sales executive – Maximizes the sale of a company's goods or services in a variety of settings. Understanding and meeting the needs of the customer are essential if a product is to be successful.

In an increasingly competitive job market for graduates, more and more students are continuing their studies and enrolling on postgraduate courses. Masters and doctoral study enables you to extend your skills and thinking, and helps differentiate yourself from the competition.

Masters courses usually require one or two years of study, and enable students to deepen their knowledge and expertise within the discipline, providing a clear progression from undergraduate education while maintaining distinctiveness from industrial training. Masters students are expected to challenge boundaries, think originally, and develop intellectual and critical approaches to the discipline of product design.

Starting your own business

The decision to start your own creative business can be a daunting step for the young designer, but this offers a creative freedom and sense of achievement that can be hard to match working for a company. It requires commitment, energy and a large amount of emotional investment. You'll need to consider if this really is the right time in your life to launch a business venture, and why you wish to do this. But if you do, you need to ensure you have the tools to design, develop, promote and control your business.

Building a business requires you to identify and define the foundations of your idea. Begin by asking yourself some challenging questions such as:

- What are your ambitions for the business?
- What are the values that underpin why you want to start a business?
- Will the business provide a product or service?
- How can you identify, protect and exploit your intellectual property?

Having identified the key attributes that your business needs to be built upon, undertake a S.W.O.T (strengths, weaknesses, opportunities and threats) analysis of your business proposal to evaluate its strategic positioning:

- What strengths do you have?
- What weaknesses do you need to address?
- What opportunities can you exploit?
- What threatens your business idea?

Once you have explored your business idea, you will need to develop a clear mission statement and decide what impact you hope to make. This will help you to pitch your idea to potential clients, customers and investors. Try to succinctly describe your idea/s through a one-minute short verbal description known as an 'elevator pitch'. When trying to compose this ask yourself:

- How does it enhance life?
- Does it revive something of the past?
- What does it make less desirable?
- Are there any possible negative backlashes to the idea?

When you have developed your business idea and defined its aspirations, you will need to identify your customers and ensure there is a viable market for your product/s and/or services. If extensive research indicates that there are enough customers prepared to purchase your business offer then you should explore the relationships you will need to help you develop your business.

Every business needs a set of relationships to take a product to market successfully, develop a viable brand identity and maintain a successful company. These can be categorized into four types:

- Customers – The people buying, using and experiencing your product/s.
- Distributors – Individuals and companies that are involved with the delivery, sales and marketing of your product/s and company.
- Generators – Individuals and companies that will help you develop new ideas, give you direction and help you grow your business.
- Realizers – Manufacturers who will produce your finished product.

When determining your business plan you should evaluate these relationships and carefully consider which activities you need to keep inside your business, and which can be outsourced. By carefully evaluating these relationships you will be in a strong position to bring your business idea and products to market.

Whatever sector of the product design industry you are entering, you will come across a unique network of must-know people. You should make a concerted effort to network as much as possible and ensure you make a positive impression on everybody you meet and have business relationships with. There is a wide range of support available for aspiring entrepreneurs, from government agencies, enterprise networks and chambers of commerce, to trade organizations and national design councils. Much of the advice is free, so ensure that you make the most of these support agencies and the advice of tutors, colleagues and peers when deciding which jobs to apply for, how to work as a freelancer, or how to set up and run your own business.

Conclusion

Product design is an extremely competitive field, and you need to show your commitment to a challenging yet exciting discipline. Getting a job, launching your own company or bringing a product to market may sound like daunting tasks, but the design world of the twenty-first century offers you great opportunities. If you study hard, take the time to review and select your work, and develop a thoughtful and innovative body of work, you will be rewarded with a successful career in product design.

Glossary

AIDA (analysis of interconnected decision areas) Method used to understand how one design decision affects the options available to other decisions in a large-scale project.

Alpha prototype An alpha prototype (also commonly referred to as a proof of principle model) is the initial attempt to evaluate some aspect of the intended design without trying to exactly simulate the visual appearance, choice of materials or intended manufacturing process. Such prototypes are used to identify which design concepts are worth pursuing and where further development and testing are required.

Analogical thinking The transfer of an idea from one context to a new one.

Anthropometric data Anthropometry, literally meaning 'measurement of humans', refers to the measurement of the human body for the purposes of understanding human physical variation. This data is collected and updated regularly and plays a vital role in establishing the ergonomic requirements for products, clothes and architecture.

Appearance model Models or visual prototypes that aim to capture the intended design aesthetic of the product, simulating the appearance, colour and surface textures but not the functional attributes of the final product. These appearance models are suitable for use in market research, design approval, packaging mock-ups and photoshoots for marketing literature.

Attribute listing A technique to help designers determine what problems a design must address. By listing the different attributes the final design must achieve, designers can evaluate different concepts against these criteria.

Axonometric projection A commonly used type of orthographic projection, used to create a pictorial drawing of an object, where the object is rotated along one or more of its axes relative to the plane of projection, to enable the viewer to see the object from a number of viewpoints.

Bar stock plastic Standard profiles of plastic bars commonly manufactured.

Base view The technical drawing term used to describe the view of an object from directly below it.

Beta prototypes A beta prototype, also known as a functional or working prototype, is a physical model that attempts to simulate the final design, aesthetics, materials and functionality of a designer's intended product. The construction of a fully working full-scale prototype is the ultimate test of concept, and enables designers and engineers to check for any design flaws and make last-minute improvements before larger production runs are ordered.

Blob architecture Blob architecture, Blobitecture and Blobism are terms used to describe a movement in architecture that began in the mid-1990s, in which the buildings display an organic, fluid form that takes advantages of the creative possibilities of advanced computer modelling software.

Blobject A product featuring smooth flowing curves, bright colours and an absence of sharp edges. The term has been used to describe the work of 1990s designers such as Karim Rashid, and products such as the original Apple iMac.

Body storming A participatory design method for demonstrating or developing ideas in a physical setting. Team members explore ideas and interactions physically, often using props to give a sense of place and context.

Bulk product Also known as a continuous engineering product, this is an ongoing standard product produced by manufacturers.

CAD (computer-aided design) The use of computer software and technology for the design of real or virtual products. As in the manual drafting of technical and engineering drawings, CAD does not merely show the form of an object but enables designers to convey symbolic information such as materials, processes, dimensions and tolerances, according to application-specific conventions.

CAM (computer-aided manufacture) The use of computer-based software tools that assist designers and engineers in manufacturing or prototyping product components and tooling.

Capability assessment This inclusive design technique enables designers to evaluate products or concepts by breaking down how they are used into a series of activities and then comparing the physical and cognitive capability levels required to use them.

Capability simulator Devices used by designers to help them empathise with those who have capability losses such as vision, hearing or mobility. While these devices offer designers a greater insight into how people might use their products, they are no replacement for talking to users with different capabilities.

Casting The manufacturing process by which a liquid material such as metal or clay is poured into a mould that contains a hollow cavity of the desired shape and is then allowed to solidify, creating the desired form.

Chip forming The inclusive term for machine tools such as lathes, drills, grinders and milling machines.

Composites Engineered materials made from two or more constituent materials with significantly different physical or chemical properties.

Concurrent design The management method of simultaneously working on the design, engineering, manufacturing and other requirements of a product to help bring it to market more quickly and efficiently.

Consumable A manufactured product that has a relatively long useful life, such as a car or a television.

Consumer product A product for personal, family or household use.

Convergent thinking Thinking that brings together information focused on solving a problem.

Cradle to cradle design A model of design that aims to create systems and products that are not merely efficient but waste-free.

Cradle to grave design Also known as life cycle assessment, this is the investigation and evaluation of the environmental impact of a given product or service from its birth and manufacture through its lifetime and to its final disposal.

Creative product design Product design that involves designers working in a creative manner to produce innovative designs.

Cutting The term used to describe machine tools such as a milling machine that remove material from a solid block of material.

Divergent thinking Method used to generate creative ideas by exploring many possible solutions, enabling the generation of multiple ideas in a spontaneous, free-flowing nature.

Ductility The extent to which materials can be deformed plastically without fracturing.

Elastomer A material such as rubber, which has the ability to return to its original shape once a load is removed.

Elevation The term used to describe a projected view of an object from the side.

Embossing The process of producing raised or sunken designs in sheet materials.

Ergonomist Someone who applies scientific data relating to humans to the design of products, systems and environments.

Ethnographer Someone who scientifically explores and describes specific human cultures and activities.

Exclusion audit An inclusive design method used to evaluate different products or concepts by comparing the proportion of the population that will be unable to use them.

Experience prototype Simulations and models used to investigate and reveal the quality of the experience being designed. Experience prototypes can be 'quick and dirty' to obtain feedback on a specific design concept, or highly crafted solutions for in-depth usability evaluation.

Exploded view A drawing that communicates how various components are assembled by illustrating how they relate to each other.

Forming The manufacturing term for moulding, shaping and bending materials.

Fusion welding A group of processes that bond metal together by heating a portion of each piece above the melting point and causing them to flow together and bond.

GA (general arrangement) drawing A drawing that describes the final layout and dimensions of a product. All of the required detail, tooling and assembly engineering drawings required for production are co-ordinated with reference to the GA.

Galvanizing The metallurgic process of coating steel with zinc to prevent corrosion.

Hard skills Key technical skills, such as drawing and modelling, that a designer requires.

Industrial equipment product Products used within a factory such as robotic assembly arms.

Industrial plant Machines and equipment used in industry such as air conditioning units.

Industry product A product designed solely for industrial use and not for use by consumers.

Informance An 'informative performance' is a method of role-playing that enables designers to communicate observations collected previously to others.

Information set The full set of engineering drawings required for production.

Injection moulding The manufacturing process for producing parts from both thermoplastic and thermosetting plastic materials. Plastic is fed into a heated barrel, mixed, and forced into a mould cavity, where it cools and hardens to the configuration of the mould cavity. Injection moulding is widely used for manufacturing a variety of parts in high volumes, from the smallest component to entire body panels of cars.

Isometric drawing A non-perspective method of pictorially representing an object. Elevations are constructed using a 30-degree set square.

Isotropic A material with physical properties that are uniform in all directions.

Joining The universal term for bonding, fixing, connecting and gluing materials and components together.

Malleability A material's ability to deform under compressive stress such as the ability to form a thin sheet by hammering or rolling.

Matrix evaluation A quantitative technique used by designers to evaluate their concepts by ranking designs against set criteria.

Metric (of a PDS) Each element of a PDS has both a metric and a value. The metric is any element that can be measured; for example, the weight or length of a piece of kit in a product.

Mock-up A form of prototype or model that simulates an object, experience or environment.

Modernism Describes both a period and movement in the history of design, starting with Bauhaus in the 1920s, and the minimalist machine aesthetic that continues to influence designers today.

Morphological chart A problem-solving technique used for addressing complex, non-quantifiable problems.

Moulds (in casting) A hollowed-out form that is filled with a liquid such as plastic, glass, metal or ceramic slurry. The liquid hardens or sets inside the mould, adopting its shape. A release agent is typically used to ease the removal of the hardened/set substance from the mould.

NDA (non-disclosure agreement) A legal contract between at least two parties that outlines confidential material, knowledge or information that the parties wish to share with one another for certain purposes, but wish to restrict access to by third parties. An NDA creates a confidential relationship between the parties to protect any type of confidential and proprietary information or trade secrets.

Neo-Modernism The aesthetic revival of Modernist design that began in the 1990s.

Oblique drawing A non-perspective method of pictorially representing an object, where the side and top views of an object are tacked on to the front elevation.

Orthographic drawing The engineering drawing method of representing 3D objects on 2D paper. A plan and two adjacent elevations of an object are projected and then unfolded so that they lie on the same plane.

Pairwise comparison method A method of evaluating products where each concept or design is matched head to head with each of the other candidates. Each alternative is scored against the other, with the design receiving the most points being declared the preferred direction.

Paper prototypes Models constructed from cardboard during the initial stages of the design process that are used to quickly resolve issues such as scale and graphics.

Patents A set of exclusive rights granted by a national government to an inventor of a demonstrably novel idea for a limited period of time in exchange for a public disclosure of an invention. Patents offer protection and the opportunity for the inventor or their assignee to have the rights to commercially exploit the idea.

PDS (Product Design Specification) A detailed briefing document that outlines all the requirements for a new product.

Perspective drawing The approximate representation of a 3D object, on a flat 2D piece of paper, as it is perceived by the eye.

Plan (in plans and elevations) The projected view from directly above an object.

Planned obsolescence The process of a product becoming obsolete and perceived by consumers as non-functional after a certain period of time or use in a way that is planned or designed by the manufacturer. This process has been widely criticized, as it enables manufacturers to

encourage sales of new products by creating an irrational desire for new products, despite there being substantial life left in the old products.

Post-Modernism A 1970s and 1980s design movement and aesthetic marked by the re-emergence of surface ornament, historical reference in decorative forms and playful rejection of Modernist dogma.

Product liability The area of law in which designers, manufacturers, distributors, suppliers, retailers and others who make products available to the public are held responsible for the injuries those products cause.

Projection symbol The symbol that communicates whether a set of drawings has been drawn in first or third angle.

Proof of principle models A proof of principle model, also known as an alpha model, is the initial attempt to evaluate some aspect of the intended design without attempting to exactly simulate the visual appearance, choice of materials or intended manufacturing process. Such models are used to identify which design concepts are worth pursuing and where further development and testing are required.

Prototype A physical model that represents the aesthetic and/or functional attributes of a design, enabling the designer to evaluate these attributes and refine them during the design process.

Rapid prototyping The automatic construction of 3D objects using additive computer-aided manufacturing technology.

Ready-made products Already manufactured objects that are used as components to create new designs.

Relative importance survey A method of determining the importance of design criteria.

Rendering The term used to describe a visual coloured representation of an object, either a hand rendering of an object using pens, pencils and pastels, or a rendered CAD image of a wireframe drawing.

Rod stock plastic Standard profiles of plastic rods commonly manufactured.

Routine product design Everyday non-challenging design.

Scenario modelling The method of creating a scenario in which a design concept will be used.

Scenario testing The method of evaluating an imagined scenario.

Schematic sketches Drawings that illustrate how a design may work and/or have its internal mechanical components arranged.

Section The term used to describe a slice through an object to illustrate a profile or interior detail not apparent from a plan view or elevation. Complex forms require multiple sections to accurately represent them.

Sketch model A simply and quickly made representation of an idea in three dimensions.

Soft skills The term used to describe the personal and intellectual skills required of a designer, such as empathy and creativity.

Solid modellers A CAD system that produces a complete 3D model of a product or component that can be cut, weighed and checked for interferences with other objects. This is in contrast to a surface modeller, which provides only the external appearance of an object.

Solid state welding A series of processes, in which two components are joined under pressure and at a temperature below the melting point of the parent material.

Special purpose product A specific design solution to a specific design problem that is not for universal use or consumption.

Stereolithography An additive manufacturing rapid prototyping process for producing models, prototypes and, in some cases, production parts. Stereolithography uses a vat of liquid UV-curable photopolymer resin and a UV laser to build parts one layer at a time.

Storyboard Storyboards use a series of illustrations or images displayed in sequence for the purpose of pre-visualizing a sequential story or activity.

Surface modeller A surface modeller provides a mock-up of the external appearance of a product.

Synectics Synectics is a commonly used group problem-solving technique that starts with brainstorming ideas before participants develop clear sets of actions through the use of analogies.

Test rig An engineering prototype devised to test a specific physical or functional task.

Thematic sketches Drawings that explore how a proposed design may look.

Thermoplastics A polymer that melts when heated. Unlike a thermoset, it can be reheated and remoulded.

Thermosets A polymer that is cured through heat or chemical reaction to create a stronger form. Once cured, thermosets cannot be reheated and remoulded, unlike thermoplastics.

Title block The technical drawing term for the graphical box on a drawing that contains details, such as what the drawing is of, what it relates to, who it is for, who it has been drawn by and when it was drawn.

Tools (in casting) The universal term used to describe a machined mould used to manufacture components.

Top view The technical drawing term used to describe the view of an object from directly above it.

Trademark A distinctive sign or indicator such as a name, word, phrase, logo, symbol, design or image used by an individual, business organization, or other legal entity to identify that the products or services to consumers with which the trademark appears originate from a unique source, and to distinguish its products or services from those of other entities.

Triple bottom line A method of describing the social and environmental impact of an organization's activities, in a measurable way, to its economic performance in order to show improvement or to make evaluation more in-depth.

Vacuum forming A process of forming sheets of thermoplastic to create complex forms. The sheet is heated to a forming temperature, stretched onto or into a single-surface mould, and held against the mould by applying a vacuum between the mould surface and the sheet, to create the finished component.

Value (of a PDS) The benefit of knowing exactly what you are trying to achieve during the design process.

Variant product design Design that replicates the general function and form of a successful product, and merely alters it in a minor way to widen consumer choice.

Bibliography

Albrecht, D. et al, *Design Culture Now*, Laurence King Publishing, London, 2000

Antonelli, P., *Humble Masterpieces: 100 Everyday Marvels of Design*, Thames & Hudson, London, 2006

Antonelli, P., *Supernatural: The Work of Ross Lovegrove*, Phaidon Press, London, 2004

Antonelli, P. and Aldersey-Williams, H., *Design and the Elastic Mind*, The Museum of Modern Art, New York, 2008

Arad, R. et al, *Spoon*, Phaidon Press, London, 2002

Asensio, P., *Product Design*, teNeues Publishing Group, New York, 2002

Baxter, M., *Product Design*, Chapman Hall, London, 1995

Bohm, F., *KGID: Konstantin Grcic Industrial Design*, Phaidon Press, London, 2007

Bone, M. and Johnson, K., *I Miss My Pencil*, Chronicle Books, San Francisco, 2009

Bouroullec, R. and Bouroullec, E., *Ronan and Erwan Bouroullec*, Phaidon Press, London, 2003

Bramston, D., *Basics Product Design: Idea Searching*, AVA Publishing, Lausanne, 2008

Bramston, D., *Basics Product Design: Material Thoughts*, AVA Publishing, Lausanne, 2009

Bramston, D., *Basics Product Design: Visual Conversations: 3*, AVA Publishing, Lausanne, 2009

Brown, T., *Change by Design: How Design Thinking Creates New Alternatives for Business and Society: How Design Thinking Can Transform Organizations and Inspire Innovation*, Collins Business, London, 2009

Bryman, A., *Social Research Methods*, Oxford University Press, Oxford, 2001

Burroughs, A., *Everyday Engineering*, Chronicle Books, San Francisco, 2007

Busch, A., *Design is...Words, Things, People, Buildings and Places*, Metropolis Books, Princeton Architectural Press, 2002

Byars, M., *The Design Encyclopaedia*, John Wiley & Sons, New York, 1994

Campos, C., *Product Design Now*, Harper Design International, London, 2006

Castelli, C.T., *Transitive Design*, Edizioni Electa, Milan, 2000

Chua, C.K., *Rapid Prototyping*, World Scientific, London, 2003

Cooper, R. and Press, M., *Design Management: Managing Design*, John Wiley & Sons, London, 1995

Cross, N., *Engineering Design Methods*, John Wiley & Sons, Chichester, 1989

Dixon, T. et al, *And Fork: 100 Designers, 10 Curators, 10 Good Designs*, Phaidon Press, London, 2007

Dormer, P., *Design since 1945*, Thames & Hudson, London, 1993

Dormer, P., *The Meanings of Modern Design*, Thames & Hudson, London, 1991

Dunne, A., *Hertzian Tales: Electronic Products, Aesthetic Experience, and Critical Design*, The MIT Press, Cambridge, Mass., 2008

Dunne, A. and Raby, F., *Design Noir: The Secret Life of Electronic Objects*, Birkhauser, Munich, 2001

Fairs, M., *Twenty-first Century Design*, Carlton Books, London, 2006

Fiell, C. and Fiell, P., *Design Handbook (Icons)*, Taschen, Koln, 2006

Fiell, C. and Fiell, P., *Design Now: Designs for Life – From Eco-design to Design-art*, Taschen, Koln, 2007

Fiell, C. and Fiell, P., *Design of the 20th Century*, Benedikt Taschen Verlag, Koln, 1999

Fuad-Luke, A., *The Eco-Design Handbook: A Complete Sourcebook for the Home and Office*, Thames & Hudson, London (3rd edition), 2009

Fukasawa, N., *Naoto Fukasawa*, Phaidon Press, London, 2007

Fukasawa, N. and Morrison, J., *Super Normal: Sensations of the Ordinary*, Lars Muller Publishers, Baden, Switzerland (2nd extended edition), 2007

Fulton Suri, J., *Thoughtless Acts?*, Chronicle Books, San Francisco, 2005

Heskett, J., *Toothpicks and Logos*, Oxford University Press, Oxford, 2002

Hudson, J., *Process: 50 Product Designs from Concept to Manufacture*, Laurence King Publishing, London, 2008

Hudson, J., *1000 New Designs and Where to Find Them: A 21st Century Sourcebook*, Laurence King Publishing, London, 2006

IDEO, *IDEO Methods Cards*, William Stout Architectural Books, San Francisco, 2002

Jones, J.C., *Design Methods: Seeds of Human Futures*, John Wiley & Sons, Chichester, 1970

Jordan, P., *An Introduction to Usability*, Taylor and Francis, London, 1998

Jordan, P., *Designing Pleasurable Products*, Taylor and Francis, London, 2002

Julier, G., *The Culture of Design*, Sage Publications, London, 2000

Kahn, K.B. (ed.), *The PDMA Handbook of New Product Development*, John Wiley & Sons, New York, 2004

Lawson, B., *How Designers Think, The Design Process Demystified*, Butterworth Architecture, Oxford, 1990

Lefteri, C., *Making It: Manufacturing Techniques for Product Design*, Laurence King Publishing, London, 2007

Lefteri, C., *Materials for Inspirational Design*, Rotovision Publishers, Hove, 2006

Lorenz, C., *The Design Dimension: Product Strategy and the Challenge of Global Marketing*, Blackwell Publishers, Oxford, 1986

Manzini, E., *The Material of Invention*, Arcadia, Milan, 1986

Moggridge, B., *Designing Interactions*, The MIT Press, Cambridge, Mass., 2006

Morris, R., *The Fundamentals of Product Design*, AVA Publishing, Lausanne, 2009

Morrison, J., *Everything But the Walls*, Lars Muller Publishers, Baden, Switzerland (2nd extended edition), 2006

Myerson, J., *IDEO: Masters of Innovation*, Laurence King Publishing, London, 2004

Noble, I. and Bestley, R., *Visual Research: An Introduction to Research Methodologies in Graphic Design*, AVA Publishing SA, 2005

Parsons, T., *Thinking: Objects – Contemporary Approaches to Product Design*, AVA Publishing, Lausanne, 2009

Pink, S., *Doing Visual Ethnography: Images, Media and Representation in Research*, Sage Publications., London, 2001

Potter, N., *What Is a Designer: Things, Places, Messages*, Hyphen Press, London (4th revised edition), 2008

Proctor, R., *1000 New Eco Designs and Where to Find Them*, Laurence King Publishing, London, 2009

Pye, D., *The Nature and Aesthetics of Design*, A. and C. Black Publishers, London, 2000

Redhead, D., *Products of Our Time*, Birkhauser Verlag AG, Munich, 1999

Rodgers, P., *Inspiring Designers*, Black Dog Publishers, London, 2004

Rodgers, P., *Little Book of Big Ideas: Design*, A. and C. Black Publishers, London, 2009

Rowe, P.G., *Design Thinking*, The MIT Press, Cambridge, Mass., 1987

Schön, D.A., *The Reflective Practitioner: How Professionals Think in Action*, Basic Books, New York, 1983

Schouwenberg, L. and Jongerius, H., *Hella Jongerius*, Phaidon Press., London, 2003

Slack, L., *What is Product Design?*, Rotovision Publishers, Hove, 2006

Sudjic, D., *The Language of Things*, Allen Lane Publishers, London, 2008

Thackara, J., *Design after Modernism: Beyond the Object*, Thames & Hudson, London, 1988

Thompson, R., *Manufacturing Processes for Design Professionals*, Thames & Hudson, London, 2007

Troika, *Digital by Design: Crafting Technology for Products and Environments*, Thames & Hudson, London, 2008

Ulrich, K.T. and Eppinger, S.D., *Product Design Development*, McGraw Hill, Cambridge, Mass., 2000

Whitely, N., *Design for Society*, Reaktion Books, London, 1993

Further resources

Magazines

Abitare
www.abitare.it

Arcade
www.arcadejournal.com

AXIS
www.axisinc.co.jp/english

Blueprint
www.blueprintmagazine.co.uk

Creative Review
www.creativereview.co.uk

Design Engineer
www.engineerlive.com/Design-Engineer

Design Week
www.designweek.co.uk

Domus
www.domusweb.it

Dwell
www.dwell.com

Elle Decor
www.pointclickhome.com/elle_decor

Eureka
www.eurekamagazine.co.uk

Frame
www.framemag.com

FX
www.fxmagazine.co.uk

Icon
www.iconeye.com

Interni
www.internimagazine.it

Metropolis
www.metropolismag.com/cda

Neo2
www.neo2.es

New Design
www.newdesignmagazine.co.uk

Objekt
www.objekt.nl

Ottagano
www.ottagono.com

Surface
www.surfacemag.com

Wallpaper*
www.wallpaper.com

Websites

3D Modelling, Rapid Prototyping
Manufacturing Technology
www.3dsystems.com

100% Design
www.100percentdesign.co.uk

Architonic
www.architonic.com

Better Product Design
www.betterproductdesign.net

British Inventors Society
www.thebis.org/index.php

Centre for Sustainable Design
www.cfsd.org.uk

Cooper-Hewitt National Design Museum, USA
www.cooperhewitt.org

Design & Art Direction (D&AD)
www.dandad.org

Design Boom
www.designboom.com

Design Classics Resource
www.tribu-design.com

Design Council
www.designcouncil.org.uk

Design Discussion Forum
www.nextd.org

Design Engine
www.design-engine.com

Design Magazine and Resource
www.core77.com

Design Management Institute
www.dmi.org

Design Museum, London
www.designmuseum.org

Design News for Design Engineers
www.designnews.com

Design Philosophy Papers
www.desphilosophy.com

Design Resource
www.designaddict.com

Design*Sponge
www.designsponge.blogspot.com

Designers Block
www.verydesignersblock.com/2009

Designers' Guide to Materials and Processes
www.designinsite.dk/htmsider/home.htm

Dexigner
www.dexigner.com

Ecology-derived Techniques for Design
www.biothinking.com/slidenj.htm

Educational Resource for Designers
www.thedesigntrust.co.uk

How Stuff Works
www.howstuffworks.com

Inclusive Design Toolkit
www.inclusivedesigntoolkit.com

Information/Inspiration Eco Design Resource
www.informationinspiration.org.uk

Institute of Nano Technology
www.nano.org.uk

International Contemporary Furniture Fair
www.icff.com/page/home.asp#

London Design Festival
www.londondesignfestival.com

Milan Furniture Fair (Salone Internazionale del Mobile)
www.cosmit.it/tool/home.php?s=0,1,21,27,28

MoCo Loco
www.mocoloco.com

Modern World Design Eco-Design Links
www.greenmap.com/modern/resources.html

New Designers
www.newdesigners.com

Participatory Design Methods
interliving.kth.se/publications/thread/index.html

Places and Spaces
www.placesandspaces.com

Red Dot Design Museum
en.red-dot.org/design.html

Royal Society of Arts
www.rsa-design.net

Showroom of UK Designers' Work
www.designnation.co.uk

The Story of Stuff
www.storyofstuff.com

Stylepark
www.stylepark.com

Victoria and Albert Museum
www.vam.ac.uk

Vitra Design Museum
www.design-museum.de

Webliography of Design
www.designfeast.com

Design competitions

Braun Prize
www.braunprize.com

Design & Art Direction (D&AD),
Student Awards
www.dandad.org

Good Design Award
www.g-mark.org

IF Concept Award
www.ifdesign.de

Materialica Design Award
www.materialicadesign.com

Muji Award
www.muji.net/award

Promosedia International
www.promosedia.it

Red Dot Design Award
www.red-dot.de

Royal Society of Arts
Design Directions Student Awards
www.rsa-design.net

Useful addresses

Australia

Powerhouse Museum
500 Harris Street, Ultimo
PO Box K346, Haymarket
Sydney, NSW 1238
www.powerhousemuseum.com

Belgium

Design Museum
Jan Breydelstraat 5
9000 Ghent
design.museum.gent.be

Canada

DX: The Design Exchange
234 Bay Street, PO Box 18
Toronto Dominion Centre
Toronto, ON M5K 1B2
www.dx.org

Denmark

The Danish Museum of Art & Design
Bredgade 68/1260, København K
www.kunstindustrimuseet.dk

Germany

Bauhaus-Archiv Museum of Design
Klingelhöferstrasse 14
D-10785 Berlin
www.bauhaus.de/english/index.htm

Die Neue Sammlung
Barer Strasse 40
80333 Munich
www.die-neue-sammlung.de

Red Dot Design Museum
Gelsenkirchener Strasse 181
45309 Essen
en.red-dot.org/371.html

Vitra Design Museum
Charles-Eames-Str. 1
D-79576 Weil am Rhein
www.design-museum.de

Mexico

Mexican Museum of Design
Francisco I. Madero No. 74
Colonia Centro Histûrico
Delegaciûn CuauhtÈmoc
Mèxico D.F, C.P. 06000
www.mumedi.org

Singapore

Red Dot Design Museum
28 Maxwell Road
Singapore, 069120
www.red-dot.sg/concept/museum/main_page.htm

United Kingdom

Chartered Society of Designers
1 Cedar Court, Royal Oak Yard
Bermondsey Street
London, SE1 3GA
www.csd.org.uk

Design Museum
28 Shad Thames
London, SE1 2YD
www.designmuseum.org

Geffrye Museum
Kingsland Road
London, E2 8EA
www.geffrye-museum.org.uk

Institution of Engineering Designers
Courtleigh, Westbury Leigh, Westbury
Wiltshire, BA13 3TA
www.ied.org.uk

Victoria and Albert Museum
Cromwell Road
London, SW7 2RL
www.vam.ac.uk

United States

Cooper-Hewitt, National Design Museum
2 East 91st Street, New York
NY 10128
www.cooperhewitt.org

The Eames Office
850 Pico Boulevard, Santa Monica
CA 90405
www.eamesoffice.com

Industrial Designers Society of America
45195 Business Court, Suite 250, Dulles
VA 20166-6717
www.idsa.org

Museum of Arts and Design
2 Columbus Circle, New York
NY 10019
www.madmuseum.org

Museum of California Design
P.O. Box 361370, Los Angeles
CA 90036
www.mocad.org

Museum of Design, Atlanta
285 Peachtree Center Avenue
Marquis Two Tower, Atlanta
Georgia 30303-1229
www.museumofdesign.org

New Museum
235 Bowery, New York
NY 10002
www.newmuseum.org

Smithsonian Institution
PO Box 37012
SI Building, Room 153, MRC 010
Washington D.C. 20013-7012
www.si.edu

UC Davis Design Museum and Design Collection
145 Walker Hall, University of California
One Shields Avenue, Davis
CA 95616
www.designmuseum.ucdavis.edu/index.html

Index

Page numbers in *italics* refer to illustrations

A

Aalto, Alvar 52: vase (Iittala) *26*
Ad Hoc (Jean-Marie Massaud for Viccarbe) *118*
Add-On Radiator (Satyendra Pakhalé for Tubes) *48*
AEG (Allgemeine Elektricitäts Gesellschaft) 25
Aeron Chair (Don Chadwick and Bill Stumpf for
    Herman Miller) 174, *175*
'After Hours' installation (Krannert Art Museum, Illinois) *139*
Aga Stove (Gustaf Dalén) 52
Airbus A380 *11*
Aladdin (Amber) (Stuart Haygarth) *70*
Alessi 34, *38*, 39, 41, 44, 53, *84*, 197, *199*
Alessi, Alberto 48, 196
Algue (Ronan & Erwan Bouroullec for Vitra) *136*
Alkalay, Shay see Raw-Edges Design Studio
All Occasion Veneerware® (bambu LLC) *172*
aluminium 120
Amisa door handle (Satyendra Pakhalé) *48*
analogical thinking 80, *80*
Andy Murray Design 60
Anemone wallpaper (William Morris) *23*
anthropologists 14
Anti Copying in Design (ACID) 209
Anti-Design, Italy 33, 38, 39
Anti-theft Bike/Car Device (Dominic Wilcox) *153*
Apollo (Ross Lovegrove for Driade) *134*
Apple 44, 46, 50, 53, 65, 162–3
    iMac 44, 162, *162*, 163
    iPhone 53; iPhone 3GS *6*
    iPod 9, *44*, 65, 163, *163*, 199, 200
    Macintosh 48, 88, 162, *162*
Arad, Ron 40, 44; Bookworm *40*; Rover Chair 40, 42;
    Tel Aviv Opera House 40; Tinker Chair 40
Archizoom Associati 33, 38
Art Deco 28
Art Nouveau 23–4
Artecnica *131*, *170*
Artek 177
Artemide 36, *36*, 39
Arts and Crafts Movement 22–3
Asia, design in 36–7, 46
Ast, Jorre van: Jar Tops (for Royal VKB) *123*
Atelier de Nîmes 50
Atfield, Jane: RCP2 Chair *178*
attribute listing 80
Avanti car (Raymond Loewy) 159
Avvanzini, Paolo (Erreti) 48

B

B.M. Horse Chair (Satyendra Pakhalé) *48*
Baccarat: Crystal Candy Set (Jaime Hayon) *44*
Baekeland, Leo 29, 52
Bakelite 29, 52
Bakker, Gijs 41, 42
Bamboo bike (Ross Lovegrove) *177*
bambu LLC: All Occasion Veneerware® *172*
Barber Osgerby: De La Warr Pavilion Chair 99, *99*
Barcelona Chair (Ludwig Mies van der Rohe) *27*
Bardagjy, Joan (with Niels Diffrient and Alvin R. Tilley):
    Humanscale 1/2/3 *193*
Bauhaus 26, 27, 52
Béhar, Yves (fuseproject): One Laptop Per Child,
    XO Laptop 100, *100*
Behrens, Peter 25, 52; fan *25*
Bel Geddes, Norman 29, 30
Bell, Alexander Graham 21
Bellini, Mario: Divisumma 18 electric calculator *32*
Bent (Stefan Diez and Christophe De La Fontaine

for Moroso) *130*
BeoSound 9000 (David Lewis for Bang & Olufsen) *34*
Berlin, Boris (with Poul Christiansen/Komplot Design):
    Gubi Chair *146*
Bey, Jurgen: Gardening bench (for Droog) 172, *172*;
    Tree-trunk Bench (for Droog) *42*
Bohmer, Jon: Kyoto Box *171*
Bhömer, Marloes ten: Rotationalmouldedshoe *139*
Bialetti, Alfonso: Moka Express coffeemaker 52
Bill, Max 31
Bin Bag Bear (Raw-Edges Design Studio) *175*
biodegradable materials 172
Biomega MN bike (Marc Newson) *148*
Blanke Ark (Blueroom Designstudio, Innovativoli
    Industridesign & Kadabra Productdesign) *6*
Bling Bling (Frank Tjepkema for Chi Ha Paura) *157*
blob architecture 41
blobjects 51, 54
blow moulding 136
Blown (Nendo) *96*
Blueroom Designstudio: Blanke Ark *6*
Bobbin Lace Lamp (Nils van Eijk/Studio Van Eijk
    & Van der Lubbe) *116*
body storming 102
Boffi 34, 42
Bokka table lamp (Karim Rashid for Kundalini) *51*
Bone Armchair and Bone Chair (Joris Laarman) *80*
Bookworm (Ron Arad) *40*
Boontje, Tord 42, 44; Garland Light (for Habitat, Artecnica)
    131; Rough and Ready 42, *42*
Booth, Hubert Cecil 52
Boulanger, Pierre: Citroen brief 66
Bouroullec, Ronan & Erwan: Algue (for Vitra) *136*
Boym, Constantin and Laurene: World Trade Center *185*
brainstorming 79, *79*
branding 156–9
    branding and marketing terms 156
    designers as brands 159
    research 62
Branzi, Andrea 39
Braun 31, 32, *32*, 163, *163*
Breuer, Marcel 26, 27; Wassily Chair *26*
briefs 64–6
Brionvega radio and portable televisions (Richard Sapper
    and Marco Zanuso) *36*
Brody, Neville 51
Brown, Julian 50
Brown, Tim: interview 212; see also IDEO
Buchan, Katy 224
Bugatti Veyron Pur Sand edition *114*
Burton, Scott 44
Buxton, Sam: Micro World *131*

C

Cabbage chair (Nendo) *96*
CAD 88, *88*, 90
Cambridge Materials Selector (CMS) 112
camera journals 60
Campana, Fernando and Humberto 44; Corallo Chair *44*;
    TransNeomatic (for Artecnica) *170*
capability assessment and simulators 192
Cappellini 31, 42, 44, 50
Cappellini, Giulio 48
carbon fibre 115
career opportunities 226–8
Carl Hansen & Søn 128
Carpenter, Ed: Pigeon Light (for Thorsten Van Elten) *146*
Carwardine, George: Terry anglepoise lamp 52
Casablanca sideboard (Ettore Sottsass for Memphis) *39*;
    projection drawing *92*
Casio watch *36*
Castiglione, Achille 34; Mezzadro stool *34*; Spirale ashtray

(for Alessi) 53
casting 136–43; see also individual processes
Center for Universal Design 191
ceramics 113
Ceretti, G. (with P. Derossi and R. Rosso): Pratone *33*
Chab table (Nendo) *96*
Chadwick, Don (with Bill Stumpf): Aeron Chair
    (for Herman Miller) 174, *175*
Chair 214 (Michael Thonet) *22*
Chair_One (Konstantin Grcic for Magis) *141*
Chair, Solid collection
    (Patrick Jouin for Materialise) *150*
Chartered Society of Designers 215
Chervon power tool (IDEO) *6*
Chi Ha Paura *157*
China see Asia, design in
chip forming 128
Chippendale, Thomas 21
Choi, Min-Kyu: Folding Plug *10*
Christiansen, Poul (with Boris Berlin/Komplot Design):
    Gubi Chair *146*
Cinderella (Jeroen Verhoeven/Demakersvan) *126*
Citroen 2CV 66
client–designer relationship 12–13
Coates, Wells: Radio Wireless, Ekco AD-65 *29*
Coca Cola® 9, 30, 52, 156, 159, 210
Coles, Alex 44
Colombo, 'Cesare' Joe 32, 34; Acrilica desk lamp
    for Oluce 34; stackable plastic chair 32, *34*
composites 114–15
compression moulding 141
concept design 78–106
concept maps see mind mapping
Concrete (Jonas Hultqvist for Tretorn Sweden AB) *86*
concurrent design 111
continuous engineering products 10
copper 120
copyright 210
Corallo Chair (Fernando and Humberto Campana) *44*
Cowbenches (Julia Lohmann) *17*
cradle to cradle design 176
Crane, Walter 22
critical design products 50, 53
Cronan, Nick 100
cross-cultural comparisons 58
Cross, Michael see Wokmedia
Crystal Candy Set (Jaime Hayon for Baccarat) *44*
Cuckoo Clock (Michael Sans) *188*
cultural probes 59, *59*
CVs and cover letters 217–19

D

Dalén, Gustaf: Aga Stove 52
Davies, Eleanor 222
De Bono, Edward 81
De Stijl 26, 27
Dean, Lionel T. 54; Holy Ghost Chairs (for Kartell) *54*
Decorative Style 23
Della Sala, Giuseppe 100
Demakersvan *126*
Derossi, P. (with G. Ceretti and R. Rosso): Pratone *33*
design ethics 184–8; see also green issues;
    sustainable design
design for all see inclusive design
design for manufacture and assembly (DFMA) 111
DesignArt 44
designers as brands 159
detail design 108–9
Deutscher Werkbund 25–6
Diamond Chair (Nendo) *104*
die cutting 129
die-casting 141

Diez, Stefan (with Christophe De La Fontaine):
    Bent (for Moroso) 130
Diffrient, Niels (with Alvin R. Tilley and Joan Bardagjy):
    Humanscale 1/2/3 193
Digi Clock (Maxim Velcovsky for Qubus Design) 113
Ding3000: Pimp My Billy: Billy Wilder 156
dip moulding 138
Dixon, Tom 40, 172, 177
Do Break Vase (Frank Tjepkema with Peter van der Jagt
    for Droog) 199
Doren, Harold van 29
Doshi & Levien: My Beautiful Backside
    (for Moroso) 6
drawing techniques
    drawing on computer 88, 90
    concept sketches 84
    freehand 83
    presentation visuals 88
    rendering 86
    see also technical drawing
Dresser, Christopher 24; Geometric teapot 24
Dreyfuss, Henry 29, 30; The Measure of Man 53, 193;
    model 300 telephone for Bell 52
Driade 124, 134
Drift design studio 122
Droog Design 41–2, 42, 172, 172, 199
Ducaroy, Michel: Togo (for Ligne Roset) 134, 135
Duchamp, Marcel 42
Dunne, Anthony 50; Hertzian Tales 53; (with Fiona Raby)
    Robot 4: Needy One 50
Dyson Ball™ upright vacuum cleaner DC24 13, 53, 88, 101

E

Eames, Charles and Ray 31, 67, 114, 204; Ottoman 671
    armchair and footstool 31
Edison, Thomas 21
education
    courses 202–3
    degree shows 207, 207–8, 208
    projects 204–5
Eek, Piet Hein: Scrapwood Cupboard Classic 178, 178
elastomers 115
Electroformed Copper Stool (Max Lamb) 182
emotional design 196–200
empathy tools 102
Epson Design (with Industrial Facility): Picturemate Printer 6
ergonomics and ergonomists 8–9, 75, 193
Esslinger, Hartmur (frog design): Apple Macintosh 162, 162
Established & Sons 99, 154, 223
etching 131
ethnographers and ethnography 14, 61–2
exclusion audit 194
exploded views 86

F

Ferrari 250 GTO 175
Fiat: 1957 model (Dante Giacosa) 6; 500 31;
    500C (Roberto Giolito) 6
finishing techniques 152
Flamp light (Martí Guixé for Galeria H20) 174, 175
Flood Light (Julie Mathias and Michael Cross/Wokmedia) 186
Flos 42, 186
focus groups 60—1
Folding Plug (Min-Kyu Choi) 10
Ford: Ka 86; Model T 52
forging 141
formica 52, 115
forming 144–8 see also individual processes
Fornaroli, Antonio (with Gio Ponti and Alberto Rosselli):
    La Cornuta coffee machine 52
Foster, Norman: Nomos furniture 34, 34

Franklin, Benjamin 20
frog design 50: Apple Macintosh 48, 162, 162
Front: Rat Wallpaper 188
Front Yard Company: PlantLock 118
Fukasawa, Naoto: Muji Wall-Mounted CD Player 197, 199
fused deposition modelling (FDM) 150
fuseproject: (with Yves Béhar) Leaf Lamp (for Herman
    Miller) 144; One Laptop Per Child, XO Laptop 100, 100
Future Systems 51
FutureFactories 54

G

Gaia & Gino 116
Galeria H20, Barcelona 175
Gardening bench (Jurgen Bey for Droog) 172, 172
Garland Light (Tord Boontje for Habitat, then Artecnica) 131
Gehry, Frank O.: Pito (for Alessi) 84
general arrangement (GA) drawings 84
Gestetner 30, 52
Ghost Chair (Ralph Nauta and Lonneke Gordijn/Drift) 122
Giacosa, Dante: 1957 model Fiat 6
glass 116
    glassblowing 138, 138
    slumping 148
Glass Reinforced Plastic (GRP) 114
Good Form 32
Google 53
Gordijn, Lonneke (with Ralph Nauta): Ghost Chair 122
Graves, Michael 38; 9093 water kettle (for Alessi) 38
Gray, Angela: mind map 82
Grcic, Konstantin: Chair_One (for Magis) 141
Great Reform movements 21–2
green issues 168–81
Gropius, Walter 26, 27
Gruppo 33
Gruppo Strum 33, 38
Gubi Chair (Boris Berlin & Poul Christiansen/Komplot
    Design) 146
Gugelot, Hans (with Dieter Rams): Braun SK55 stereo
    radiogramme 32
Guixé, Martí: Flamp light (for Galeria H20) 174, 175
Gun Lamp (Philippe Starck for Flos) 186

H

Habitat 131, 182
Hadid, Zaha 44; Z. Island 9
Haier: HD-31100EGW Microwave 46
Hanabi (Nendo) 120
hard skills 12
Harper, Tom 223; mood board 63; sketchbooks
    and models 223
Haygarth, Stuart: interview 70; Aladdin (Amber) 70;
    Raft (Dogs) 70; Tail Light (Fat) 70; Tide 178
Hayon, Jaime: Crystal Candy Set 44; The Tournament 13
Helen Hamlyn Research Centre (RCA, London) 192
Henningsen, Poul: PH5 light fitting 53
Herman Miller 144, 174, 175
high-tech design 34
Hollein, Hans 28
HONDA 53
honeycomb 114
Horta, Victor 24
Humanscale 1/2/3 (Niels Diffrient, Alvin R. Tilley
    and Joan Bardagjy) 193
Hustwit, Gary: Objectified: A Documentary Film 53

I

i2i (IDEO with Steelcase) 212
IDEO: Chervon power tool 6; (with Steelcase) i2i 212;

    My Passport 212; Positivo 212
Iittala: Alvar Aalto vase 26
IKEA 52; hacking 156, 156
inclusive design 190–4
Indartu 172
Industrial Designers Society of America 193, 215
Industrial Facility: (with Epson Design) Picturemate
    Printer 6; 2nd Phone (for Muji) 180, 180
Industrial Revolution 6, 20–1
informance 104
information set 109, 128
injection moulding 136
Innovativoli Industridesign: Blanke Ark 6
intellectual property 209–10
International Style 28
Internet 53
internships 216
interviews
    research 58
    job 225
investment casting 142
Issigonis, Alec: Morris Mini Minor 53; prototype drawing 83
Itten, Johannes 27
Ive, Jonathan 44, 162; iMac 162, 162; iPhone 3GS 6;
    iPod touch 44

J

Jacobsen, Arne: Ant chair for Fritz Hansen 53
Jagt, Peter van der (with Frank Tjepkema for Droog):
    Do Break Vase 199
Jaguar E-Type (Malcolm Sayer) 53, 196
Japanese art 23–4
Jar Tops (Jorre van Ast for Royal VKB) 123
Jencks, Charles 28
jet engine 11
Jobs, Steve 44, 162
joinery 134
Jonas Hultqvist Design: Concrete (for Tretorn Sweden AB) 86
Jones, Matt 216
Jongerius, Hella 41, 44
Jordan, Pat 196
Jouin, Patrick 104; Chair (for Materialise) 150
Judd, Donald 44
Jugendstil 23
Juicy Salif (Philippe Starck for Alessi) 53, 159, 197, 199

K

Kadabra Productdesign: Blanke Ark 6
Kandinsky, Wassily 26, 27
Kari Traa AS: Girl's Ski Helmet 6
Kartell 31, 34, 36, 54
Kartono, Singgih S.: Magno Wooden Radio 125
Kawakubo, Rei 51
Kelloe, Jenny: Noise Bomb 59
Kelp Constructs (Julia Lohmann) 17
Kelvin 40 concept Jet (Marc Newson) 132
Kerridge, Tobie 215
Kiesler, Frederick 48
Kihara, Nobutoshi: Walkman for Sony 36
King, Perry A. (with Ettore Sottsass): Olivetti Valentine
    typewriter 32, 32, 53
Knoll International 39, 50
Kodak 31, 52
Komplot Design: Gubi Chair 146
KR5 Arc Hollow Wrist robotic arm (Kuka Automation
    + Robotics) 11
Kuka Automation + Robotics: KR5 Arc Hollow Wrist
    robotic arm 11
Kundalini: Bokka table lamp (Karim Rashid) 51
Kuramata, Shiro 40, 48
Kyoto Box (Jon Bohmer) 171

L

L'Eau d'Issey, Edition Ettore Sottsass 161
Laarman, Joris: Bone Armchair and Bone Chair 80
Ladycross Sandstone Chair (Max Lamb) 182
Lamb, Max: interview 182; Electroformed Copper Stool
    182; Ladycross Sandstone Chair 182; Pewter Stool 143,
    182, 182; Sheet Steel chair 145
laminates 115
laser cutting 130, 168
lateral thinking 81
Le Corbusier: Le Modular man 193
lead 120
Leaf Lamp (Yves Béhar with fuseproject for Herman Miller) 144
Lego 40, 52
Levy, Arik: Mistic vase/candleholder for Gaia & Gino 116
Lewis, David: BeoSound 9000 (for Bang & Olufsen) 34
LG Electronics 37, 46
Lievore, Alberto: Rothko Chair (for Indartu) 172, 172
Ligne Roset 134, 135
LINEA Collection for PDC Brush NV (pilipili) 86
literature review 58
Livi, Vittorio (Fiam) 48
Loewy, Raymond 29, 30, 52 ,159; Avanti car 159; Coca
    Cola® bottle 159; MAYA design principle 161; Pencil
    Sharpener 30; Time magazine cover 159, 161
Lohmann, Julia: interview 16; Cowbenches 17; Kelp
    Constructs 17; Ruminant Bloom 17, 177
London Design Festival 9, 13
lost-wax casting see investment casting
Louis 20 chair (Philippe Starck) 178, 178
Louis Ghost chair (Philippe Starck) 41, 54
Louis Vuitton 41, 50
Lovegrove, Ross 50, 51; Apollo (for Driade) 134; Bamboo
    bike 177; Figure of Eight chair (for Cappellini) 50;
    Study for the Eye Digital Camera 50; Supernatural
    chair (for Moroso) 50; Ty Nant water bottle 196, 199
Lucchi, Michele de 39

M

machining 128–9
Magis 42, 48, 141
magnesium 120
Magno Wooden Radio (Singgih S. Kartono) 125
Maldonado, Tomás 31
manufacturing 14, 111–12, 128–52; see also green issues;
    individual materials, processes
marketing 14, 164–6
    branding and marketing terms 156
    marketing mix 165–6
    market research 63, 164
Marx, Karl: Das Kapital 21
Massaud, Jean-Marie: Ad Hoc (for Viccarbe) 118
materials 112–27
    biodegradable 172
    recyclable/recycled 178
    see also individual names
Mathias, Julie see Wokmedia
matrix evaluation 106
Matsumoto, Hadeki 51
MAYA ('Most advanced yet acceptable') design principle
    (Raymond Loewy) 161
Memphis 39, 53
Mendini, Alessandro 38, 39
Menstral, Georges de: Velcro 80
Mer, Yael see Raw-Edges Design Studio
Mermaid (Tokujin Yoshioka for Driade) 124
metrics 73
Meyer, Hannes 27
Mezzadro stool (Castiglioni brothers) 34, 42
Micro World (Sam Buxton) 131
Mies van der Rohe, Ludwig 27; Barcelona Chair 27

Milton, Alex (with Will Titley): Outgang XP 139
mind mapping 82
Mistic vase/candleholder (Arik Levy for Gaia & Gino) 116
Miyake, Issey 48, 96, 96; L'Eau d'Issey, Edition Ettore
    Sottsass 161
modelling 98
Modernism 28
Modernista 23
Mods 157, 200
Moooi 42, 113
Morenstein, Josh 100
Morita, Akio (Sony) 36, 37
Moroso 6, 50, 130
Morris Mini Minor (Alec Issigonis) 53
Morris, William 22, 23; Anemone wallpaper 23
Morrison, Jasper 40; Ply Chair (for Vitra) 181, 181
Muji 180, 180, 197, 199
Muthesius, Hermann 25
My Beautiful Backside (Doshi & Levien for Moroso) 6
My Passport (IDEO) 212

N

narration 60
Naumann, Friedrich 25
Nauta, Ralph (with Lonneke Gordjin): Ghost Chair 122
Negroponte, Nicholas 100
Nelson, George 169
Nendo: interview 96; Blown 96; Cabbage chair 96;
    Chab table 96; Diamond Chair 104; Hanabi 120
Neo-Modernism 41
New Design 40
Newson, Marc 51; Biomega MN bike 148; Kelvin 40
    concept Jet 88, 132
nickel 120
Nissan Figaro car 53
Nizzoli, Marcello: Lettera typewriter for Olivetti 53
Noguchi, Isamu 48
Nomos Desking System (Foster and Partners with Tecno) 34
non-disclosure agreement (NDA) 209–10
Norman, Donald 196
Nouvel, Jean 50
Nucleo: Terra! 169

O

Ohl, Herbert 31
Olivetti & Co. 32, 32, 39, 53
Olivetti, Camillo 52
orthographic drawing 92, 92
Osthaus, Karl Ernst 25
Ottoman 671 armchair and footstool
    (Charles and Ray Eames) 31
Outgang XP (Alex Milton and Will Titley) 139
OXO Good Grips (Smart Design) 195, 195

P

packaging 161
Packard, Vance 168; The Waste Makers 169
pairwise comparison method 68–9
Pakhalé, Satyendra: interview 48; Add-On Radiator 48;
    Amisa door handle 48; B.M. Horse Chair 48
panel beating 144
Panton, Verner: Panton chair 32
Papanek, Victor 168; Design for the Real World 53, 169
paper sizes 94
Pardo, Jorge 44
Parenthesis 40
Pasquier, Nathalie du 39
patents 211
Pencil Sharpener (Raymond Loewy) 30

Per Finne: Girl's Ski Helmet 6
Perazza, Eugenio (Magis) 48
perceptual mapping 164
Perrier water bottle 10
personas 62, 62
perspective drawings 83, 91, 91
Petursdottir, Katrin Olina (with Michael Young):
    Tree wall coat hanger (for Swedese) 125
Pewter Stool (Max Lamb) 143, 182, 182
Picturemate Printer (Industrial Facility with Epson Design) 6
Pigeon Light (Ed Carpenter for Thorsten Van Elten) 146
pilipili: LINEA Collection for PDC Brush NV 86
Pimp My Billy: Billy Wilder (Ding3000) 156
Pito (Frank O. Gehry for Alessi) 84
planned obsolescence 169
PlantLock (Front Yard Company) 118
Plastic Nostalgic (Raw-Edges Design Studio) 154
plastics 122–4
Ply Chair (Jasper Morrison for Vitra) 181, 181
plywood 115; forming 146
Poltronova 39
Pompidou Centre, Paris 34
Ponti, Gio 36; (with Antonio Fornaroli and Alberto Rosselli):
    La Cornuta coffee machine 52
Pools & Pouf! (Robert Sandler) 134
Porsche 158, 158
Porsche, Ferdinand: Volkswagen Beetle car 48
portfolios 220–2
Positivo (IDEO) 212
Post-Modernism 38
Pratone (G. Ceretti, P. Derossi and R. Rosso) 33
Pre-Raphaelites 22
precious metals 120
presentation visuals 88
Product Design Specification (PDS) 15, 72–6, 105
product liability 186
product types 8–11
Propeller: Kapsel Media Centre brainstorming session 79
prototyping 101–4, 109; Alpha prototypes 109; Beta prototypes
    109, 128; rapid prototyping (RP) 104, 104, 150
Pugh method 106
punching and blanking 129

Q

Qubus Design 113
questionnaires and surveys 59, 59

R

Raby, Fiona 50; (with Anthony Dunne) Robot 4: Needy One 50
'radical design', Italy 33, 38, 39
Radice, Barbara 39
Radio Wireless, Ekco AD-65 (Wells Coates) 29
Raft (Dogs) (Stuart Haygarth) 70
Ramakers, Renny 41, 42
Rams, Dieter 32, 163; (with Hans Gugelot) Braun SK55
    stereo radiogramme 32; Braun T3 Pocket Radio 163, 163
Rashid, Karim 51, 159; Bokka table lamp for Kundalini 51
Rat Wallpaper (Front) 188
Raw-Edges Design Studio 154; Bin Bag Bear 175;
    Plastic Nostalgic 154; Tailored Wood 154
reaction injection moulding (RIM) 138
ready-made products 42
Recor, Bret 100
recycling 171, 172, 175, 178
Register, Nicolas 88
registered and unregistered design rights 201
Remy, Tejo: Milk Bottle lamp 42
research 14, 56–63
    market research 63, 164
Rietveld, Gerrit: Red and Blue Armchair 27, 52
rights 209–11

Roadkill Rug (Studio Oooms) *186*
Robot 4: Needy One, Technological Dreams Series (Anthony Dunne and Fiona Raby) *50*
role-playing 102
Rolls Royce Flying Lady mascot *142*
Rosselli, Alberto 36; (with Antonio Fornaroli and Gio Ponti): La Cornuta coffee machine 52
Rossetti, Dante Gabriel 22
Rosso, R. (with G. Ceretti and P. Derossi): Pratone *33*
rotational moulding 139
Rotationalmouldedshoe (Marloes ten Bhömer) *139*
Rothko Chair (Alberto Lievore for Indartu) 172, *172*
Rough and Ready furniture (Tord Boontje) 42, *42*
Royal VKB *123*
rubber 115
Ruminant Bloom (Julia Lohmann) *17*, 177
Ruskin, John 22

S
Saarinen, Eero 114
Samuel, Alexander: Coca-Cola® bottle 52
Samsung Electronics 37, *46*
sand casting 143
Sandler, Robert: Pools & Pouf! *134*
Sans, Michael: Cuckoo Clock *188*
Sapper, Richard 36; Tizio Table Lamp (for Artemide) 32, 36, *36*, 53
Sato, Oki 96
Sayer, Malcolm: Jaguar E-Type 53, *196*
scenario modelling and testing 103
Schick, Jacob: electric razor 52
Schneider, Peter 32
Scott, Ridley 162
Scrapwood Cupboard Classic (Piet Hein Eek) 178, *178*
'Second Nature' exhibition (21_21 Design Sight, Japan) *149*
2nd Phone (Industrial Facility for Muji) 180, *180*
selective laser sintering (SLS) 150
Sezessionsstil 23
shadowing 61
Sheet Steel chair (Max Lamb) *145*
Sheraton, Thomas 21
Siemens Grillo telephone (Richard Sapper and Marco Zanuso) 36
silicones 115
Singer, Isaac Merrit 21
Sipek, Borek 40
Skov Holt, Steven 51
slip casting 141
Smart Design: OXO Good Grips 195, *195*
soft skills 12
soldering and brazing 132
Sony 37, 52, 53; Walkman 36, 37, 50, 53
Sottsass, Ettore 38, 39, 48; Casablanca sideboard *39* and projection drawing *92*; L'Eau d'Issey *161*; (with Perry A. King) Olivetti Valentine typewriter 32, *32*, 39, 53; Yemen blown glass vase *39*
Sowden, George 39; Acapulco clock sketch *92*
spinning 142
Sponge Vase (Marcel Wanders for Moooi) *113*
Stam, Mart 52
stamping 144
Starck, Philippe 41, 50, 51, 159; *Design for Life* 53; Gun Lamp (for Flos) *186*; Juicy Salif (for Alessi) 53, 159, 197, *199*; Louis Ghost chair *41*, 54; Louis 20 chair (for Vitra) 178, *178*
steam bending 146
steel 118
Steelcase Design Studio (with PearsonLloyd): Cobi Chair 110, *110*; i2i (with IDEO) *212*
stereolithography (SLA) 104, 150
Stile Liberty 23
Stokke: Tripp Trapp chair 173, *173*

storyboards 60, 103, *103*
streamlining 29
Studio Alchimia 33, 39
Studio Oooms: Roadkill Rug *186*
Studio Van Eijk & Van der Lubbe: Bobbin Lace Lamp *116*
Studio X 50
Stumpf, Bill (with Don Chadwick): Aeron Chair (for Herman Miller) 174, *175*
superforming 148
Superstudio 33, 38
Surrealism 38
surveys 59
relative importance surveys 69
sustainable design 170–81
Suzuki, Daisetz 48
Swedese *125*
Swiss Army Knife (Wenger) *25*

T
Tail Light (Fat) (Stuart Haygarth) *70*
Tailored Wood (Raw-Edges Design Studio) *154*
Tangerine 44
Teague, Walter Dorwin 29
technical drawing 91–4
Tecno: Nomos Desking System (with Foster and Partners) *34*
Terra! (Nucleo) *169*
Terry anglepoise lamp (George Cawardine) 52
thermoforming 146
thermoplastics 122–3
thermosets 124
Thonet, Michael 22; Chair 214 22
Thorsten Van Elten 146
Thun, Matteo: Container Cabinet 34
Tide (Stuart Haygarth) *178*
Tilley, Alvin R. (with Niels Diffrient and Joan Bardagjy): Humanscale 1/2/3 *193*
Time magazine: Raymond Loewy cover 159, *161*
tin 120
titanium 120
Titley, Will (with Alex Milton): Outgang XP *139*
Tizio Table Lamp (Richard Sapper for Artemide) 32, 36, *36*, 53
Tjepkema, Frank: Bling Bling (for Chi Ha Paura) *157*; (with Peter van der Jagt for Droog) Do Break Vase *199*
Togo (Michel Ducaroy for Ligne Roset) *134*, 135
tooling 128
The Tournament (Jaime Hayon) *13*
Toyota Prius *199*, 200
trademarks 211
Trannon 177
TransNeomatic (Fernando and Humberto Campana for Artecnica) *170*
Tree-trunk Bench (Jurgen Bey for Droog) *42*
trend forecasting 165
triple bottom line 170–1
Tripp Trapp chair (Stokke) 173, *173*
Turrell, James 44
Ty Nant water bottle (Ross Lovegrove) 196, *199*

U
Ulm Academy for Design 31, 32
Unique Selling Proposition (USP) 165
universal design *see* inclusive design
upholstery 135

V
Valentine typewriter (Ettore Sottsass and Perry A. King for Olivetti & Co.) 32, *32*, 39, 53
values 73

Velcovsky, Maxim: Digi Clock for Qubus Design *113*
Velcro 80
Velde, Henri van de 24, 25; writing desk and chair *23*
Venturi, Robert 28, 38
VENUS chair (Tokujin Yoshioka) 149, *149*
Verhoeven, Jeroen (Demakersvan): Cinderella *126*
Vespa scooter 31, 48, 52, 200
Viccarbe 118
Vitra 41, 136, *178*, 181, *181*
Volkswagen Beetle 9, 48, 52

W
Wanders, Marcel 41, 42, 44, 104; Knotted Chair 42, *42*; Sponge Vase (for Moooi) *113*
War Bowl (Dominic Wilcox) *185*
Wassily Chair (Marcel Breuer) *26*
water-filling plant *11*
water-jet cutting 130
Watt, James 20–1
weaving 134
Wedgwood Jasperware vase *20*
Wedgwood, Josiah 20, 21
Wegner, Hans J.: Wishbone Chair (for Carl Hansen & Søn) *128*
Weil, Daniel 40; Bag Radio *40*
welding 132
Wenger Swiss Army Knife *25*
Wilcox, Dominic: Anti-theft Bike/Car Device *153*; War Bowl *185*
wind-up computer 53
Wishbone Chair (Hans J. Wegner for Carl Hansen & Søn) *128*
Wokmedia: Flood Light *186*
wood 125–6
work placements 216
World Trade Center (Constantin and Laurene Boym) *185*

Y
Yamamoto, Yohji 40
Yanagi, Setsu 48
Yoshioka, Tokujin: Mermaid (for Driade) *124*; VENUS chair 149, *149*
Young, Michael (with Katrin Olina Petursdottir): Tree wall coat hanger (for Swedese) *125*

Z
Z. Island (Zaha Hadid Architects) *9*
Zaha Hadid Architects: Z. Island *9*
Zanuso, Marco 32, 36
zinc 120

Picture credits

The author and publisher would like to thank the following institutions and individuals for providing photographic images for use in this book. In all cases, every effort had been made to credit the copyright holders, but should there be any omissions or errors the publisher would be pleased to insert the appropriate acknowledgement in any subsequent edition of this book:

p4: Tahon & Bouroullec; p7, top left: Norsk Form and Thomas Ekström; p7, top middle: Courtesy of IDEO; p7, top right: © Apple Inc. Courtesy of Apple Inc.; p7, middle left: Fiat Group Automobiles UK Ltd; p7, middle right: Per Finne; p7, bottom left: Industrial Facility, London, Epson Design, Japan; p7, bottom right: Moroso SpA, Alessandro Paderni-Eye Studio; p9: Courtesy of DuPont ™ Corian ® Photographer: Leo Torri; p10, top: © Min-Kyu Choi (www.minkyu.co.uk/www.madeinmind. co.uk) Supported by Royal College of Art, BASF, Korean Institute of Design Promotion (KIDP); p10, bottom: The Perrier brand and image is reproduced with the kind permission of Société des Produits Nestlé S.A.; p11, top left: Photonica/Getty Images; p11, top right: AIRBUS SAS, France; p11, bottom left: Imagebank/Getty Images; p11, bottom right: Kuka Automation + Robotics; p12: Dyson Ltd; p13: Susan Smart Photography; p17: © Julia Lohmann (www.julialohmann.co.uk); p20: Hulton Archive/Getty Images; p22: © Thonet GmbH; p23, top: © V&A Images, Victoria and Albert Museum; p23, bottom: Photo: Hans-Joachim Bartsch.© 2010. Photo Scala, K, Bildagentur fuer Kunst, Kultur und Geschichte, Berlin; p24: © V&A Images, Victoria and Albert Museum; p25, top: © Wenger Swiss Army Knife, Wenger SA; p25, bottom: Melva Bucksbaum Purchase Fund. Acc. n.: 24.2000.© 2010. Digital image, The Museum of Modern Art, New York/Scala, Florence; p26, top: Copyright: Iittala, Finland; p26, bottom: Gift of Herbert Bayer. Acc. n.: 229.1934 © 2010. Digital image, The Museum of Modern Art, New York/Scala, Florence; p27: © 2010. Digital image, The Museum of Modern Art, New York/Scala, Florence; p29: © V&A Images, Victoria and Albert Museum; p30: Raymond Loewy TM by CMG Worldwide, Inc. /www.raymondloewy.com; p31: © V&A Images, Victoria and Albert Museum; p32, top: © V&A Images, Victoria and Albert Museum; p32, bottom: © V&A Images, Victoria and Albert Museum; p33: Courtesy of Cassina; p34: Kartell Museum; p34, bottom: Zanotta SpA-Italy; p35, top: Bang & Olufsen; p35, bottom: Peter Strobel Photodesign/cologne-Germany; p36: Gift of the manufacturer. Acc. n.: 198.1973.© 2010. Digital image, The Museum of Modern Art, New York/Scala, Florence; p37, top: Sony Corporation; p37, bottom: Casio Electronics Co. Ltd.; p38: Alessi SpA, Italy; p39, top: Venini SpA; p39, bottom: © V&A Images, Victoria and Albert Museum; p40, top: Skidmore, Owings & Merrill Design Collection Purchase Fund. Acc.n.: SC20.1983© 2010. Digital image, The Museum of Modern Art, New York/Scala, Florence; p40, bottom: Kartell; p41: Starck Network; p42: Photography: Cappellini, Robbie Kavanagh (story board); p43, top: Courtesy Droog; p43 bottom: Photography by Tord Boontje; p44, top: © Apple Inc. Courtesy of Apple Inc.; p44, bottom: Estudio Camapana, Edra; p45: Nienke Klunder; p47, top: Haier Europe Trading Srl; p47, bottom: Copyright 2010 Samsung Electronics America; p49: Atelier Satyendra Pakhalé; p50, top: Commissioned by Jan Bolen 213, photo by Per Tingleff; p50, bottom: Courtesy Lovegrove Studio; p51: Kundalini srl; p54: Photographer: John Britton Courtesy Lionel T. Dean. with project assistance of RP bureau 3T; p57: School of Design, University of Northumbria; p59: Jenny Kelloe, University of Dundee; p60: Andy Murray Design; pp61–62: School of Design, University of Northumbria; p63: Tom Harper, Edinburgh College of Art; p66: © Citroen Communication (S.A. Automobiles Citroen); p71: Stuart Haygarth; p79: Propeller Design Team and Kapsel Multimedia AB; p80: Friedman Benda Gallery, Joris Laarman Lab; p82: Angela Gray; p83: © BMW AG; p85, top: Image provided by Gehry Partners, LLP; p85, bottom: Alessi SpA, Italy; p86: pilipili

productdesign NV; p87, top: Jonas Hultqvist- Jonas Hultqvist Design; p87, bottom: Ford Motor Company; p89, top: Dyson Ltd; p89, bottom: Marc Newson Ltd; p91: © Alan (Fred) Pipes; p92, top: Drawing by George Sowden for Memphis 1981 First Exhibition. "Acapulco" Clock in wood with silk screen printed decoration.; p92, bottom: Studio Ettore Sottsass s.r.l. and Erik and Petra Hesmerg; p93: © Alan (Fred) Pipes; p97: Nendo; p99: Barber Osgerby, Established & Sons; p100: Courtesy of Fuseproject; p103: Martí Guixé, Galeria H2O; p104: Nendo; p110: PearsonLloyd in conjunction with Steelcase Design Studio; p113, top: Qubus Design/Maxim Velcovsky; p113, bottom: Moooi; p114: A. Ford and Bugatti Owners' Club; p116: Gaia & Gino, photographer: Serdar Samli; p117: Studio Van Eijk & Van der Lubbe, photography: Studio 4/A; p118: Jean-Marie Massaud, Viccarbe; p119: PlantLocks ® Front Yard Company Ltd; p121: Nendo; p122: Ralph Nauta and Lonneke Gordijn, Drift; p123: Royal VKB; p124: Driade; p125, top: Pelle Wahlgren; p125, bottom: © Singgih S. Kartono; p126: Demakersvan; p127: Carl Hansen & Søn A/S; p130: Moroso SpA, Alessandro Paderni-Eye Studio; p131, left: Courtesy Studio Tord Boontje; p131, right: www.mikroworld.com/Sam Buxton; p133: Marc Newson Ltd; p134: Driade; p135, top: Ligne Roset, www.ligne-roset.co.uk; p135, bottom: Patrick Gries; p137: © Vitra, photographer: Paul Tahon; p138: John McGregor, Edinburgh College of Art; p139, top: Alex Milton and Will Titley; p139, bottom: Marloes ten Böhmer; p140: © Magis, photo by Tom Vack; p142: Polycast and Rolls-Royce Motor Cars Limited; p143: Photography by Max Lamb and Jane Lamb; p144: Courtesy of Fuseproject; p145: Max Lamb; p146: Ed Carpenter (www.edcarpenter.co.uk) for Thorsten Van Elten (www.thorstenvanelten.com); p147: Fabiane Möller, Thomas Ibsen, Stuart McIntyre Boris Berlin & Poul Christiansen of Komplot Design Gubi A/S Inventor of 3D veneer: Dr. Achim Möller Manufacturer of 3D veneer: Reholz GmbH; p148: Biomega; p149 Tokujin Yoshioka Design, 21_21 Design Sight (www.2121designsight.jp); p151: Thomas Duval; p153: Dominic Wilcox, www.dominicwilcox.com; p155, top left: Yael Mer & Shay Alkalay, Raw-Edges Design Studio, Arts & Co, www.arts-co.com; p155, top right and bottom: Yael Mer & Shay Alkalay, Raw-Edges Design Studio; p156: Ding3000; p157, left: © Tjep; p157, right: Hulton Archive/Getty Images; p158: © Porsche AG; p159: Roman Leo; p160: Raymond Loewy TM by CMG Worldwide, Inc. /www.raymond-loewy.com; p161: Daniel Jouanneau; p162, and 163 top left and bottom: © Apple Inc. Courtesy of Apple Inc.; p163, top, right: Gift of the manufacturer. Acc. num. 595.1965.© 2010. Digital image, The Museum of Modern Art, New York/Scala, Florence; p169: Nucleo; p170: Artecnica (www.artecnica. com); p171: Jon Bohmer, Kyoto Energy Ltd.; p172, left: Alberto Lievore, Indartu (Simeyco, S.A.L.); p172, right: bambu LLC; p173, top: Courtesy Droog; p173, bottom: Stokke ® Tripp Trapp ® www.stokke.se; p174, top: Herman Miller Inc.; p174, bottom left: Photo by Inga Knölke; p174, bottom right: Martí Guixé, Galeria H2O; p175: Yael Mer & Shay Alkalay, Raw-Edges Design Studio, Platform 10, Design Products, Royal College of Art London; p176: Alex Milton, Edinburgh College of Art; p177: Biomega; p178, left: © Vitra AG (www. vitra.com), photographer Marc Eggiman; p178, right: Nob Ruijgrok; p179: Stuart Haygarth; p180: Muji www.muji.eu; p181: © Vitra AG (www.vitra.com), Photography Hans Hansen; p183, top: Max Lamb; p183, bottom: Photography by Max Lamb and Jane Lamb; p185, top: Dominic Wilcox (www. dominicwilcox.com); p185, bottom: Boym Partners Inc; p186, top: Studio Oooms (www.oooms.nl); p186, bottom: Wokmedia; p187: Starck Network; p188, top and 189: Front; p188, bottom: Dominik Butzmann; p193: Niels Diffrient, Alvin R. Tilley, and Joan Bardagjy, Humanscale 1/2/3, figure: Female selector, © 1974 Massachusetts Institute of Technology and Henry Dreyfus Associates by permission of The MIT Press.; p195: OXO Good Grips; p198, top left: Ty Nant, Courtesy Lovegrove Studio; p198, top middle: Muji, www.muji.eu; p198, top right: Starck Network; p198, bottom: © Tjep; p199: Picture courtesy of Toyota (GB) PLC; pp202–03: John McGregor, Edinburgh

College of Art; pp205–07: School of Design, University of Northumbria; p208: School of Design, University of Northumbria, photographer: James Cunnings; p213: Courtesy of IDEO; p223: Tom Harper, Edinburgh College of Art.

Acknowledgements

Paul Rodgers and Alex Milton would like to thank all the contributing designers for their time, effort and generosity. We would also like to thank the School of Design at the University of Northumbria and Edinburgh College of Art for their support in making this book happen, our past and present colleagues for their critical advice and input, and all our design students over the years. Special mention is due to Ed Hollis, Euan Winton, Matthew Turner, and Douglas Bryden. There are, of course, many others and you know who you are!

A really big thanks to everybody at Laurence King Publishing including Jo Lightfoot, Zoe Antoniou, Melanie Walker, and Fredrika Lökholm for all their hard work.

Last but by no means least, a special thanks is due to Alison and Fiona for providing invaluable support and inspiration.